THE CULTIC MOTIF
IN THE SPIRITUALITY
OF THE BOOK OF HEBREWS

Darrell J. Pursiful

MELLEN BIBLICAL PRESS
Lewiston/Queenston/Lampeter

Library of Congress Cataloging-in-Publication Data

Pursiful, Darrell J.
  The cultic motif in the spirituality of the book of Hebrews /
Darrell J. Pursiful.
      p.   cm.
  Originally presented as the author's thesis (Ph. D.)--Southern
Baptist Theological Seminary.
  Includes bibliographical references and index.
  ISBN 0-7734-2376-1
  1. Bible. N.T. Hebrews--Criticism, interpretation, etc.
2. Spirituality--Biblical teaching. 3. Worship in the Bible.
I. Title.
BS2775.2.P876 1993
227'.8706--dc20   93-21560
                                                          CIP

A CIP catalog record for this book
is available from the British Library.

The Edwin Mellen Press   The Edwin Mellen Press
        Box 450   Box 67
  Lewiston, New York   Queenston, Ontario
     USA 14092   CANADA L0S 1L0

                   Edwin Mellen Press, Ltd.
                   Lampeter, Dyfed, Wales
                 UNITED KINGDOM SA48 7DY

           Printed in the United States of America

for

Darrell T. and Nola Pursiful

my parents

my first Bible teachers

TABLE OF CONTENTS

TABLE OF ABBREVIATIONS

I. Ancient works

1 Clem	*First Clement*	First Apol.	Justin Martyr, *First Apology*
1QH	*Hôdayôt* (*Thanksgiving Hymns*) from Qumran Cave 1	*Fuga*	Philo, *De fuga et inventione*
1QS	*Serek Hayyahad* (*Rule of the Community, Manual of Discipline*) from Qumran Cave 1	*Gig.*	Philo, *De gigantibus*
		Hag.	*Hagigah*
		Heres	Philo, *Quis rerum divinarum heres sit*
2 Apoc.Bar.	Syriac *Apocalypse of Baruch*	*Jub.*	*Jubilees*
4Q400	Text 400 from Qumran Cave 4	*LA.* I,II	Philo, *Legum allegoria*
4Q511	Text 511 from Qumran Cave 4	*Legat.*	Philo, *Legatio ad Gaium*
		Lev. Rab.	*Leviticus Rabbah*
4QFlor	*Florilegium* from Qumran Cave 4	*m.*	Tractate of the Mishnah
4QShirShabb	*Songs of the Sabbath Sacrifice* from Qumran Cave 4	*Meg.*	*Megilla*
		Mek.	*Mekilta*
4QTestim	*Testimonia* text from Qumran Cave 4	*Menah.*	*Menahot*
		Mig.	Philo, *De migratione*
Ant.	Josephus, *Antiquities of the Jews*	*Mos.* I,II	Philo, *De vita Mosis*
Asc. Isa.	*The Ascension of Isaiah*	*Num. Rab.*	*Numbers Rabbah*
b.	Tractate of the Babylonian Talmud	*Plant.*	Philo, *De plantatione*
		Prov.	Philo, *De providentia*
Benef.	Seneca, *De beneficiis*	*Pss. Sol.*	*Psalms of Solomon*
Ber.	*Berakot*	*Sabb.*	*Sabbat*
CD	Cairo (Genizah text of the) *Damascus* (*Document*)	*Som.* I,II	Philo, *De somniis*
		Spec. I,II	Philo, *De specialibus legibus*
Det.	Philo, *Quod deterius potiori insidiari soleat*	*T. Levi*	*Testament of Levi*
Dialogue	Justin Martyr, *Dialogue with Trypho*	*Ta ʿan.*	*Ta ʿanit*
		Tg.	*Targum*
Exod. Rab.	*Exodus Rabbah*	*Yebam.*	*Yebamot*

II. Modern works

AARSR	American Academy of Religion Studies in Religion	**JSNTSS**	Journal for the Study of the New Testament Supplementary Series
ANRW	*Aufstieg und Niedergang der römischen Welt*	*NTS*	*New Testament Studies*
		RevExp	*Review and Expositor*
CBQ	*Catholic Biblical Quarterly*	SBL	Society of Biblical Literature
CBQMS	CBQ Monograph Series	**SBLMS**	SBL Monograph Series
IDB	*Interpreter's Dictionary of the Bible*		
IDBSupp	*IDB Supplementary Volume*	SNTSMS	Society for New Testament Studies Monograph Series
JBL	*Journal of Biblical Literature*	*TDNT*	*Theological Dictionary of the New Testament*

PREFACE

Numerous strands of personal interest brought me to this investigation of the cultic imagery of Hebrews. First, there is the book of Hebrews itself. This enigmatic first century sermon has long been intriguing to me. Its rich symbolism and intricate argumentation often lies just beyond one's grasp. For some this fact has led to despair of ever understanding its message, but for those who love the book it is a constant invitation to plunge even deeper into its depths. No doubt part of my fascination with Hebrews is precisely in that it so successfully evades our attempts to systematize, to rationalize, to reduce to a manageable parcel. Nevertheless, it should be clear from this study that I believe a critical, scientific study of Hebrews is indeed both possible and worthwhile. My interest has been primarily with the spirituality of Hebrews, but I hope to have also added something generally to the study of this magnificent "word of encouragement."

My methodology in this study is something of a hybrid, linking phenomenology of religion (e.g., Eliade, Ringgren and Ström), anthropology (e.g., van Gennep, Turner), and the academic study of spirituality (e.g., Schneiders, Kinerk) to a foundation in historical-critical exegesis. I leave it to the reader to judge whether I have made myself clear on methodological issues and whether indeed this approach to Hebrews makes a worthwhile contribution.

The second interest that led me to this topic is Christian spirituality. By this term I mean not just the intellectual examination of certain phenomena in the Christian religion, as important as that is, but also an insider's quest to give authentic expression to one's own faith. My approach to the biblical texts has been very much in the category of *fides quaerens intellectum*--faith seeking understanding. Moreover, in grappling with the more difficult issues that Hebrews presents, especially for twentieth-century readers, I have come to a greater appreciation of the converse experience of *intellectus quaerens fidem*.

Finally, there are the closely related issues of myth and ritual as they bear upon our understandings of spiritual experience, be it ancient or contemporary. In this study ritual has been most clearly in focus, although I believe a mythopoeic reading of certain aspects of Hebrews is a possiblility. For example, I would like to have explored the eschatology of Hebrews in terms of mythic conceptions of time, but such would have quickly become a study all its own. I have not said everything that could be said about ritual in Hebrews, but I think I have at least demonstrated that such an approach yields credible conclusions about the nature of the book and about the milieu in which it was written.

This study was originally presented as a Ph.D. dissertation at the Southern Baptist Theological Seminary, and I would be remiss not to mention the great help that my committee of instruction has been to me throughout the project. Dr. John B. Polhill's constant encouragement, diligence, and humor have helped the process move quickly and easily. The other members of my committee, Drs. Gerald L. Borchert and Harold S. Songer, have likewise been conscientious critics of my work. These three have given me the freedom to pursue my own interests and argue my own conclusions while always pushing me to be the best scholar I could be. From the beginning they have modelled for me exacting scholarship, effective teaching, and authentic faith.

I would also like to express my gratitude to two former members of the Southern Seminary faculty who offered invaluable help at the beginning of this project. Dr. John N. Jonsson was helpful in introducing me to the phenomenological approach to the study of religion. Dr. E. Glenn Hinson deserves credit for augmenting and clarifying my personal interest in Christian spirituality. A paper on corporate worship in Hebrews written for Dr. Hinson's seminar on "Spirituality in Early Christian History" was the starting point from which this work has ultimately developed.

Numerous friends and colleagues have endured listening to my first attempts to express my insights as well as the excitement of those discoveries. Their patience is duly and gratefully noted. The many friends and family members who have encouraged me along the way are indeed a "cloud of witnesses," too numerous to list, to whom I remain forever grateful.

Darrell J. Pursiful

Louisville, Kentucky
Holy Week, 1993

Chapter 1

INTRODUCTION

Although many consign it to the non-working section of the New Testament canon, the book of Hebrews continues to inspire and challenge those who make the effort to engage it. Its distinctive theology, its careful argumentation, and its creative appropriation of Old Testament texts combine to make the interpretation of Hebrews a stimulating project for the most accomplished exegete. Even so, the most uncritical reader cannot help but catch something of the richness of the author's symbolism and the triumph of his rhetorical skill.

The author does not merely write; in truth he[1] preaches to us across the centuries about the sacrifice of our exalted High Priest and about how our lives should be different, better, because of Jesus. The depth and intricacy of his argument cannot be denied. At places it does not submit itself to overly rigorous canons of logic. It will lend itself to intellectual analysis; but, like a powerful, evocative sermon, sometimes it can only be experienced. The subject of this study is the spiritual wisdom of this unknown preacher and the intellectual grounding on which he expounds it. Specifically, we shall endeavor to describe the imagery in which the author of Hebrews makes his appeal to Christian commitment.

Purpose of the Study

Hebrews is in some ways one of the most anti-ritualistic books in the New Testament. Even so, the author's argument from first to last takes on a decidedly

---

[1] That the author was male is a conjecture based on the presence of the masculine participle διηγούμενον in 11:32.

ritualistic flavor. The purpose of this study will be to examine the spirituality of the book of Hebrews as it is expressed in the language of cultus and ritual. While others have dealt in great detail with the cultic symbolism of Hebrews, their focus has usually been on the theology of the book. Those who have explored the spirituality or "worship" of Hebrews have done so in only a limited fashion.

That the book of Hebrews has much to say on the subject of Christian worship has been widely acknowledged in the twentieth century. In his 1957 dissertation, Taylor states that

> The Epistle to the Hebrews provides one of the outstanding opportunities for a study of the meaning of worship. Throughout the book the effort of the writer to persuade the people concerning the value of Christ is undergirded by a consistent effort to explain his position and to support it by means of proper worship.[2]

This position is echoed from various and diverse quarters. Peterson asserts (perhaps a bit too enthusiastically) that "the theme of worship is clearly central" to Hebrews.[3] Galley suggests that Hebrews may provide insights into a unique conceptualization of Christian worship in relation to the book's reflections on the Old Testament cultus:

> The (peculiar to Hebrews) manner of examining the Old Testament priestly and sacrificial cultus as a foreshadowing of the Christ event means for our investigation that the author had a distinctive sense of worshipful event. Thence it precipitates nothing short of the question as to how he then understands Christian worship.[4]

Citations such as these could easily be multiplied, but whereas numerous scholars agree that worship is a (if not the) key emphasis in Hebrews most content themselves with vague statements of the matter and make no effort toward clarifying or describing worship as it is conceptualized or even toward defining the troublesome word "worship."

The most thorough treatments of worship in Hebrews are very brief.

---

[2]Charles Duey Taylor, "A Comparative Study of the Concept of Worship in Colossians and Hebrews" (Th.D. dissertation, The Southern Baptist Theological Seminary, 1957), pp. 1-2.

[3]David Peterson, "Towards a New Testament Theology of Worship," *Reformed Theological Review*, 43 (1984), 65.

[4]Hans-Detlof Galley, "Der Hebräerbrief und der christliche Gottesdienst," *Jahrbuch für Liturgik und Hymnologie*, 31 (1987-1988), 75. Translations from German, French, and Spanish works are the author's unless otherwise noted.

Taylor's dissertation referred to above deals more with the question of the *object* of worship (Christ, not angels) than with the broader question of how worship is conceived.[5] Galley's twelve-page article does little more than set the stage for a description of corporate worship in Hebrews in eschatological terms. The deeper and more intriguing matters of cultic reflection and the Christian life *in toto* as an act of worship are largely neglected.

We propose, then, to examine in detail the cultic motifs in Hebrews as they shed light on the spirituality therein expressed.[6] A number of concerns have been raised by the research of others into this area, which will guide the direction of this research. First, most who express an opinion on the subject indicate that there is an eschatological dimension to the conceptualization of worship in Hebrews. Second, the question must be raised as to the motif of heavenly cultus in Hebrews as it may or may not relate to spirituality on earth. Third, it must be noted that the issue of sacramentalism in Hebrews would be a book in itself and will be at best a side issue in this study.

The plan of this study will be primarily exegetical, with attention to the relevant passages of Hebrews studied in a historical-critical fashion, and taking cues where possible from both the phenomenology of religion and the academic study of spirituality. In order to set the teachings of Hebrews in their proper intellectual and religious perspective, attention will also be paid to relevant contemporary literature.

Through the process of this study, it is hoped that a contribution might be made to several aspects of the discussion of Hebrews. First there is the area of describing and classifying the spirituality expressed in Hebrews. Spirituality is an area of increasing interest in the scholarly study of religion; and it is an area in which much is still left to do, especially in the realm of biblical spirituality. A few works from various quarters have begun to examine the spirituality of the Bible

---

[5]In a 151-page dissertation, Taylor does not begin to discuss "common ideas in worship" between Colossians and Hebrews until page 115. Most of the foregoing pages are devoted to discussions of religion in Asia Minor and key features of the so-called "Colossian heresy."

[6]The term "motif" is used loosely throughout this study to signify the broad cluster of themes in Hebrews that touch on the matter of cultus. For a more exact treatment of literary motifs, see William Freedman, "The Literary Motif: A Definition and Evaluation," *Novel*, 4 (1971), 123-131.

4

itself rather than just the spiritual classics of later centuries,[7] but there is much work yet to be done. An examination of the cultic motif in Hebrews promises fruitful insights into the spirituality of Hebrews as a whole. We shall, in fact, argue that the depiction of spirituality in Hebrews is cultic through and through and that the author's usage of cultic imagery is in fact central to his pastoral goals.

Beyond the immediate concern of spirituality, this study may contribute in general to the understanding of Hebrews. This is particularly the case with regard to the author's cultic mode of argumentation. Since any spirituality must rest upon theological and/or philosophical assumptions, these must be part of this study's concern. Attention will thus be given to understanding the internal logic of the author's cultic depiction of spiritual realities. Due attention will thus be paid to the cultic depiction of Christ and his saving work as over against the ritual system of Judaism.

Finally we shall from time to time offer suggestions toward reuniting what in scholarly study of Hebrews has too often been separated, i.e., the motif of "pilgrimage," most closely associated with the work of Ernst Käsemann[8] and centering in the paraenetic sections of Hebrews, as opposed to the reflection on "cultus" most clearly seen in the central expository section of the book, 8:1-10:18. Johnsson has described this bifurcation and notes that for many scholars the unspoken assumption is that either (timeless, eternal) cult or Käsemann's (futuristic, eschatological) wandering people of God motif must be central to the understanding of the book.[9] A preliminary study suggests that the author may understand cultus as itself a kind of participation in eschatological realities. This may in fact be what Dukes perceives with reference to the "sacramental" principle in

---

[7]The *Message of Biblical Spirituality* series edited by Carolyn Osiek is the most thorough attempt to date. A small handful of dissertations on the topic of biblical spirituality have also begun to appear in the past two decades, among them Sandra Marie Schneiders, "The Johannine Resurrection Narrative: An Exegetical and Theological Study of John 20 as a Synthesis of Johannine Spirituality," 2 vols. (S.T.D. dissertation, Pontificia Universitas Gregoriana, 1975); and Mitzi Lynn Minor, "The Spirituality of the Gospel of Mark" (Ph.D. dissertation, The Southern Baptist Theological Seminary, 1989).

[8]Ernst Käsemann, *The Wandering People of God*, trans. Roy A. Harrisville and Irving L. Sandberg (Minneapolis: Augsburg, 1984).

[9]William G. Johnsson, "The Cultus of Hebrews in Twentieth-Century Scholarship," *Expository Times*, 89 (1978), 105.

the eschatology of Hebrews.[10]

A Survey of Research into the
Spirituality of Hebrews

The most recent contribution to the study of the spirituality of Hebrews is found in McDonnell's *The Catholic Epistles and Hebrews*.[11] It is a good, albeit brief, synthesis of various strands of spiritual reflection from Hebrews; but McDonnell's tendency is to jump to modern applications before laying a firm exegetical foundation. A more thorough undertaking is the collection of articles in Pitts' *The Way of Faith*.[12] This intentionally diverse collection of sermons and essays is a bit uneven in quality and focus, but it at least deals with most of the major passages of Hebrews with a degree of exegetical rigor. Few other works set out specifically to understand the spiritual teaching of Hebrews, but many studies have contributed incidentally to that endeavor.[13] A few of these are worthy of mention.

The Pilgrimage Motif

Many works which have contributed to understanding the spirituality of Hebrews have drawn on Käsemann's *The Wandering People of God*. In particular, Barrett's study of the eschatology of Hebrews makes reference to "the

---

[10]James Graydon Dukes, "Eschatology in the Epistle to the Hebrews" (Th.D. dissertation, The Southern Baptist Theological Seminary, 1956), pp. 132-139. By "sacramentalism," Dukes means the sacrificial act of Jesus as high priest. He sees this act as the means of integrating the temporal concepts of eschatology in Hebrews (i.e., the present age and the age to come) with the spatial concepts (i.e., the earthly and heavenly realms).

[11]Rea McDonnell, *The Catholic Epistles and Hebrews*, Message of Biblical Spirituality 14 (Wilmington: Glazier, 1986).

[12]James M. Pitts, ed, *The Way of Faith* (Wake Forest: Chanticleer, 1985).

[13]On the pastoral intent of the author, see especially Otto Kuss, "Der Verfasser des Hebräerbriefes als Seelsorger," in *Auslegung und Verkündigung*, vol. 1 (Regensburg: Friedrich Pustet, 1963); and Gaspar Mora, *La Carta a los Hebreos como escrito pastoral* (Barcelona: Herder, 1974).

pilgrim's progress" as an eschatological theme.[14] A treatment of this theme takes up a significant part of Spicq's introduction to the theology of Hebrews.[15] Johnsson has more carefully defined the concept of pilgrimage in a 1978 study and finds that the phenomenological elements of Muslim pilgrimage are also to be found in the book of Hebrews.[16]

Jewett's *Letter to Pilgrims* is also worthy of mention.[17] It is unfortunate that Jewett applies audience criticism to Hebrews in the highly circular way that he does. His central thesis, that the book was written against angel-worshiping heretics in the Lycus Valley, is unconvincing. Jewett does, however, offer some striking insights into the message of Hebrews for present-day Christians' pilgrimage through a threatening, secular world.

In Brown's treatment of the spiritual life in Hebrews he operates exclusively under the rubric of pilgrimage.[18] Even in discussing passages with obvious cultic overtones, Brown notes only the author's emphasis on the Christian life as a journey. While the pilgrimage motif in Hebrews cannot be denied, it is not the exclusive matrix within which to understand the book.[19]

The Cultic Motif

While this pilgrimage imagery has received a great proportion of the effort and interest in describing the spirituality of Hebrews, the cultic motif has not been

---

[14]C. K. Barrett, "The Eschatology of the Epistle to the Hebrews," in *The Background of the New Testament and Its Eschatology*, ed. D. Daube and W. D. Davies (Cambridge: University Press, 1956).

[15]Ceslaus Spicq, *L'Épitre aux Hébreux*, vol. 1 (Paris: Gabalda, 1952), pp. 269-280.

[16]William G. Johnsson, "The Pilgrimage Motif in the Book of Hebrews," *JBL*, 97 (1978), 239-251.

[17]Robert Jewett, *Letter to Pilgrims* (New York: Pilgrim, 1981).

[18]Raymond Brown, "Pilgrimage in Faith: The Christian Life in Hebrews," *Southwestern Journal of Theology*, 28 (1985), 28-35.

[19]L. D. Hurst, *The Epistle to the Hebrews*, SNTSMS 65 (Cambridge: University Press, 1990), p. 99, in fact suggests that the author of Hebrews is not nearly as interested in the themes of pilgrimage and homelessness as is often assumed.

entirely neglected. Spicq only devotes four pages to the cultic dimensions of the people of God, but therein he makes the important observation that:

> the image of nomadism is insufficient for designating the Christian life. It is necessary to make it more precise through the liturgical metaphor of the approach to God. If faith makes one advance, it is the cultus that permits the faithful to attain to God, or rather it does not deal only with proceeding and progressing spiritually, but religiously.[20]

One must still ask, of course, whether this "cultus" is to be understood in literal or metaphorical terms, and what relationship it has to spirituality. The case can be made in any event that the author to the Hebrews conceives of the people of God in cultic terms. López Fernández observes that the "wanderings" of believers on earth are always expressed in Hebrews in cultic images.[21] Furthermore, these images describe believers as priests who have received a kind of priestly anointing which allows them to render cultic service to God.[22] Williamson has also suggested a priestly identity for believers in Hebrews in his article on the background of Hebrews by drawing on Merkavah mysticism as a possible history-of-religions current behind the book.[23]

A word must also be offered about Johnsson's study of the cultic imagery of defilement and purgation in Hebrews.[24] Johnsson applies a phenomenological methodology to these concepts in order to understand better their specifically *religious* significance. While Johnsson touches on the matter of cultus, his concern is more narrowly focused on the language of blood and sacrifice as it is developed in chapters 9 and 10 of Hebrews. Johnsson has contributed greatly to Hebrews

---

[20]Spicq, *Hébreux*, vol. 1, p. 280.

[21]Enrique López Fernández, "Sacerdocio ministerial y eucaristía en la Carta a los Hebreos," *Studium Ovetense*, 5 (1977), 107. This would, of course, give support to Johnsson's more systematic understanding of what "pilgrimage" means.

[22]Ibid., p. 108.

[23]Ronald Williamson, "The Background of the Epistle to the Hebrews," *The Expository Times*, 87 (1975-1976), 232-237. The suggestion of a Merkavah background was first made by Hans-Martin Schenke, "Erwägungen zum Rätsel des Hebräerbriefes," in *Neues Testament und christliche Existenz*, ed. Hans Dieter Betz and Luise Schottroff (Tübingen: Mohr, 1973).

[24]William G. Johnsson, "Defilement and Purgation in the Book of Hebrews" (Ph.D. dissertation, Vanderbilt University, 1973).

research by demonstrating that the language and thought patterns of the author to the Hebrews are "religious" before they are "theological."

Two further matters often present themselves in the discussion of the cultic motif of Hebrews. One issue is that of Hebrews' depiction of a heavenly cultus and the other is the issue of sacramentalism.

The heavenly cultus in Hebrews has been explored in a number of studies, but with limited application to the spirituality of the book. Dibelius' essay on the heavenly cultus in Hebrews actually deals more with the "perfection" of Christ as a kind of consecration or ordination which is then passed on to believers.[25] Peterson's *Hebrews and Perfection*[26] largely refutes Dibelius' position, but the possibility remains that the perfection of believers has something to do with readiness to render fitting worship to God. Cody's *Heavenly Sanctuary and Liturgy in the Epistle to the Hebrews*[27] remains a valuable resource in setting out the basic parameters of this motif, especially his chapter on the thematic background. Unfortunately, Cody's treatment of the heavenly liturgy is limited to Christ's expiatory liturgy and does not clarify the nature of the liturgy of praise of the angels and saints described for example in 1:5-13 and 12:22-24. The precise relationship between the cultic activities of Christ, angels, and human believers is thus neglected. MacRae has explored the heavenly temple speculation in Hebrews as it relates to the book's eschatology, concluding that the perceived tensions in the eschatological presentation reflect a difference between the presuppositions of the author and his audience.[28]

In general, scholars who see in Hebrews a strong sacramental emphasis are more likely to posit a relationship between earthly and heavenly cultus. For example, Crichton, who argues that New Testament worship in general is

---

[25]Martin Dibelius, "Der himmlische Kultus nach dem Hebräerbrief," *Botschaft und Geschichte*, vol. 2 (Tübingen: Mohr, 1956).

[26]David Peterson, *Hebrews and Perfection* (Cambridge: University Press, 1982).

[27]Aelred Cody, *Heavenly Sanctuary and Liturgy in the Epistle to the Hebrews* (St. Meinrad, IN: Grail, 1960).

[28]George W. MacRae, "Heavenly Temple and Eschatology in the Letter to the Hebrews," *Semeia*, 12 (1978), 179-199.

eschatologically focussed, states of Hebrews that the earthly liturgy is "but the counterpart" of the heavenly.[29] When Williamson argues against the sacramental view of Hebrews, he betrays the close connection between sacramentalism and eschatology by dismissing both in a single sentence:

> In this present life the bliss of glory is still an object of faith and hope, though by faith the throne of grace may be approached even here; but there is no suggestion anywhere in the epistle [to the Hebrews] that at regular intervals, in eucharistic worship, the believer anticipates on earth what will be his fully only in heaven.[30]

It seems that Williamson has here confused the question of the eucharist in Hebrews with that of an eschatological focus in worship generally. In truth, the issue of sacramentalism in Hebrews remains unsettled, and may never be settled. In opposition to Williamson's contention that Hebrews may in fact be the most anti-sacramental book in the New Testament, others, notably Roman Catholic Scholars, argue for a profound sacramentality in the book.[31]   In any case, such considerations are secondary to this proposal. Following Moule, our working hypothesis regarding the eucharist in Hebrews is that specific allusions are "uncertain and at best scanty."[32] We must therefore content ourselves with the question of worship in general.

Definition of Key Terms

Words like ritual, cultus, worship, and spirituality imply different things to

---

[29]J. D. Crichton, "A Theology of Worship," in *The Study of Liturgy*, ed. Cheslyn Jones, Geoffrey Wainwright, and Edward Yarnold (New York: Oxford, 1978), p. 17.

[30]Ronald Williamson, "The Eucharist and the Epistle to the Hebrews," *NTS*, 21 (1975), 310.

[31]For example, Paul Andriessen, "L'Eucharistie dans l'Epître aux Hébreux," *Nouvelle Revue Théologique*, 94 (1972), 269-277, and James Swetnam, "Christology and the Eucharist in the Epistle to the Hebrews," *Biblica*, 70 (1989), 74-95. Søren Ruager's claim ("'Wir haben einen Altar' [Heb 13.10]: Einige Überlegungen zum Thema: Gottesdienst/Abendmahl im Hebräerbrief," *Kerygma und Dogma*, 36 [1990], 72-77) that the Lord's Supper in Hebrews can be understood in terms of an Old Testament communal meal may represent something of a *via media* between the two extremes.

[32]C. F. D. Moule, *Worship in the New Testament* (Richmond: John Knox, 1961), p. 39.

different people. Ritual may mean empty formalism to one and meaningful symbolic action to another. One person may think of spirituality as a synonym for the devotional life while someone else understands by the term weird, mystical speculations. At the outset, therefore, we must address the problem of definitions.

Ritual

There are likely as many definitions of ritual as there are anthropologists.[33] Those definitions which carry a disparaging connotation, for example, that ritual is a kind of irrational or even neurotic behavior,[34] are summarily dismissed. Since the author of Hebrews chose to describe the work of Christ in ritualistic terms, our presupposition is that he held in some sense a favorable regard for the category of ritual.

Zuesse provides a more positive, or at least value-neutral, assessment of ritual: "For our purposes, we shall understand as 'ritual' those conscious and voluntary, repetitive and stylized symbolic bodily actions that are centered on cosmic structures and/or sacred presences."[35] Under the rubric of "bodily actions" Zuesse also includes such verbal behavior as chant, song, and prayer. Underhill sees ritual as having to do with the social and sensory embodiment of humanity's response to the divine.[36] For her a religious ritual is "an agreed pattern of ceremonial movements, sounds, and verbal formulas, creating a framework within which corporate religious action can take place."[37] This definition adds the necessary element of social or cultural norms. One can interpret a ritual in a

---

[33]Christopher Crocker, "Ritual and the Development of Social Structure: Liminality and Inversion," in *The Roots of Ritual*, ed. James Shaughnessy (Grand Rapids: Eerdmans, 1973), p. 49.

[34]As described, for example, by Edmund Leach, "Ritual," *International Encyclopedia of the Social Sciences*, vol. 13, ed. David L. Sills (New York: Macmillan, 1968), p. 521; and Evan M. Zuesse, "Ritual," *The Encyclopedia of Religion*, vol. 12, ed. Mircea Eliade (New York: Macmillan, 1987), p. 405.

[35]Zuesse, "Ritual," p. 405.

[36]Evelyn Underhill, *Worship* (New York: Harper, 1937), p. 20.

[37]Ibid., p. 32.

somewhat objective manner precisely because it is constructed out of raw material that culture supplies in the form of generally accepted myths and symbols.

This observation about the corporate aspect of ritual leads to the common assertion that ritual is a form of communication.[38] Ritual not only does something; it says something as well.[39] What a culture says about itself in ritual often represents the ideals to which the culture aspires and the most fundamental tenets of its collective faith.[40]

Though researchers produce various working definitions appropriate to their own particular interests, there is still a considerable amount of agreement on certain basic characteristics of ritual. Among these are that rituals express fundamental categories by which people attempt to understand and control their social existence, that they seek to deal with situations of transition and change, and that they are essentially about communication.[41]

For our purposes, ritual is understood to be any external, embodied religious expression that is prescribed or informed by cultural norms. A given religious expression may often be subdivided into numerous discrete acts. For example, the levitical Day of Atonement observance includes the dressing of the high priest, casting of lots, two distinct animal sacrifices, disposition of sacrificial blood, and so on. Lest it become confusing to discuss a ritual (singular) made up of various rituals (plural), the word "liturgy" will be employed where necessary to signify a collection of ritual acts that occur as part of the same ritual observance.

Cultus

Cult and cultus are used with no discernable difference in the literature

---

[38]Leach, "Ritual," pp. 523-526; Edward Fischer, "Ritual as Communication," in *The Roots of Ritual*, ed. James Shaughnessy (Grand Rapids: Eerdmans, 1973).

[39]Crocker, "Ritual and the Development," p. 47, suggests that ritual is "a statement in metaphoric terms about the paradoxes of human existence."

[40]According to Jonathan Z. Smith, *Imagining Religion* (Chicago: University Press, 1982), p. 63, ritual is "a means of performing the way things ought to be in conscious tension to the way things are in such a way that this ritualized perfection is recollected in the ordinary, uncontrolled, course of things."

[41]Crocker, "Ritual and the Development," p. 49.

surrounding ancient Jewish religious practices in general and Hebrews in particular. The terms are combined in the adjectival form "cultic."[42] Mowinckel defines cultus as the visible, socially established and regulated forms that are conducive to communal religious experience.[43] Interaction with the divine is an important element in the definitions of both Mowinckel and Underhill. Underhill in fact places a premium on worship, ritual, and cultus as response to and acknowledgement of the Transcendent. According to her, the means available by which humans may respond to the Spirit are ritual, symbol, sacrament, and sacrifice. However they are combined, these four categories are the chief elements of cultus, which is "the agreed embodiments of [God's] worship."[44] This definition suggests that cultus is a broader concept of which ritual is one part. We suggest that cultus be defined as a system of visible and culturally established religious acts or symbols conceived as a coherent whole. One may thus speak, for example, of the ancient Israelite cultus made up of various discrete elements (priesthood, temple, sacrifices, dietary laws, sabbath observance, and so forth), some of which may be called rituals.

Worship

According to *Webster's Third New International Dictionary*, worship may be defined as

> ... the reverence or veneration tendered a divine being or supernatural power; *also*: an act, process, or instance of expressing such veneration by performing or taking part in religious exercises or ritual ...[45]

Following such a definition, worship is very close to what is commonly called "spirituality." In fact, many who have written on "worship" in Hebrews are quick to remind us that the term carries with it connotations that move beyond the

---

[42]In this study the adjectives "cultic" and "ritualistic" are used synonymously.

[43]Sigmund Mowinckel, *Religion und Kultus* (Göttingen: Vandenhoeck & Ruprecht, 1953), p. 13.

[44]Underhill, *Worship*, p. 20.

[45]Philip Babcock Grove, et al., eds., *Webster's Third New International Dictionary* (Springfield, MA: Merriam, 1976), p. 2637.

activities of Christians gathered on the first day of the week.[46]

Many in fact use the word "worship" to indicate the whole of a person's devotional life. For Underhill, worship is "the response of the creature to the eternal."[47] According to McElrath and Leonard, worship is above all "a response to the gracious initiative of a loving and merciful God."[48] Conceived broadly, worship encompasses the entire faith commitment of the believer.

Nevertheless, the definition of worship often slips subtly into the realm of Sunday morning activities. As but one example, a recent issue of *Review and Expositor* took up the theme of worship. In his preface to the issue Culpepper defined worship as "our response to God's self-disclosure that gives order to our lives."[49] Other contributors described worship in similar terms.[50] Even so, most if not all the articles in the issue dealt with matters of liturgical practice and philosophy. Thus at one end of the spectrum worship can be practically synonymous with spirituality while at the other it more closely resembles what we have described as cultus or ritual. We conclude that "worship" is generally too slippery a term to use with great precision in this investigation. The word will thus be used sparingly, and where necessary it will be qualified with adjectives such as "corporate" or "interior" so as not to confound the reader.

Spirituality

The definition of spirituality is closely tied with the methodological question of how to study it. The discussion of methodology will be the subject of the following chapter. In general, we may say here that spirituality is defined in broad terms to include all that has to do with giving expression to one's commitment to

---

[46]David Peterson in "Theology of Worship" emphatically concludes that the attitude of the heart and the activities of a committed Christian lifestyle are an integral part of what the New Testament (and Hebrews in particular) means by the word "worship."

[47]Underhill, *Worship*, p. 3.

[48]Hugh T. McElrath and Bill J. Leonard, "Spirituality and Worship," in *Becoming Christian*, ed. Bill J. Leonard (Louisville: Westminster/John Knox, 1990), p. 47.

[49]R. Alan Culpepper, "Editorial Introduction," *RevExp*, 85 (1988), 5.

[50]For example, Paul A. Richardson, "The Primacy of Worship," *RevExp*, 85 (1988), 10.

God. By this definition we thus reveal our grounding in and favorable assessment of the theistic traditions of the West. While acknowledging that there are other religious traditions for which this definition is unsuitable, our concern in Hebrews is with a particular expression of a particular theistic religion. A broader definition would add nothing to our discussion and in fact would tend to confuse matters unnecessarily. Underhill's discussion of "worship" offers what would seem to be a good definition of theistic spirituality: "Thus worship will include all those dispositions and deeds which adoration wakes up in us, all the responses of the soul to the Uncreated, all the Godward activities of man."[51]

Overview of the Study

The methodological questions involved in this study will be the focus of the following chapter. These questions involve the nature of the study of spirituality in general as well as matters of introduction with respect to the book of Hebrews itself.

The following three chapters will focus on the various cultic systems in the book of Hebrews. In chapter three we shall examine the foundations of the author's cultic thought as they are depicted in the ritual performances of Jesus and of the levitical priests. The subject of chapter four will be the cultus of the angels and righteous dead. Finally, the Christian life on earth as expressed in cultic terms will occupy our attention in chapter five.

In chapter six we shall summarize the conclusions of this study and offer some suggestions as to their modern relevance to Christian spirituality.

---

[51]Underhill, *Worship*, p. 9.

Chapter 2

METHODOLOGICAL CONSIDERATIONS

The methodological questions for this study may be conveniently described under two broad headings. First, we intend to approach Hebrews from a particular vantage point: the academic study of spirituality. It is therefore necessary to describe some of the presuppositions underlying what is meant by such a study. Spirituality as an academic discipline is currently in the middle of an awkward adolescence in which questions of definition and methodology have not yet been answered in ways that will be agreed upon by all researchers in the field. The methodology proposed for this study remains primarily exegetical in nature while acknowledging the benefits to be gained from the contributions of those in other fields. This is particularly true in the formulation of a method for the study of cultus in general which must necessarily be an aspect of our investigation.

Second, given our focus on a particular biblical document, it is necessary to state from the outset some of the critical conclusions about that document which will inform the exegesis. The text known as "To the Hebrews" presents its own unique set of problems to those interested in matters traditionally called "questions of introduction." These questions are not unimportant, but whatever answers arise in the course of investigation must be understood to be partial and speculative solutions.

The Study of Spirituality

The concern of this study is to describe and clarify the spirituality of the book of Hebrews as that spirituality is expressed in cultic language. The tools, methods, and assumptions which have arisen in the past thirty years for the study of spirituality should provide a constructive framework in which to explore and describe the cultic motif in Hebrews.

A Brief History of the Discipline

As an academic discipline, spirituality is very much a newcomer. Schneiders traces the beginnings of modern research in spirituality to the late 1950's.[1] As a new science, spirituality has developed over time as have other new sciences. Schneiders describes a three-stage process in the development of a new science. In the first stage individual researchers deal with particular problems of interest to them, but without the necessary language and categories which would make their work truly accessible to a wider audience.

In the second stage of development, individual researchers begin trying to put the results of their research in common by means of discussion, intra-disciplinary publication, common practice, and the beginning of the effort to initiate new students into the field. The activity of this stage reveals the need for "definitions, common methodology, and common vocabulary which is eventually recognized as the need for generalized theory."[2] In 1975, this stage was where Schneiders located the scientific study of spirituality;[3] and, though progress has been made, the new science has not yet developed a widely accepted theoretical framework, which would be the threshold into the third and final stage of development.

Spirituality as an academic discipline has experienced rapid growth over the past thirty years. The power and direction of the discipline are demonstrated by two important indicators.[4] The first of these is the great proliferation of courses and programs in spirituality now available and the number of graduates of these

---

[1]Sandra Marie Schneiders, "The Johannine Resurrection Narrative," vol. 1 (S.T.D. dissertation, Pontificia Universitas Gregoriana, 1975), p. xvii.

[2]Ibid.

[3]Ibid., p. xxi.

[4]Sandra M. Schneiders, "Spirituality in the Academy," in *Modern Christian Spirituality*, AARSR 62 (Atlanta: Scholars, 1990), p. 19.

programs being invited to teach in their area of specialization. The second indicator is the increasing number of publications devoted to some aspect of spirituality. Among these publications are a growing number of research tools.[5]

Despite ongoing debates regarding the nature and methods of the study of spirituality, the momentum of the discipline within academia shows no signs of waning. Whatever the future may hold for the discipline, the present, if somewhat confused, is also very exciting.[6]

The Object of the Study
of Spirituality

The problems researchers encounter in attempting to define spirituality are corollary to the more basic question of the object of study. Once the subject matter is clearly defined, reasonable progress toward a generally agreeable definition can be made. Schneiders has defined the object of the study of spirituality as "spiritual experience as such,"[7] using the expression "spiritual experience" to indicate that the subject matter transcends the purely religious experience in the technical sense of the term to embrace non-religious and even anti-religious kinds of experience.[8] In her dissertation, Schneiders did use the term "religious experience" to describe the object of spirituality as a discipline,[9] and for our purposes this designation will prove sufficient.

Most researchers acknowledge the experiential dimension of what they mean by "spirituality." Principe posits three different but related levels of meaning for the term "spirituality," the first of these being the real or existential level, which

---

[5]Such as Gordon S. Wakefield, ed., *Westminster Dictionary of Christian Spirituality* (Philadelphia: Westminster, 1983); Cheslyn Jones, Geoffrey Wainwright, and Edward Yarnold, eds., *The Study of Spirituality* (Oxford: University Press, 1986); and the Crossroad *World Spirituality* series.

[6]Schneiders, "Spirituality in the Academy," p. 37.

[7]Ibid., p. 31.

[8]The term "spirituality" is, in fact, commonly used with adjectives like "feminist" and "Marxist" with no reference to the religious stances of persons so designated.

[9]Schneiders, "Johannine Resurrection Narrative," p. 622.

has to do with the lived quality of a person.[10] McGinn has defined Christian spirituality as "the lived experience of Christian belief in both its general and more specialized forms."[11]

The question naturally arises as to what should be included in an analysis of a particular spirituality. To call spirituality a type of experience would seem to preclude all phenomena independent of the individual person.[12] In fact these phenomena, including such things as religious structures, institutions, moral codes and liturgical rites, do enter into the investigation as the expressions of religious experience.[13] In the study of spirituality, one can deal only with what is expressed. Kinerk makes a great point of the nature of spirituality as something expressed in his article on methodology:

> First of all, a definition of spirituality for the purpose of study should limit the material to what is expressed. Nothing can be studied unless it is communicated in some way. . . . we can only examine what is expressed and yet we know that the expression is never exhaustive of the reality.[14]

Because spirituality, being a form of experience, is a purely subjective phenomenon, it can only be studied in and through its manifestations. As Schneiders concludes, it "must always attain its object indirectly by the analysis of the expressions of religious experience."[15]

A Methodology for the Study
of Cultic Spirituality

The study of spirituality has largely been developed to deal with the writings

---

[10]Walter Principe, "Toward Defining Spirituality," *Sciences religieuses/Studies in Religion*, 12 (1983), 135.

[11]Bernard McGinn, "Introduction," *Christian Spirituality*, vol. 1, ed. Bernard McGinn, John Meyendorf and Jean Leclerq, World Spirituality (New York: Crossroad, 1989), p. xv.

[12]Schneiders, "Johannine Resurrection Narrative," p. 623.

[13]Ibid.

[14]Edward Kinerk, "Toward a Method for the Study of Spirituality," *Review for Religious*, 40 (1981), p. 5.

[15]Schneiders, "Johannine Resurrection Narrative," p. 624.

of past spiritual directors such as Ignatius Loyola. [16] These "classics of spirituality" are written in the first person and directly address the issues of spiritual growth and experience. The question must therefore be asked as to how much direct knowledge we can have of the spirituality of Hebrews.

Two other New Testament traditions might be fruitfully compared and contrasted as a means of better understanding the task ahead. With the letters of Paul, the scholar deals directly with Paul's religious outlooks and concerns as well as the concerns and religious outlooks of the communities to which he writes. Pauline spirituality is thus generally acknowledged to be accessible to research without serious methodological problems. [17] On the other hand, in the gospels we have no direct information. The researcher must analyze how an evangelist tells the story of Jesus and infer the evangelist's basic outlook from that presentation. [18]

With Hebrews one encounters something of a hybrid. While the sermon is a direct address to a community with particular instructions regarding that community's spiritual life, the ambiguous nature of the background of Hebrews keeps us from getting a clear picture of the spirituality being expressed. In the case of the Gospel of Mark, Minor addressed the methodological problem through attention to the narrative mode of communication in which Mark presented his spirituality.[19] To study the spirituality of Hebrews, it will likewise be necessary to pay close attention to the author's habitual modes of expression. The most distinctive aspect of the author's mode of communication is his heavy reliance on the language of cultus. We therefore propose a method for the study of cultic spirituality which will take into account this particular aspect of the author's thought world.

The study of cultus. The early historians of religion tended to view cult as a symptom of religious degeneration. Now, however, it is generally agreed that "all

---

[16]Mitzi Lynn Minor, "The Spirituality of the Gospel of Mark" (Ph.D. dissertation, The Southern Baptist Theological Seminary, 1989), p. 21.

[17]Thomas Tobin, *The Spirituality of Paul*, Message of Biblical Spirituality 12 (Wilmington: Glazier, 1987) p. 13.

[18]Minor, "Spirituality of Mark," p. 18.

[19]Ibid., pp. 29-32.

religion finds expression in the cult as its principal means of expression."[20] Investigation into the ritual life of past and present cultures has been greatly advanced by phenomenology of religion. This approach has been applied to the language of defilement and purgation in Hebrews by Johnsson, who sees himself as essentially making explicit Westcott's methodology for dealing with the cultic language of Hebrews.[21]

Phenomenology of religion has its roots in Husserlian phenomenology, but has assumed a distinct character in exponents like Mircea Eliade, Joseph Kitagawa, and others. It is a comparative study of religious ideas and their manifestations which draws its material from the history of religions, but arranges these data "from a systematic rather than a historical point of view."[22] Otto Kaiser's essay on Old Testament exegesis warned against the danger of being misled by structural similarities such as phenomenology hopes to find, but even so he concludes that "there can be no doubt that the phenomenological approach offers definite assistance in constructing a bridge from a text belonging to the distant past to the living questions it reflects."[23]

The statements of Schneiders and others about a global perspective and anthropological (rather than theocentric) focus in the study of spirituality argue for a phenomenological approach to the subject. The principal characteristics of such a methodology are *epoche* and eidetic vision.[24] *Epoche* has to do with the attitude of the phenomenologist. It is "a deliberate mental 'bracketing' of the data under

---

[20]Helmer Ringgren and Åke V. Ström, *Religions of Mankind*, ed. J. C. G. Grieg, trans. Niels L. Jensen (Edinburgh: Oliver and Boyd, 1967), p. xxxvi.

[21]William G. Johnsson, "Defilement and Purgation in the Book of Hebrews," (Ph.D. dissertation, Vanderbilt University, 1973).

[22]Ringgren and Ström, *Religions*, p. xviii.

[23]Otto Kaiser and Werner Georg Kümmel, *Exegetical Method*, trans. E. V. N. Goetschius (New York: Seabury, 1963). The revised edition (1981) regretably deletes much of Kaiser's treatment of this matter.

[24]Johnsson, "Defilement," p. 98.

consideration so that questions of reality or truth are put aside."[25]   Thus the phenomenologist approaches the data with all seriousness and does not dismiss anything as "primitive" or "crude," as has often been done with the sacrificial imagery in Hebrews. The fundamental question for phenomenology is not "is this statement true?" but rather "why is it said in that particular way?"[26]

Eidetic vision involves the search for essences or "structures" which emerge from the data of religion. It is presupposed that careful examination yields coherent existential and religious patterns that show how human beings see themselves in relation to other people, to God, and to the cosmos.[27]

What, then, does such an approach to the study of cultus tell us? First, a study of cultic language must take into account the centrality of ritual in religious experience. Ringgren and Ström note this vital role of cult, observing that absence of cult most frequently produces a moral rigorism destructive of religious content.[28] In religion, cultus is often what brings humanity into contact with the transcendent, filling human existence with divine strength.[29]

Cultus has this effect because it taps into the mythic springs of a culture or group on an existential level.[30] Kerényi suggests that "ceremonial is the translation

---

[25]Ibid., p. 99.

[26]John N. Jonsson, conversation on October 2, 1991.

[27]Johnsson, "Defilement," p. 100.

[28]Ringgren and Ström, *Religions*, p. xxxvi.

[29]Ibid., p. xxxviii.

[30]The appropriateness of discussing biblical traditions in terms of the category of myth has been challenged by many. See, for example, Brevard S. Childs, *Myth and Reality in the Old Testament* (London: SCM, 1960); and John N. Oswalt, "A Myth Is a Myth Is a Myth: Toward a Working Definition," in *A Spectrum of Thought*, ed. Michael L. Peterson (Nashville: Parthenon, 1982). Nevertheless, the word is firmly entrenched in the technical vocabulary of ritual studies. We use the term in this study in the positive sense of a culturally significant story intended to reveal ultimate truths. Our defintion is thus closer to that suggested by William G. Doty, "Mythophiles' Dyscrasia: A Comprehensive Definition of Myth," *Journal of the American Academy of Religion*, 48 (1980), 531-562.

of a mythological value into an act."[31] Eliade has been a major figure in this mythopoeic conceptualization of ritual. He would, in fact, argue that every ritual has its divine model or archetype and that every ritual is in some way related to the myth of creation.[32] Through cultus, humans are able to reach back into the "sacred Time of myth" both to construct reality and to be freed from the weight of "dead Time," thus permitting a re-creation of the world.[33] Without necessarily agreeing that every ritual has a "mythic model" behind it, there are certainly mythic values conveyed in ritual. This mythic significance is what many researchers mean by the term "mythologem," which refers to "the participation within the enactment of the myth in ritual."[34] Such an enactment cultivates the experiential and religious dimension of human existence in both the participant and the community.[35]

The search for structures, however, must never detract from the individuality of distinct religious expressions. This concern has been a constant emphasis of phenomenologists of the so-called Scandinavian School, who have rejected dialectical and comparative approaches to religious phenomena out of "a compelling interest in the specific and the concrete."[36] Beyond whatever common patterns may be discerned in cultus, the particularity of the empirical evidence must be highlighted.

A ritual is a form of communication, but it is communication on a highly symbolic plane. While it may be argued that almost all human activity is in some sense symbolic, what sets ritual apart is that it underlines and makes emphatic its

---

[31]C. G. Jung and C. Kerényi, *Essays on a Science of Mythology* (Princeton: University Press, 1969), p. 10.

[32]Mircea Eliade, *Cosmos and History*, trans. Willard R. Trask (New York: Harper, 1959), pp. 21-23.

[33]Mircea Eliade, *Myth and Reality*, trans. Willard R. Trask (New York: Harper, 1963), p. 140.

[34]John N. Jonsson, *Worlds within Religion* (Louisville: Nilses, 1987), p. 23.

[35]Ibid.

[36]John N. Jonsson, "Reflection on Geo Widengren's Phenomenological Method: Towards a phenomenological hermeneutic of the Old Testament," *Scriptura*, 2 (1986), 28.

symbolic intention.[37]   The author to the Hebrews has provided a cultic "vocabulary" by which to understand Christian religious experience.   A phenomenological approach to the text may very well give us some insights into the "grammar" of his message.   Of course, this approach must never replace other tested methods of exegesis, but must consistently be corrected and shaped by what can be known of the text through historic, linguistic, literary, and other analyses.

An important question has to do with controlling the vast amount of data available for research. One management strategy is suggested by Grimes' *Research in Ritual Studies*.[38]   Grimes organizes the first section of his bibliography according to various components of ritual:

1.1 Action (movement, dance, performance, mime, music, rhythm, gesture, play, work)
1.2 Space (geography, environment, architecture, cosmology, shrines, sacred places)
1.3 Time (season, holiday, repetition, calendar)
1.4 Objects (masks, costumes, fetishes, icons, art)
1.5 Symbol, metaphor
1.6 Group (role, kinship, class, caste, family, hierarchy, ethnicity, acculturation)
1.7 Self (body, feeling, states of consciousness, gender)
1.8 Divine beings (gods, demons, spirits, animals, saints, ancestors)
1.9 Language (sound, song, poetry, word, story, myth)
1.10 Quality (e.g., color or shape), quantity, theme (e.g., evil)[39]

Of these components, only a few are actually relevant in a study of Hebrews. Action, particularly sacrificial action, is important in the development of the argument in Hebrews. Another key component is that of space, especially in terms of sanctuaries for the performance of the cultus and the cosmological (and axiological) distinctions made between heavenly and earthly realities. Given the importance of priesthood as a category for Hebrews, the group component (including considerations such as class and hierarchy) becomes primary. For purposes of this study Grimes' categories of group, self, and divine beings may be taken together as the various performers or celebrants of cultic acts. Other aspects

---

[37]Evan M. Zuesse, "Ritual," *The Encyclopedia of Religion*, vol. 12, ed. Mircea Eliade (New York: Macmillan, 1987), p. 406.

[38]Ronald L. Grimes, *Research in Ritual Studies* (Metuchen: Scarecrow, 1985).

[39]Ibid., pp. 1-2.

of cultus which are not as central as these three will receive only the most cursory treatment. The fuller implications of cultic studies for this study will be discussed after dealing more generally with the study of spirituality.

The study of spirituality. We have previously dealt with spirituality as a species of lived experience. Now our attention must focus on spirituality as an academic discipline intended to study that experience. Of course, not all aspects of this discipline will be germane to the present investigation. The subdivisions of spirituality "are as numerous as the aspects of religious experience multiplied by the number of religious traditions and historical periods in which that experience is realized."[40] Some subdivisions of spirituality would thus be history of spirituality, spiritual psychology, systematic spirituality, biblical spirituality, comparative spirituality, and pastoral spirituality.[41]

The focus of this study is in the area of biblical spirituality, and even this term may be used in a number of ways. Biblical spirituality may imply beginning with a problem in current spirituality and attempting to clarify or solve that problem by bringing to bear relevant biblical material. Others may take it to mean the use of Scripture in the spiritual life. Finally, biblical spirituality may signify the study of spirituality expressed in Scripture. Such studies might focus on the development of some theme over time or might simply study some particular part of the Bible.[42] This study falls under the last of these definitions of biblical spirituality and intends to study a particular biblical book, Hebrews, without attempting a systematic study of cultus as a theme in biblical spirituality in general.

Since spirituality is the study of outward manifestations of religious experience, one must ask as to what kinds of manifestations ought to be considered. A frequent tendency in early studies was to take a narrow view focussing on the practice and teachings of a spirituality about virtues and vices,

---

[40]Schneiders, "Johannine Resurrection Narrative," p. xxi.

[41]Ibid.

[42]Ibid., p. xxiii.

prayer, mystical experiences and the like.[43] In his *History of Christian Spirituality* Bouyer sought a wider perspective, insisting that spirituality must take account of the link between objects of faith and reactions aroused by those objects in the religious consciousness.[44] For Bouyer, therefore, one must at least refer to the belief systems of practitioners of a spirituality. Principe objects that Bouyer does not yet go far enough in his database and asks "whether any person's or group's spirituality--or the dynamics and causes of that spirituality--can be grasped without understanding that person or group in their total context."[45]

Principe thus calls for an even broader view of spirituality in which the total context of the individual or group must be examined. Not only theological and religious attitudes, but the whole gamut of psychological, historical, anthropological, sociological, philosophical, linguistic, and other influences must be taken into account because each of these shape one's spiritual ideal and one's response to that ideal.[46] For Schneiders as well, spirituality is a "field-encompassing field"[47] interested in all dimensions of human life and how they interrelate in the realm of religious experience.

In actuality, any particular study in the field of spirituality will employ only such aspects of this totality as are appropriate. Spirituality is multidisciplinary, but the disciplines one calls upon must be suitable for the manifestations to be considered.[48] The methodology followed in Schneiders' own dissertation may be broken down into three phases. She engaged first in an exegesis of the text, leading to theological reflection, and concluding in an interpretation of the

---

[43]Principe, "Toward Defining," p. 137.

[44]Louis Bouyer, *History of Christian Spirituality*, vol. 1 (London: Burns and Oates, 1960), pp. viii-ix.

[45]Principe, "Toward Defining," p. 138.

[46]Ibid.

[47]Schneiders, "Spirituality in the Academy," p. 32.

[48]Schneiders, "Johannine Resurrection Narrative," p. 624.

spirituality of the Fourth Evangelist.[49] Schneiders understood her task to be

> to *isolate* the central experience of Johannine spirituality in its experiential particularity as it is expressed in ch. 20; then to attempt to *discern* its organizing function in respect to the other major elements of his spirituality; and finally to *describe* the resultant constellation or moving equilibrium which constitutes Johannine spirituality.[50] (emphasis added)

Kinerk has provided some helpful methodological cues. Drawing on his definition of spirituality as "the expression of a dialectical personal growth from the inauthentic to the authentic,"[51] he suggests two basic questions for the analysis of a spirituality and two other questions dealing with comparison and contrast of different spiritualities. He also suggests three criteria for evaluation of a spirituality.

Of sole importance for this study are the two questions for analysis that Kinerk proposes. The first of these is: "what are the expressions of the authentic and inauthentic?"[52] That is, What is valued in this spirituality? What is rejected? The second question for analysis is: "what is the wisdom of a particular spirituality?"[53] By wisdom Kinerk means the special manner in which a spirituality proposes to respond to God. It is thus a question of techniques of encounter growing out of the lived experience of practitioners which in simplest terms might be expressed: what does one *do*? With this question, Kinerk brings us into contact with the practical side of spirituality research. This aspect may in fact be the one distinctive that separates spirituality from other types of religious studies. Hanson, for example, calls attention to the strongly existential relation to the subject matter common in spirituality studies.[54] The concern to grow in faith and the discernment in texts of encouragement and direction for that growth are therefore appropriate to

---

[49]Ibid., pp. xxvii-xxix.

[50]Ibid., pp. 633-634.

[51]Kinerk, "Toward a Method," p. 6.

[52]Ibid., p. 7.

[53]Ibid., p. 10.

[54]Bradley C. Hanson, "Spirituality as Spiritual Theology," in *Modern Christian Spirituality*, AARSR 62 (Atlanta: Scholars, 1990), pp. 49-50.

the discipline of spirituality and should be made explicit in its methodology.

Kinerk's work is of great importance in the methodology proposed for this study. In particular, there is much to be gained from an approach to the discipline which distinguishes spirituality not by the methods of research as such but by the questions one puts to the data. Kinerk's method will be augmented and critiqued by the contributions of others in the field as well as by the particular problems already discussed concerning an examination of the cultic motif in Hebrews generally.

The method proposed for this study. One may only study a spirituality through its concrete expressions. For Hebrews, the only expression available for examination is the text itself. In short, then, the method of this study will be an exegetical method intended to isolate relevant data and set it in an appropriate framework so as to draw out the spirituality of Hebrews as it is communicated in the language of cultus.

The first phase must therefore be the isolation and exegesis of relevant texts. A preliminary reading of Hebrews suggests four distinct cultuses which would be profitable to explore in terms of Christian spirituality. The first might be called the *Old Covenant Cultus*, that which has to do with the Aaronic priesthood, animal sacrifices, and an earthly sanctuary. This cultus is the springboard for the author's development of the better priesthood and sacrifice of Christ, and in many ways becomes a paradigm for inauthentic religion. The second important phase is the *Christ Cultus*, the priestly, cultically-conceived activities of Jesus Christ for the expiation of human sins. With the great emphasis on Jesus as the πρόδρομος and ἀρχηγός of Christians, his depiction in cultic terms will likely prove fruitful in discerning patterns of empowerment for believers.[55] These two constellations of cultic material are foundational to the author's understanding of cultus. As the cultic foundation of Hebrews, they will form a necessary background to the work which will follow.

Another important cultic movement occurs explicitly in only a few verses of Hebrews, but it is still important to this study. This motif may be called the

---

[55]The question of an "imitative" form of spirituality naturally arises. According to Johnsson, the idea of imitation is a minor aspect of the phenomenological "structure" of pilgrimage ("Defilement," pp. 408-409). The possibility of an *imitatio Christi* current in Hebrews' spirituality is at least worth exploring.

Heavenly Cultus, by which is meant the acts of worship that angels and deceased believers perform in the heavenly realm. The significance of this aspect for the spirituality of Hebrews becomes clear at 12:22: "But you have come to . . . the heavenly Jerusalem, and to myriads of angels in festive assembly."[56] In what sense may the pilgrim believers on earth be said to have come to an angelic celebration? Finally, of course, there is what may be called the *New Covenant Cultus*, including whatever acts or attitudes of devotion are enjoined upon Christian believers throughout the course of their earthly existence, to the extent that these are described in cultic terms.

This textual material is to be handled both phenomenologically and historico-critically. The phenomenological attitude of *epoche* is necessary to avoid any denigration of the cultus in Hebrews as "superstitious" or "primitive." The goal is to see how cultic language functions and discern why the author chose to express himself in these terms. An attempt must also be made to discern how the data of Hebrews in their particularity conform to and diverge from the broader religious "structures" of cultus. While phenomenological insights will be introduced where they shed light on the text, the primary focus of the exegesis will remain firmly grounded in historical-critical methods that pay close attention to the historical, textual, and linguistic concerns by which one may discern the particular message of Hebrews.

Once the exegesis of key texts has been completed, a reflective phase of the methodology will attempt to distill from the accumulated data the expressions of authentic and inauthentic spirituality that they communicate. Particular attention will be devoted to searching for any broad organizing forms which may be discerned in the author's presentation of the spiritual life, as well as the possibility of different stages of spiritual growth.[57]

On the basis of this reflection, the techniques of encounter growing out of the lived experience of the practitioners of this spirituality will be examined. We shall thus undertake, if only in a cursory fashion, to examine the contemporary relevance of Hebrews for the spiritual life.

---

[56]Unless otherwise noted, all New Testament quotations represent the author's translations.

[57]Kinerk, "Toward a Method," pp. 8-10.

This methodology conforms in general with the three-dimensional approach suggested by Schneiders for the study of spirituality.[58] The study will be in the first instance descriptive, in that the first priority will be to surface the relevant data through historical, textual, and comparative studies. It is also analytical or critical, in that it intends to explain and evaluate the collected data. Finally, the method proposed is synthetic and constructive to the extent that it leads to an appropriation of what is learned for the continuing spiritual tradition of the church.

Introduction to Hebrews

The book of Hebrews presents a challenge to modern exegetes that is unlike that of nearly any other part of the New Testament canon. Though he did not write anonymously or pseudonymously, the author remains unknown to us. Nor do we know for sure much about the conceptual world from which the book was written. Even the matters of destination, provenance, and date are elusive and open to widely divergent speculations. Before dealing with the methodology proposed for this study in detail, it is therefore necessary to address matters of introduction regarding Hebrews itself.

Authorship, Date, Provenance and Destination

Modern scholars have largely abandoned the attempt to name a specific New Testament personage as the author of Hebrews. This is to be commended on a number of counts. First of all, the available data are nowhere near enough to raise any such theory of authorship above the level of mere conjecture. The list of proposed authors to the Hebrews reads like a "Who's Who" of the New Testament world, including such figures as Paul, Apollos, Barnabas, Priscilla (with or without assistance from Aquila), Epaphras, Mary the mother of Jesus, and seemingly everyone else. That such a diverse collection of names can all be applied to the same document is evidence enough that more information is needed before the author might be so precisely identified.

Tabling the attempt to name the author is also to be commended because it has allowed the question of authorship to evolve into a much more fruitful exercise

---

[58]Schneiders, "Spirituality in the Academy," p. 35.

of describing as precisely as possible what can be known in general about the author. In this area a consensus does seem to be forming. Most would agree, for example, that the author was a well-educated Hellenistic Jew.[59] Many have noted the rhetorical skill of the writer, and presume that he was a highly educated person by Hellenistic standards, although few if any would agree with Spicq that we have here a philonian converted to Christianity. The author was obviously trained in the exegesis of the Greek Old Testament, from which he quotes exclusively and extensively. The great deal of attention paid to the levitical cultic system suggests that the author was someone with a deep personal interest in this aspect of Jewish life. One may conclude that he was a deeply religious man for whom, before his conversion, cultus as such was a central aspect of his spirituality.

The date of Hebrews remains uncertain. A rough *terminus a quo* would be around A.D. 60. The author writes to believers who had heard the gospel from others (2:3) and had been Christians themselves for some time (5:12). Furthermore, the first leaders of their congregation had already died (13:7--the outcome of their life is held up as an example to the audience). The *terminus ad quem* is apparently established by the use of Hebrews by *1 Clement*, but Attridge points out the difficulties in dating that document. The conventional date of *1 Clement* at 96 is based primarily on the assumption that the phrase "the sudden and repeated calamities and reverses which are befalling us" (1:1) is a reference to the persecution of Christians under Domitian. Attridge classifies the evidence for such an assumption as "extremely weak."[60] Some help in establishing an upper limit is provided in the mention of Timothy in 13:23. If this is the same Timothy mentioned in connection with Paul elsewhere in the New Testament, Hebrews must have been written during the lifetime of Paul's protégé: probably no later than the first decade of the second century.

The destruction of the Temple in Jerusalem has been suggested as a much earlier *terminus ad quem* for Hebrews. This proposal is made largely on the evidence that the author refers to cultic activity in the present tense (e.g., 8:3-5; 9:7-

---

[59]See, for example, Harold W. Attridge, *The Epistle to the Hebrews*, Hermeneia (Philadelphia: Fortress, 1989), p. 5, and William L. Lane, *Hebrews*, vol. 1, Word Biblical Commentary (Waco: Word, 1991), pp. xlvii-li.

[60]Attridge, *Hebrews*, p. 7.

8; 10:1-3). It must be noted, however, that throughout Hebrews the author speaks exclusively of the pentateuchal tabernacle, and never of the temple.[61] Furthermore, the use of similar "timeless" presents to describe the Temple can be found in Josephus (*Ant.* 4:224-257), Clement (*1 Clem.* 41:2), *Barnabas* (7-8), and the *Epistle to Diognetus* (3).[62] More will have to be said about the date of Hebrews, but first the question of the destination of the book will be addressed.

Where was the audience to which the author to the Hebrews wrote? The ambiguous phrase "those from Italy send you greetings" represents the totality of internal evidence on the matter of the book's destination. Although the phrase might be taken to mean that the author is in Italy and writing to a congregation elsewhere, it must be remembered that the only New Testament parallel to ἀπὸ τῆς Ἰταλίας (Acts 18:2) refers to people "from Italy" but now residing somewhere else.

To this evidence must be added the strands of literary and conceptual dependence in which Hebrews is intertwined. The book's connections to *1 Clement* have already been noted. Within the New Testament itself, the text most closely related to Hebrews is 1 Peter.[63] Both 1 Peter and *1 Clement* originated in Rome and bear a striking resemblance to Hebrews in concepts and imagery. Bruce enumerates certain verbal allusions to Hebrews from other first and second century Roman texts such as the *Shepherd of Hermas* (Vision 2.3.2.),[64] Justin Martyr (*First Apol.* 12:9; 63:5,10,14; *Dialogue* 116:1),[65] and Valentinus' *Gospel of Truth*

---

[61]Gerald L. Borchert, "A Superior Book: Hebrews," *RevExp*, 82 (1985), 324, notes that the book's primary motifs are all pre-Solomonic and non-temple: the patriarchs, Moses, the wilderness generation, etc.

[62]Lane, *Hebrews*, vol. 1, p. lxiii.

[63]Ceslaus Spicq, *L'Épître aux Hébreux*, vol. 1 (Paris: Gabalda, 1952), pp. 139-144, summarizes the parallels between 1 Peter and Hebrews.

[64]F. F. Bruce, *The Epistle to the Hebrews*, rev. ed., New International Commentary on the New Testament (Grand Rapids: Eerdmans, 1990), p. 100, n. 61; p. 262.

[65]Ibid., p. 24.

(Jung Codex 20:10).[66]

On the basis of this external evidence, the presupposition of this study will be that Hebrews is addressed to Rome, where it quickly became an important document in the religious thinking of Christians. Since the author desired to be "restored" very soon to his audience (13:19), we further conclude that the author was himself a member of the congregation in Rome, but separated from them for reasons unknown to us. As Lane has suggested, the Roman church was in all likelihood made up of independent house churches even relatively late in the first century.[67] This suggests a certain diversity and tendency toward independence within Roman Christianity, of which there is evidence in Hebrews. A congregation of Jewish Christians for whom the presentation of Jesus as the great High Priest and fulfillment of the levitical sacrifices is certainly possible in the city of Rome.

Some have interpreted certain cryptic comments within Hebrews to suggest a date in the 60's apart from any argument about the Temple. Most recently, Lane has advanced the theory that the reference to previous hardships in 10:32-34 is actually a description of the hardships Jewish Christians faced with the Edict of Claudius in A.D. 49.[68] If this assumption can be made, then it is not unreasonable to assume that the present crisis described in Hebrews may be related to the oncoming persecution under Nero. Such an assumption does justice to all the available evidence, but it cannot be pressed in this study.

To summarize, the critical assumptions underlying this study are that Hebrews was written by an educated Hellenistic Jew who was a member of a Jewish-Christian house church in Rome. The book was written to that house church because of the author's absence (whether through imprisonment, missionary travels or some other circumstance cannot be determined), most likely because word had gotten to him of the congregation's lackluster response to persecutions which had not yet reached the height of their severity. These persecutions may have been those instigated in the last years of Nero's reign.

---

[66]Ibid., p. 88, n. 86.

[67]Lane, *Hebrews*, vol. 1, pp. lix-lx.

[68]Ibid., pp. lxiii-lxvi.

Genre

The growing consensus among scholars is that Hebrews is a sermon. The author characterizes his work as a "word of exhortation" (13:22), and this phrase is also found in Acts 13:5 with reference to a synagogue address. Mora classifies Hebrews as a pastoral writing in the broadest sense, with which nearly all commentators would agree. [69] Underneath this umbrella term, scholars arrive at different conclusions about the exact nature of Hebrews: is it a letter,[70] a pastoral epistle to the whole church,[71] the earliest example of artistic Christian literature,[72] or a sermon or homily set to writing?[73]

Scholars are arriving at the conclusion that Hebrews is in fact a product of rhetorical art, designed primarily to be heard rather than read. Although Maxey has recently suggested that Hebrews 12:4-13 is in fact the elaboration of a *chreia*,[74] a position with implications for the genre of Hebrews in general, the view that Hebrews is in fact a Hellenistic sermon is predominant. Wills has argued for a particular genre of Hellenistic Jewish and early Christian sermon which he calls the "word of exhortation," borrowing the phrase from Hebrews 13:22 and Acts 13:5.[75] He finds examples of this rhetorical format in several early Hellenistic documents. These "words of exhortation" include (1) an indicative or exemplary section

---

[69]Gaspar Mora, *La Carta a los Hebreos como escrito pastoral* (Barcelona: Herder, 1974), p. 1, n. 1.

[70]Spicq, *Hébreux*, vol. 1, pp. 21-25.

[71]Martin Dibelius, "Der himmlische Kultus nach dem Hebräerbrief," in *Botschaft und Geschichte*, vol. 2 (Tübingen: Mohr, 1956.), p. 160.

[72]Adolf Deissmann, *Light from the Ancient East*, trans. Lionel R. M. Strachan (New York: Harper, 1927), pp. 243-244.

[73]Bruce, *Hebrews*, p. xlviii; Lane, *Hebrews*, vol. 1, pp. lxx-lxxi.

[74]Lee Zachary Maxey, "The Preacher as Rhetorician: The Rhetorical Structure and Design of Hebrews 12:4-13," Paper read at the Society of Biblical Literature Annual Meeting, November 24, 1991.

[75]Wills, Lawrence, "The Form of the Sermon in Hellenistic Judaism and Early Christianity," *Harvard Theological Review*, 77 (1984), 277-299.

consisting of either scripture quotations or authoritative examples (from the past or present) or a reasoned exposition of theological points, (2) a conclusion based on these *exempla*, indicating their significance to the addressees and often employing οὖν, διό, διὰ τοῦτο, or some other connector, and (3) an exhortation, usually expressed with an imperative or hortatory subjunctive and often accompanied by οὖν.

In general, one may speak of Hebrews as a sermon or homily. In this study the genre of Hebrews will not be pursued any more specifically. Whether or not Hebrews is, for example, a "word of exhortation" as defined by Wills or a "homiletic midrash" as Buchanan contends,[76] or any other subspecies of religious address, is beyond our concern. As with any master rhetorician, the author (or better, "the preacher") to the Hebrews expresses himself creatively, quite apart from any wooden slavishness to the rhetorical manuals or preaching conventions of his day.

To claim that Hebrews is a sermon sets it in the context of a worshipping community. This insight must be given its full weight in exegesis. Kuss has ably argued for the practical, pastoral inclination of Hebrews.[77] While admitting that this unknown writer belongs among the most significant theologians of the New Testament, Kuss is quick to point out that one of his most prominent characteristics is in fact that his basic attitude is chiefly pastoral.[78] He is not a theologian for theology's sake, but rather he brings his theological acumen to bear for the sake of the community for which he feels accountable in its particular time of crisis.[79] As Mora has expressed, Hebrews is not intended to be a theoretical discourse to be

---

[76]George Wesley Buchanan, *To the Hebrews*, The Anchor Bible (Garden City: Doubleday, 1981), p. xxi.

[77]Otto Kuss, "Der Verfasser des Hebräerbriefes als Seesorger" in *Auslegung und Verkündigung*, vol. 1 (Regensburg: Pustet, 1963).

[78]Ibid., p. 330.

[79]Ibid.

understood but rather a proclamation of the Christian message to be believed.[80] The matter of genre relates to the suitability of an investigation of the spirituality of Hebrews. By its very nature, a sermon is a pastoral exercise closely related to the issue of spiritual direction.

Religious-Intellectual Milieu

A discussion of the conceptual framework in which the author to the Hebrews undertook to compose his sermon should begin by a frank admission of the difficulties of the question. Thompson alerts us to the fact that "the thought world of Hebrews is . . . as difficult to disentangle as the literature of antiquity in general."[81] As with any great mind, the author culled concepts and attitudes from various traditions which he interpreted within his own world view.[82]

Some have sought the key to unlock the author's conceptual milieu in the Greek world. As Brown notes *vis-à-vis* the Fourth Gospel, what is of interest must be only what has come to the author without the mediation of Judaism, what is formative rather than what is purely a surface feature.[83] In addressing the question of the Hellenistic background(s) of Hebrews, one must first admit that all first-century Judaism was in fact hellenized.

Ernst Käsemann is perhaps the best known proponent of the view that the thought world of Hebrews has its roots in gnostic mythology. Käsemann's basic thesis was that the central motif of Hebrews, that of "the wandering people of God," can be understood as an aspect of gnostic thought about the spiritual journey to heaven. This view thus sees in Hebrews a depiction of Jesus in terms of the redeemed Redeemer myth. Käsemann has been rightly criticized on a number of points. First of all, his book deals with themes that are not specifically gnostic. Related to this criticism is the further observation that Käsemann often lacks clarity

---

[80]Mora, *Hebreos*, p. 1, n. 1.

[81]James W. Thompson, *The Beginnings of Christian Philosophy*, CBQMS 13 (Washington: Catholic Biblical Association of America, 1982), p. 154.

[82]The most comprehensive study to date on the background issues surrounding Hebrews is L. D. Hurst, *The Epistle to the Hebrews*, SNTSMS 65 (Cambridge: University Press, 1990).

[83]Raymond Brown, *The Gospel according to John*, vol. 1, The Anchor Bible (Garden City: Doubleday, 1966), p. lvi.

in identifying gnostic materials. It must be remembered that the first edition of *Das wanderende Gottesvolk* was published before the discovery of the Nag Hammadi documents. Käsemann includes much data from sources that simply are not gnostic (e.g., Philo and apocalyptic literature). Other interpreters have interpreted such motifs as "rest," "curtain," and "pilgrimage," in Hebrews without any reference to a supposed gnostic background.[84]

Another, better balanced, approach to the Greek background of Hebrews is provided by Thompson's *The Beginnings of Christian Philosophy*. Thompson emphasizes the role of Middle Platonism in the first century world in general and within this context seeks to point out the influences of this philosophical school in the argument of Hebrews. Thompson documents the wide influence of Middle Platonic thought in the first century and finds that this influence can account for the similarities that many have noted in Hebrews with Philo, Gnosticism, and Christian Platonism in that they all derived some of their thought and categories from Middle Platonism. Thompson sees Hebrews standing at the transition to Christian philosophical thought--at the turning from an apocalyptic world view to the metaphysical categories of the Greeks.[85] The appeal to Middle Platonism provides an interesting and somewhat convincing framework in which to understand Hebrews, but ultimately Thompson's thesis looks very much like the old, discredited philonic consensus (see below).[86] There is more to the picture of Hebrews' religious and intellectual milieu, and to supply the missing piece one must look to the book's Jewish roots.

The author's intimate acquaintance with Jewish tradition need not be questioned. Throughout the document he displays a knowledge of Jewish religion and thought, including familiarity with the Old Testament in its Greek translation, with the levitical sacrificial system, and with Jewish techniques of scriptural exposition. The author was a Jew, but what kind of Jew was he?

---

[84]For example, in C. K. Barrett, "The Eschatology of the Epistle to the Hebrews," in *The Background of the New Testament and Its Eschatology*, ed. D. Daube and W. D. Davies (Cambridge: University Press, 1956), such motifs are interpreted not in gnostic but in eschatological terms.

[85]Thompson, *Beginnings*, pp. 152-162.

[86]Such is the assessment of Hurst, *Hebrews*, p. 10.

Until approximately the mid-twentieth century something of a consensus had identified the author to the Hebrews with Philo of Alexandria and the highly assimilated, philosophically oriented Judaism of the Diaspora. The major proponent of this view is Spicq, whose two-volume commentary on Hebrews provides a virtual encyclopedia of supposed parallels to Philo. Sowers has written on the hermeneutics of Philo and the author of Hebrews.[87] After surveying the options he concludes that Philo is the best religio-historical material we have for Hebrews, pointing to a common septuagintal text, similar reflection on the Logos, and the same explanation of exegetical issues such as God's oath to Abraham. According to Sowers, while the author didn't allegorize, he did know the conclusions of the Alexandrian allegorists; and the traces of his interaction with them are evident.

Williamson has effectively refuted the theory of direct dependence on Philo.[88] In fact, according to Borchert he has closed the door on anything more than verbal similarity between Philo and Hebrews.[89] Thompson, however, claims that both Spicq and Williamson have exaggerated their positions. Attridge, while pointing out dissimilarities, agrees that there are "undeniable parallels,"[90] and concludes that the two are indebted at points to similar traditions of Greek-speaking and Greek-thinking Judaism.

Another major contender for pride of place in the constellation of background traditions is the intensely eschatological and sectarian Judaism of Qumran. An Essene connection to Hebrews has been argued by scholars such as Yadin and, more recently, Hughes.[91] Proponents of this view point to the

---

[87]Sidney G. Sowers, *The Hermeneutics of Philo and Hebrews*, Basel Studies of Faculty 1 (Richmond: John Knox, 1965).

[88]Ronald Williamson, *Philo and the Epistle to the Hebrews* (Leiden: Brill, 1970).

[89]Borchert, "Superior Book," p. 322.

[90]Attridge, *Hebrews*, p. 29.

[91]Yigael Yadin, The Dead Sea Scrolls and the Epistle to the Hebrews," *Scripta Hierosolymitana*, 4 (1958), 36-55; Philip Edgecombe Hughes, "The Epistle to the Hebrews," in *The New Testament and Its Modern Interpreters*, ed. Eldon Jay Epp and George W. MacRae

38

speculation in both Hebrews and the Dead Sea Scrolls on the divine world and its inhabitants, and on the eschatological agent or agents of God's intervention into human affairs. Here, too, theories of direct influence can be easily refuted. The speculation on these matters regularly outstretches the documentary evidence. There is cause for reserve on this matter, however, until the new documents from Qumran that have recently become available are translated and interpreted.

A number of conclusions may be drawn which will form the critical presupposition of this study regarding the religious-intellectual milieu of Hebrews. As with practically every other matter in an "introduction to Hebrews," these conclusions are tentative and subject to further reflection and revision. Nevertheless, we conclude that the language and thought-forms of Hebrews arose from a primarily Jewish milieu and that no single strand of Judaism provides a clear, simple matrix within which to understand the author or his text.[92] While it seems undeniable that the author was acquainted with Alexandrian Judaism and Greek philosophical categories, the strong eschatological current within Hebrews is equally undeniable. The healthy tension between eschatology and metaphysics in Hebrews is thus to be maintained. Furthermore, Thompson's point is well taken that one cannot explain the author's thought world by comparison to discrete traditions or categories. These point to a recurring set of metaphysical assumptions; and Thompson may be right in suggesting dualism as a major theme, though it is certainly not the only one.

Furthermore, the deep appreciation for cultus in Hebrews must be always in mind. The author's own religious development no doubt was heavily influenced by concern for and devotion to the cultic practices of Judaism, and he may in fact have had some personal connection to the Jerusalem temple. The author, then, is not merely a (Hellenistic) Jewish philosopher, but a pious Jew who held the cultus of his ancestors in high esteem. That much is clear despite his occasional inconsistency with the known practices of the temple in the first century.[93] We

---

(Atlanta: Scholars, 1989).

[92]Attridge, *Hebrews*, pp. 29-30.

[93]e.g., the arrangement of the furniture in 9:3-4. Even here, however, it is possible to

thus see that manifold religious and intellectual currents flow through this unknown preacher. But as Thompson himself has noted, the author of Hebrews has interpreted various traditions according to his own world view; and that world view is pre-eminently neither Jewish nor Greek, but Christian.[94]

---

suppose a knowledge of Jewish tradition. See *2 Apoc. Bar.* 6:7; 2 Macc 2:4-8.

[94]It is thus significant that Hurst finds the closest parallels with Hebrews' thought world in the Stephen tradition of Acts 7 (*Hebrews*, pp. 89-106) and notes other points of contact with the Pauline corpus and 1 Peter (Ibid., pp. 107-130).

Chapter 3

THE CULTIC FOUNDATION

The cultic element in Hebrews is undoubtedly pronounced, and this has led many to disparage or ignore the middle sections of the sermon where ritualistic imagery predominates. Such a view of ritual is unwarranted despite its lengthy pedigree. Turner makes note in *The Ritual Process* of a Native American critique of Lewis Henry Morgan's study of Iroquois religion to the effect that Morgan utterly missed the point of his subject matter:

> To my mind, the Seneca comments are related to Morgan's distrust of the "imaginative and emotional," his reluctance to concede that religion has an important rational aspect, and his belief that what appears "grotesque" to the highly "evolved" consciousness of a nineteenth-century savant must be, *ipso facto*, largely "unintelligible."[1]

This study proceeds on the assumption that cultus as a form of discourse must be accepted on its own terms to be understood accurately. Turner's observations cited above indicate three important guideposts for the student of ritual: account for the imaginative and emotional (one might even say existential); look for a rational element, even when that reasoning proceeds on culturally-prescribed assumptions that the researcher may not share; and finally, proceed with due humility, assuming that the ritual is intelligible within its own frame of reference.

Such an approach to cultus naturally tends to produce a more favorable assessment of the value of cultic practices within a society. Smith, for example, sees ritual in preindustrial societies as a means "of performing the way things ought

---

[1] Victor Turner, *The Ritual Process* (Ithaca: Cornell University, 1969), p. 2.

to be"[2] which tends to sacralize even the everyday, uncontrolled aspects of life. Ritual is the "quintessential culture"[3] in which a group reveals its deepest shared values. In this light Wilson has suggested that the study of ritual contains "the key to an understanding of the essential constitution of human societies."[4]

Our first task must be to examine the foundations of cultic thought for the author of Hebrews. This will be accomplished by exploring the cultic framework in which the author of Hebrews specifically discusses the levitical cultus ("Old Covenant Cultus") and sets it in contrast to the salvific work of Christ conceived as a cultic performance ("Christ Cultus"). We shall do this in the context of a survey of the cultic practices and interpretations of Israel.

Cultus in Hebrews

Israelite religion found in its cultus the "milieu" of its experience of God.[5] As Levenson points out, in the Old Testament Sinai tradition the goal of the Exodus is not so much the promised land as intimacy with Yahweh.[6] This intimacy is realized in the tabernacle as God's vehicle for communication and communion with his chosen people.[7] Gyllenberg goes so far as to suggest that the cultus is the locus

---

[2]Jonathan Z. Smith, *Imagining Religion* (Chicago: University Press, 1979), p. 63.

[3]Victor Turner, *Process, Performance, and Pilgrimage* , Ranchi Anthropology Series 1 (New Delhi: Concept, 1979), p. 128.

[4]Monica Wilson, "Nyakusa Ritual and Symbolism," *American Anthropologist*, 56 (1954), 241, quoted in Turner, *Ritual Process*, p. 6.

[5]Rafael Gyllenberg, "Kultus und Offenbarung," in *Interpretationes ad Vetus Testamentum Pertinentes Sigmund Mowinckel Septuagenario Missae*, quoted by William Oliver Walker, Jr, "Cultus and Tradition: A Contribution to the Problem of Faith and History in the Old Testament" (Ph.D. dissertation, Duke University, 1962), p. 387.

[6]Jon D. Levenson, "The Jerusalem Temple in Devotional and Visionary Experience," in *Jewish Spirituality*, vol. 1, ed. Arthur Green, World Spirituality (New York: Crossroad, 1987), p. 37.

[7]Ibid.

of God's revelation to Israel.[8]

Such an approach to Israel's cultus continues into the New Testament era. In this period the temple in Jerusalem and its cultus was the center of Jewish piety and the locus of the presence of God.[9] Furthermore, one is free to suppose a good bit of conservatism as far as Israel's practice and interpretation of its cultus.[10] When critiques against the temple are raised, as in the Old Testament prophetic tradition, the criticism is generally not against the temple or cult as such but against abuses of the cultic system.[11]

Of course, the concern in Hebrews is with the tent, not the temple. Levenson makes a good case for a harmonization of tent and temple in later Old Testament traditions, although he admits that references to the former *may* have at times implied a critique of the latter.[12] In general, this observation holds true: what is said of the tent may be interpreted and applied in terms of the temple. Turning specifically to the cultic imagery of Hebrews, one finds that the foundational and primary cultic passages deal with the activity of Jesus as the Great High Priest in the heavenly sanctuary. This salvific work is explicitly compared and contrasted with the cultic practices of the Mosaic covenant. Since these two cultuses are so intertwined in the text of Hebrews itself, we will treat them together in this study as well.

The author of Hebrews establishes the categories under which he intends to discuss his cultic formulation of the work of Christ. In 9:1 he introduces the closely related concepts of δικαιώματα λατρείας τό τε ἅγιον κοσμικόν, "regulations for worship and an earthly sanctuary." These two categories, liturgy

---

[8]Gyllenberg, "Kultus und Offenbarung," quoted by Walker, "Cultus and Tradition," p. 385.

[9]Although the Qumran covenanters did not participate in the Jerusalem cultus, its symbolism remained central to the expression of their spirituality.

[10]Baruch A. Levine, "Biblical Temple," *The Encyclopedia of Religion*, vol. 2, ed. Mircea Eliade (New York: Macmillan, 1987), p. 205.

[11]See for example *1 Enoch* 89:73-74; *T. Levi* 14:5-8; *Pss. Sol.* 2:1-3; 8:8-21; CD 4:12-5:9.

[12]Levenson, "Jerusalem Temple," pp. 32-34.

and sanctuary, form the basis of the author's exposition in 9:2-28. To these aspects of the cultus must be added the idea of priesthood which by the author's own admission is central to his message (8:1).

After surveying the data of Hebrews concerning priesthood, sanctuary, and liturgy, we shall suggest a model for understanding the cultic foundation of Hebrews in broad terms. We shall then conclude with an assessment of how these data impact our understanding of the spirituality of Hebrews.

Cultic Personnel: The Priesthood

The ministry of the priest controlled and regulated Israel's cultic life and through it the whole of the people's relationship with Yahweh. Vanhoye enumerates the wide variety of functions that the ancient priests performed, including caring for the sanctuary and its sacra, offering sacrifices, uttering oracles, and giving blessings.[13]

The most important and essential duty of the Old Testament priest was to offer sacrifices to God, and this was his exclusive domain:

> The layman prepared the sacrifice, but it was the cultic official who presented it and proclaimed the "law of sacrifice." Just as he could impose the curse and decree of exclusion from the Yahweh community, so also he was responsible for the ceremony of blessing. Everything in the cultic sphere was supervised, regulated and carried out by him.[14]

Answering to the internal dynamic of the cultic system as a whole, the internal dynamic of the priesthood was the idea of holiness. The conviction that one must be holy to approach God necessarily raised the problem of impurity. In response, the ancient cultus posited as a ritual solution mediation through a holy priest.[15]

Also significant for the Old Testament understanding of priesthood is the

---

[13]Albert Vanhoye, *Old Testament Priests and the New Priest*, trans. J. Bernard Orchard (Petersham, MA: St. Bede's, 1986), p. 20.

[14]Hans-Joachim Kraus, *Worship in Israel*, trans. Geoffrey Buswell (Richmond: John Knox, 1966), p. 101.

[15]Vanhoye, *Old Testament Priests*, pp. 26-34. Harold S. Songer, "A Superior Priesthood: Hebrews 4:14-7:28," *RevExp*, 82 (1985), 345, also highlights the importance of providing access to God (or gods) and guaranteeing the wellbeing of the people in both Jewish and pagan thought.

close relationship that priests maintained with the sanctuary.[16] The authority of the priest is distinguished from that of the tribal chief or the prophet precisely by this close connection to a holy place: "... whereas the chief and the prophet obtained their authority through the inner power which their spiritual inspiration gave them, the priest acted as the servant of the spirit at some sanctuary where it was present."[17] The priest is thus distinct in that he is a servant of the sanctuary.[18]

At the head of the priestly hierarchy was the high priest, who was the subject of great respect and even awe in first century Judaism. In the Hellenistic era the priesthood was the class with the highest status among the people. Foreigners in fact considered the high priest to be the head of the Jewish people.[19] Sirach 50:5-21 records a hymn in praise of the high priest Simon II, who was clearly a subject of deep emotional attachment for the author. Philo depicts the high priest as a quasi-divine figure whose very humanity is suspended when he enters the holy of holies on the Day of Atonement (e.g., *Spec.* I, 116).

The author suggests a cultic role for Jesus as early as 1:3 ("having accomplished cleansing from sins ..."). Jesus is specifically called a high priest in 2:17 and 3:1, and in 8:1 the author announces that the chief point (κεφάλιον) of his message is that "we have such a high priest." The first major exposition of the theme of Jesus as high priest is found in 4:14-5:10. Since this passage also reveals a great deal about the author's perception of the levitical priesthood, it is an appropriate starting point for our discussion.

Although Lane links 4:14 with what has come before as its intended

---

[16]Aelred Cody, *A History of Old Testament Priesthood* (Rome: Pontifical Biblical Institute, 1969), p. 29; Roland de Vaux, *Ancient Israel*, trans. John McHugh (New York: McGraw-Hill, 1961), pp. 348-349.

[17]Johannes Pedersen, *Israel: Its Life and Culture*, vols. 3-4 (London: Oxford University, 1940), p. 150.

[18]Ibid., p. 157. In this light, see Hebrews 8:2, where Jesus is described as τῶν ἁγίων λειτουργὸς καὶ τῆς σκηνῆς τῆς ἀληθινῆς.

[19]Menahem Haran, et al., "Priests and Priesthood," *Encyclopaedia Judaica*, vol. 13 (New York: Macmillan, 1971), p. 1086.

conclusion,[20] Westcott takes the last three verses of chapter 4 as a transition into the high priest exposition beginning at 5:1.[21] It has long been noted that 3:1-5:10 develops the thought of 2:17 of Jesus as a "merciful" and "faithful" high priest. Working in inverse order, the author first explains the faithfulness of Jesus in 3:1-4:13 before turning to Jesus' mercy in 4:15-5:10. The mention of ἀρχιερέα in 4:14 may therefore be an inclusion of 3:1, or it may stand as the introduction to the second major point. Lane is probably to be favored in this regard, but the idea that Jesus has "passed through the heavens" will occupy our attention at a later point.

Lane is certainly correct that 4:15-5:10 lays the foundation for the central exposition of Jesus as high priest in 7:1-10:18.[22] While in that central section the author's emphasis is on the dissimilarities between Jesus and Aaron, in this introductory exposition the emphasis is more on the similarities.[23] These similarities between the priesthood of Christ and of the old covenant priest center around the ideas of solidarity and humility and are determined by the description of Christ in 4:15-16.[24]

In 4:15 one learns that Jesus is able (δυνάμενος) to sympathize with sinners. In 5:2 one further learns that he is generally required to do so because of his office.[25] Two important factors in the priestly career of Jesus come out in 4:15. The first is his ability to sympathize with sinners and the second is his sinlessness. To "sympathize" (συνπαθῆσαι) expresses not merely the compassion of an outside observer, but also "the feeling of one who enters into the suffering and

---

[20]William G. Lane, *Hebrews*, vol. 1, Word Biblical Commentary (Dallas: Word, 1991), p. 105. So also Albert Vanhoye, *La Structure littéraire de l'épître aux Hébreux* (Paris: Brouwer, 1963), p. 104.

[21]B. F. Westcott, *The Epistle to the Hebrews*, 2nd ed. (Grand Rapids: Eerdmans, 1955), p. 105. So also Harold Attridge, *The Epistle to the Hebrews*, Hermeneia (Philadelphia: Fortress, 1989), p. 138, who sees the paragraph as a block of paraenetic material beginning with a resumptive οὖν.

[22]Lane, *Hebrews*, vol. 1, p. 111.

[23]Ibid.

[24]Ibid., p. 123.

[25]Westcott, *Hebrews*, p. 119.

makes it his own."26 Lane suggests that the word always includes the element of active help for the one sympathized with (see 10:34; 4 Macc. 4:25; 13:23).27 Such sympathy for the weak is understandable in terms of the Old Testament witness to the humanity of the Aaronic high priest, who was required to offer sacrifices for his own sins and for those of his household, although the motif of a sympathetic high priest as such is rare in Judaism.

Despite Jesus' ability to sympathize, the author asserts his sinlessness: "[he was] in every respect tempted like us, yet without sin." The phrase χωρὶς ἁμαρτίας refers here to the outcome of Jesus' temptations and not to any kind of limitation on the temptation itself.28 While the rabbis had the ideal of a sinless high priest (*Lev. Rab.* 5:6), they were perfectly aware that this ideal was not reached (*m.Yoma* 3:8). The Old Testament never imagined a sinless high priest (Lev. 4:3; 9:7; 16:6, 17), nor did Sirach, the *Testament of the Twelve Patriarchs*, the Dead Sea Scrolls, or Josephus.29 Philo is unique in Judaism in claiming that the high priest's humanity was "suspended" while he discharged his duties in the holy of holies (*Spec.* I, 116; *Heres*, 84; *Som.* II, 189, 231). Philo equated the high priest with the divine Logos (*Mig.*, 102; *Gig.*, 52; *LA*. III, 82), and his doctrine of a sinless high priest "must have sounded blasphemous to many Jews."30

The theme of a new priesthood is developed in *Testament of Levi* 18 and linked to the priesthood of Melchizedek. This whole passage should most likely be bracketed as a Christian interpolation, given the astounding connections with the New Testament found there; but according to Stewart there is still a case for a least a basic Jewish pedigree.31

Because believers have such a high priest, they are urged to draw near

---

26Ibid., p. 107.

27Lane, *Hebrews*, vol. 1, p. 114.

28Ibid.

29R. A. Stewart, "The Sinless High-Priest," *NTS*, 14 (1967-1968), 126-131.

30Ibid., p. 126.

31Ibid., p. 129.

(προσερχώμεθα) to the heavenly throne and there experience intimate communion with God. This is the first time the author uses the cultic term προσέρχομαι. Significantly, it is applied not to Christ or to priests under the old covenant but to Christian believers. We shall explore this point more fully in our treatment of the New Covenant Cultus in chapter five.

Hebrews five begins with a description of the qualifications of a high priest (5:1-4), after which the author explains how Jesus has satisfied these requirements and fulfilled the office. (5:5-10).[32] The exposition proceeds in an inverted parallel structure which may be summarized as follows:[33]

> A 5:1 general description of priesthood
> B 5:2-3 requirement of solidarity with the weak
> C 5:4 requirement of divine appointment
> C' 5:5-6 Christ's divine appointment
> B' 5:7-8 Christ's solidarity with the weak
> A' 5:9-10 description of Christ's priesthood

The two requirements that the author proposes for a high priest are (1) that he have sympathy with human beings in their weakness (5:2-3) and (2) that he receive his appointment from God rather than taking it for himself (5:4). Of course, these are not the only requirements of a high priest. Here the author only includes those characteristics relevant to his theme of Jesus as high priest.[34] The author does not consider genealogy a prerequisite for priesthood, as comes out clearly in his exposition on Melchizedek in chapter seven. In 7:13-14 the author explicitly admits that Jesus does not belong to the proper priestly line, but this is never a problem because his concept of priesthood is broader than that of the Mosaic regulations. The πᾶς ἀρχιερεύς of 5:1 would for the author almost surely extend to include Melchizedek himself. His concern is with what is true for "every" high priest, and he considers the levitical high priest a good example of this general principle.[35]

The primary requirement for a high priest then is his humanity, as evident

---

[32]Westcott, *Hebrews*, p. 121.

[33]Ibid.; Lane, *Hebrews*, vol. 1, p. 111.

[34]Attridge, *Hebrews*, p. 142.

[35]Lane, *Hebrews*, vol. 1, p. 116. See also Westcott, *Hebrews*, p. 117.

not only in his solidarity with human beings but in his humble acquiescence to God's call. As a human being the high priest can act "for human beings" (ὑπὲρ ἀνθρώπων, 5:1). This diverges from the Old Testament emphasis that the high priest is appointed "for God" (e.g., Exod. 28:1,3; 29:1) and points again to the high priest's solidarity with the people. Christ in Hebrews was not a priest from eternity, but rather he became one: his high priesthood, though it is divine, is bound up with his *human* nature.[36]

In 5:2 the author asserts the high priest's ability to "feel gently towards" (μετριοπαθεῖν) human beings in their ignorance. Μετριοπαθέω suggests restraining or moderating one's feelings so as to deal gently or considerately with another.[37] Rather than the impassibility of the Stoics and Philo, the author to the Hebrews elevates gentle consideration as a virtue. To this assessment of the high priest there are no clear parallels in contemporary Judaism.[38] His statement is likely influenced by his previous reflection on Jesus as high priest.[39] It may be, however, that here we find an inkling of the author's own conception of priesthood. Might the author here be revealing his own fond remembrances of sympathetic priests that he has known?

The high priest is required to deal gently with sinners because he himself is beset with weakness, and it is because of his own weakness that he must offer sacrifices not only for the people but for his own sins (5:3). It is the lot of high priests that their weakness actually results in sin; therefore, a sacrifice is necessary for them. In this statement we find a departure from the usual high dignity attached

---

[36]Aelred Cody, *Heavenly Sanctuary and Liturgy in the Epistle to the Hebrews* (St. Meinrad, IN: Grail, 1960), p. 97.

[37]Lane, *Hebrews*, vol. 1, p. 116. See also Wilhelm Michaelis, "πάσχω, κ.τ.λ." *TDNT*, vol. 5, p. 938.

[38]Lane, *Hebrews*, vol. 1, p. 116. There is, however, a less positive description of this quality in *T. Levi* 2:4. There Levi relates that because of the sins and injustices of the people, "I kept grieving over the race of the sons of men, and I prayed to the Lord that I might be delivered." All quotations from Pseudepigrapha are from James H. Charlesworth, ed, *The Old Testament Pseudepigrapha*, 2 vols. (Garden City: Doubleday, 1985).

[39]William Manson, *The Epistle to the Hebrews* (London: Hodder and Stoughton, 1951), pp. 107-108.

50

to the office of high priest;[40] but as has been seen, the fallibility of the high priest was openly admitted in Judaism despite his higher standard of holiness (Lev. 21).

With verse 4 the author turns to his second major requirement of a high priest: he must receive his appointment from God. Because of sin a human being could not presume to draw near to God. Therefore God himself must appoint an intermediary.[41] By stressing the high priest's refusal to arrogate the honor to himself, the author once again stresses the necessary humility of the office holder. The high priest is dependent upon God for his appointment.[42] Although the author is certainly aware of the genealogical requirements of the Mosaic priesthood, he chooses to emphasize the example of Aaron, who attained the office of high priest by divine appointment (Exod. 28:1). Of course, throughout the first century the appointment of the high priest was highly politicized.[43] By appealing to the origins of the Aaronic priesthood, the author may have intended an implicit criticism of the *status quo*.

In 5:1-10 we see the same strategy as in 3:1-6, where the author first demonstrated the similarities between Moses and Jesus before asserting Jesus' superiority.[44] The same pattern appears as well in 9:1-28. Verses 5-10 of chapter 5 comprise a single periodic sentence in which the author masterfully exposes not only the continuity of Christ with all other high priests but his superiority over them. The period 5:5-10 may be arranged around the three finite verbs applied to Jesus: "he did not glorify himself," (5:5) "he learned obedience," (5:8) and "he became the source of eternal salvation" (5:9).

Like Aaron, Jesus did not presume upon himself the honor of the high priesthood, but was called by God. The element of discontinuity between Aaron

[40]As found, for example, in Sirach 45, 50, as well as in the Philo passages already cited.

[41]Westcott, *Hebrews*, p. 120.

[42]Lane, *Hebrews*, vol. 1, p. 117.

[43]The people hated the rise of well-born priestly families and a high priestly aristocracy from Herod on (*b.Yoma* 18a; *b.Yebam.* 61a), but the high priesthood generally retained its exalted, hallowed status. See Haran, "Priests," p. 1087.

[44]Lane, *Hebrews*, vol. 1, p. 117.

and Jesus comes into focus with the citation of Psalm 110:4 in 5:6. In context, both Psalm quotations in 5:5-6 have to do with Jesus' installation in the priestly office and his investiture with power.[45] The author makes much of Jesus' priesthood "according to the order of Melchizedek" (5:6), particularly in 7:1-28. The full significance of the Melchizedek motif cannot concern us here, but it is worth stating that two central features of the Old Testament Melchizedek tradition seem important to the author: (1) that his priesthood is connected to his kingly office (7:1-2), and (2) that his priesthood is not dependent on any fleshly descent or limited by conditions of time (7:3).[46] Melchizedek is important in the author's argument because "he represented a non-Jewish, a universal priesthood."[47] In this light Psalm 110:4 becomes a central interest of Hebrews because it provides a scriptural basis for a non-Aaronic priestly christology.[48]

To state that Jesus "learned obedience from what he suffered" (5:8) establishes his solidarity with the human condition. Westcott is correct in stating that the expression "in the days of his flesh" (5:7) has to do with the general condition of humanity in the changing circumstances of the present life.[49] It is because of Christ's involvement with the human condition that he offers up tearful petitions and entreaties to God. By using the cultic term προσφέρω in 5:7 the author depicts Jesus' prayer as a kind of sacrifice, parallel to the sacrifices offered by high priests in 5:3.[50]

It is in this context that one must understand the assertion that "he was heard" (εἰσακουσθείς). There was no guarantee that God would respond to the high priests' sacrifices *ex opere operato*. That Jesus' petition was directed to "the One able to deliver him from death" has seemed paradoxical to many. Were it not

---

[45]Ibid., p. 118.

[46]Westcott, *Hebrews*, p. 123.

[47]Ibid.

[48]Lane, *Hebrews*, vol. 1, p. 118.

[49]Westcott, *Hebrews*, p. 125.

[50]*Contra* Attridge, *Hebrews*, p. 149.

for the emphasis on the mortality of the levitical priests elsewhere in Hebrews, one might be tempted to dismiss the phrase as a circumlocution to avoid direct mention of God. One must wonder if the content of Jesus' petition is hinted at in these words; and if so, in what sense can it be said that Jesus "was heard?" Although the author finds fault with their sacrifices in that they cannot achieve definitive cleansing from sin, he seems to make only one negative assessment of the old covenant priests themselves: they are "prevented by death from continuing in office" (7:23).[51] In contrast, Jesus holds his priestly office forever (1:11-12; 5:6; 7:17,24-25; 13:8) by the power of his "indestructible life" (7:16). At the first level, then, the participle εἰσακουσθείς simply recounts the fact that Jesus' sacrifice was acceptable before God. In contrast to previous high priests, whose rituals may or may not have been favored, Jesus' sacrifice proved effective. At a deeper level, however, God did indeed "hear" the prayer of Jesus and ultimately deliver him from death.

The culmination of Jesus' high priestly office is described in 5:9-10. Christ's "perfection" as a priest (τελειωθείς) seems to relate to his previous experience of suffering which taught him obedience. For Jesus to be perfected assures the audience that he is fully equipped to approach God for priestly action.[52] It has been debated as to whether Hebrews depicts a priestly "ordination" of Jesus. This question will be addressed below.

The final two verses of this passage announce the major themes of the central section of Hebrews. Jesus is described as the source of eternal salvation (10:1-18) and his qualifications for the office of high priest are presented (8:1-9:28). Finally, the passage closes with another reference to the high priesthood of Melchizedek (7:1-28).[53]

As becomes clear in 9:7, Hebrews considers the work of the high priest to be the climax of the Old Covenant Cultus. This work is contrasted in 9:11-28 with the work of Christ.

---

[51]The author also mentions how their moral weakness leads to sin and requires its own sacrifice (5:2-3; 9:7), but in 5:2-3 this assessment seems to contribute to the priest's solidarity with the people.

[52]Lane, *Hebrews*, vol. 1, p. 122.

[53]Ibid., pp. 111-112.

Cultic Place: The Sanctuary

From its very beginning Israel's tribal confederacy had the institution of a central sanctuary as the basis of its cultic life.[54] Scholars generally do not doubt the presence of other sanctuaries in ancient Israel, but contend nevertheless that wherever the Ark of the Covenant rested was the première cultic center in Israel.[55] Even a cursory glance at the narratives of the Pentateuch reveals the importance of *place* in ancient Israelite religion. This emphasis is reinforced in the deuteronomic emphasis on the central sanctuary where Yahweh causes his name to dwell.

The unanimous witness of the Old Testament is that sacred places become sacred because people have met God there. Jerusalem possessed value and meaning because God had chosen it as his preferred residence on earth.[56] The temple was the place where an Israelite came into the presence of Yahweh (1 Kgs. 8:27-34; Isa. 6:1-5), and in fact even a "vision of God" was a possibility for the visitor at the sacred site.[57] Psalm 134 records a blessing associated with the temple which moves in a twofold direction: God is blessed and blesses, that is, the people both give and receive a benediction. Levenson interprets this and other statements in the Psalms to indicate the focal nature of Mount Zion. Zion is the "conduit" from which God's blessing goes out into the world.[58] The temple is furthermore a "divine palace" designated to replicate on earth Yahweh's heavenly residence.[59]

This developed temple-theology indicates that the presence of God is "the

---

[54]Kraus, *Worship in Israel*, p. 127.

[55]Ibid.

[56]Sarah Ann Sharkey, "The Background of the Imagery of the Heavenly Jerusalem in the New Testament," (Ph.D. dissertation, The Catholic University of America, 1986), p. 76.

[57]Levenson, "Jerusalem Temple," p. 43. Levenson suggests that "to see the face of YHWH" (for example at Deut. 16:16) is an idiom indicating a visit to the Temple. See also Psalm 11:4-7.

[58]Ibid., p. 38.

[59]Levine, "Biblical Temple," p. 211.

core of spiritual meaning" in Israel.[60] One might justifiably add that God's presence more often as not is conceived in more or less physical terms. God reveals himself in particular places: Bethel, Shiloh, Jerusalem. Throughout its history, Israel has had a strong interest in sacralized space, be it a distinct, permanent structure like the temple, or a mobile arrangement like the tent in the wilderness. In the Conquest traditions, the promised land itself is seen as a kind of sacred space. The Ark of the Covenant was clearly understood to be a channel for the presence of God.[61]

The place where God chooses to dwell thus becomes a transition point between the earthly world and the heavenly.[62] It is the area in which God and humanity can meet.[63] It is, in the language of religious phenomenology, the *axis mundi* or "hub of the world." This is certainly true of Mount Zion, which was conceived of in the first century as the highest point on earth and the center of the world, thus conforming to the foremost symbol of an *axis mundi* in the world's religions.[64] Such a place is where the cosmic regions intersect. It is the sacred place above all others: "It defines reality, for it marks the place where being is most fully manifest."[65] This aspect is seen, for example, in the vision recorded in Isaiah 6, where the earthly temple provides access to the heavenly.[66]

The idea that some places are somehow more holy or numinous than others is widespread in the world's religions, and often this idea takes on a central

---

[60]Levenson, "Jerusalem Temple," p. 37.

[61]Kraus, *Worship in Israel*, p. 126.

[62]Levenson, "Jerusalem Temple," p. 49.

[63]Marie Isaacs, *Sacred Space*, JSNTSS 73 (Sheffield: Academic Press, 1992), p. 77.

[64]Lawrence E. Sullivan, "Axis Mundi," *The Encyclopedia of Religion*, vol. 2, ed. Mircea Eliade (New York: Macmillan, 1987), p. 20.

[65]Ibid., p. 21.

[66]George W. E. Nickelsburg and Michael E. Stone, eds., *Faith and Piety in Early Judaism* (Philadelphia: Fortress, 1983), p. 57. According to them, the idea of the earthly Temple as the counterpart of the heavenly is based on Exodus 25:9 and the elaborate vision of Ezekiel 40-48.

importance. Bolle, for example, suggests that the symbolism of "being there" is a key factor in Indian civilization and goes a long way towards understanding the emphasis on pilgrimage in that culture.[67] While it is not absent in Western religions, Bolle concludes that this symbolism is not central in the Judeo-Christian tradition as it is in India.[68] Of course, Bolle is referring to modern Judaism and Christianity, not the Judaism of the first century with its standing temple.[69] Indeed Hebrews harkens back to an even earlier time in Israelite history when it seems that the idea of sacred space was paramount. Two Old Testament traditions link the relationship between Israel and Yahweh with sacred space. In the settlement tradition the land of Israel itself symbolizes and manifests the presence of God, while in the the Sinai tradition it is the tent of meeting with its sacred rites that performs this function.[70] What Bolle describes of Indian family deities could easily apply to the God of the patriarchs and of the wilderness generation:

> The family deity is what he is because he is local. This simple point is the most difficult to understand. He is essentially a local deity, but at the same time universal. When a family moves, they take their god along, or, more accurately, they take God along. God too moves . . . . *God is universal because he is there.*[71]

By this understanding a local sanctuary holds in tension the transcendence and immanence of God. It is the point of contact and transition between the mundane world and the mythic world of ultimate reality.

Nowhere in Hebrews does the importance of cultic place come out more

---

[67]Kees W. Bolle, "Speaking of a Place," in *Myths and Symbols*, ed. Joseph M. Kitagawa and Charles H. Long (Chicago: University, 1969), p. 129.

[68]Ibid., p. 138.

[69]Of course, the pilgrimages of Judaism were much more central for Jews in Palestine than in the Diaspora. Nevertheless, even Philo describes a visit to Jerusalem to pray and sacrifice (Prov. 2, 64).

[70]Levenson, "Jerusalem Temple," p. 35.

[71]Bolle, "Place," pp. 128-129.

clearly than in chapter nine.[72] As throughout the sermon, the concern here is with the tent of the wilderness generation rather than with the temple in Jerusalem, although it is difficult to imagine his audience not making the logical connection between the two.[73] As in chapter five, the author here develops his argument about the sanctuary and liturgy in an inverted parallelism:

> A   9:1   the conditions of the Old Covenant Cultus
> B   9:2-5   the old covenant sanctuary
> C   9:6-10   the old covenant liturgy
> C' 9:11-22 Christ's heavenly liturgy
> B' 9:23-26a Christ's heavenly sanctuary
> A' 9:26b-28 the conditions of the Christ Cultus

Verses 2-5 describe the old covenant sanctuary as consisting of two tents, the "holy place" (ἅγια) and the "holy of holies" (ἅγια ἁγίων). These were in fact two compartments of the same structure, but the author stresses emphatically the distinction between the front and rear compartments.[74] This prepares the reader for the argument in 9:6-10 about the meaning of the cultic actions the priests performed in the sanctuary.[75] The author shows no great interest in the furniture of the tent, although he mentions several items before confessing that he does not have the time nor inclination to discuss them in detail (9:5). The one detail that he emphasizes is the division of the sanctuary into two halves, a division which "appears to be fundamental for the interpretation of 9:1-10."[76]

The significance of the two compartments becomes clear in 9:6-8. While the priests go "continually" into the outer compartment to perform their cultic activities, only the high priest may enter the inner sanctum, and then only once per year and by means of blood. This arrangement suggests a "graded right of

---

[72]Although Isaacs, *Sacred Space*, uses the term "sacred space" to include places that are not, strictly speaking, cultic (e.g., the promised land itself), our concern here is more specifically with the sanctuary as the place of cultic action.

[73]The Jerusalem temple is described as a "tent" in Pss. 15:1; 27:5; 61:5; and 78:60. See Kraus, *Worship in Israel*, p. 134.

[74]Lane, *Hebrews*, vol. 2, p. 217.

[75]Ibid.

[76]Lane, *Hebrews*, vol. 2, p. 219.

approach" in which direct access to God is not yet a reality (9:8).[77] Entering the divine presence is not an easy matter.[78] As long as the outer compartment stands, it serves as a reminder that one may only go so far in approaching God.

Some choose to switch the meaning of the symbolism here in a more explicitly eschatological direction, making the "outer tent" now the Mosaic institution in its entirety as opposed to the heavenly sanctuary.[79] But it is not necessary to see in the reference to the "outer tent" in 9:8 anything more than what the author intended earlier. Under the old covenant, the customary place of worship was the holy place, not the holy of holies that represented the divine presence itself. Architecturally, one might say that under the old covenant worship took place in the vestibule. The inner sanctum was off limits, which most impressively demonstrated the limits placed upon the worshiper.[80]

The eschatological symbolism of the passage emerges only in 9:9 where the author describes the first tent (ἥτις, referring to ἡ πρώτη σκηνή in 9:8) as a παραβολή of the present time with its sacrifices of limited effectiveness. Thus, the spatial relationships within the Mosaic sanctuary become the basis for a temporal metaphor of two ages. As the outer compartment is a symbol of the externals of the old covenant which is tied up with a present age doomed to pass away (1:2), the inner compartment becomes the "greater and more perfect tent" through which Christ achieves unmediated access to God. This is the true, heavenly sanctuary (8:2, 9:24). It is the original of which the earthly version (9:1, 11) is but the antitype (9:24) and copy (8:5; 9:23).

The prepositional phrase διὰ τῆς μείζονος καὶ τελειοτέρας σκηνῆς ("through the greater and more perfect tent") must be taken locally rather than instrumentally. The instrumental interpretation, given by many Roman

---

[77]Westcott, *Hebrews*, p. 249.

[78]Lane, *Hebrews*, vol. 2, p. 226.

[79]"There can be access only after the front compartment has been set aside," Ibid., p. 223.

[80]Westcott, *Hebrews*, p. 252.

58

Catholic scholars[81] and evident in patristic exegesis,[82] runs counter to the immediate argument and to parallel passages in Hebrews.[83] Up to this point, σκηνή consistently refers either to the heavenly sanctuary (8:2) or the tent in the wilderness (8:5).

In all of Hebrews only in 9:11-12 does the author suggest a division of the heavenly sanctuary into two parts.[84] There is a tent *through which* Christ passes as well as a tent *into which* he enters. Cody observes that the "tent through which" does not seem to be identical or coextensive with the heavenly holy of holies, which he equates with heaven itself in light of 9:23-24,[85] and thus finds room to equate the former with the body of Christ. This is probably splitting too many hairs, and in any event Cody's interpretation gets in the way of the passages in Hebrews which speak of Jesus passing through the heavens (4:14) or the curtain (6:19; 10:20) to attain to the divine presence. The gallery of word-pictures that the author paints is what matters; and it should not surprise us if he occasionally mixes metaphors, especially in reference to the unseen realm of heavenly geography.

Much of this chapter is best understood in terms of cultic activities rather than cultic space, but a final matter of concern in terms of the sanctuary is the puzzling reference to the purification of the heavenly things in 9:23. In what sense do the heavenly things (τὰ ἐπουράνια) require purification? Two predominant interpretations assume that these heavenly things are to be taken symbolically. With reference to 9:9, some commentators believe τὰ ἐπουράνια to be human consciences.[86] Others prefer to relate the heavenly things to the new age

---

[81]See, for example, James Swetnam, "Christology and the Eucharist in the Epistle to the Hebrews," *Biblica*, 70 (1989), 74-95, and Cody, *Heavenly Sanctuary*, pp. 155-165.

[82]As noted and expanded upon by Westcott, *Hebrews*, pp. 257-258.

[83]Lane, *Hebrews*, vol. 2, p. 237.

[84]Cody, *Heavenly Sanctuary*, p. 150.

[85]Ibid., p. 156.

[86]F. F. Bruce, *The Epistle to the Hebrews*, rev. ed, New International Commentary on the New Testament (Grand Rapids: Eerdmans, 1990), p. 218; Hugh Montefiore, *A Commentary*

inaugurated by Christ's sacrifice.[87] Both of these interpretations are less concerned with spatial considerations than with an eschatological, temporal perspective. Others relate the "cleansing" to Christ's victory over Satan,[88] while Moffatt dismisses the idea entirely without attempting to find an adequate solution.[89]

Watering down purification until it is mere inauguration is not a valid approach to the issue. The author specifically uses the verb καθαρίζω, not ἐγκαινίζω as he does in 10:20. Such usage is in keeping with the central motif of the Day of Atonement, which is in fact the cleansing of the sanctuary and its furnishings.[90] The overriding assumption of the Day of Atonement rite and of this passage is that sin is contagious and requires expiatory purification.[91] All human means of approach to God must therefore be cleansed with blood.[92] That sin is capable of defiling the earthly sanctuary is clear from the Old Testament (Lev. 16:16; 20:3; 21:23; Num. 19:20); and the author of Hebrews himself claims that sin has repercussions on society (12:15-16) and, under the old covenant, on the cultic vessels (9:21).[93]

Milgrom argues that Israel presumed that impurity is a "dynamic (but not

---

on *The Epistle to the Hebrews* (London: Black, 1964), p. 159.

[87]Spicq, *Hébreux*, vol. 2, p. 267; N. H. Young, "The Gospel According to Hebrews 9," NTS, 27 (1980-1981), 198-210.

[88]For example, Otto Michel, *Der Brief an die Hebräer*, Kritisch-Exegetischer Kommentar über das Neue Testament (Göttingen: Vandenhoeck & Ruprecht), pp. 213-214.

[89]James Moffatt, *A Critical and Exegetical Commentary on the Epistle to the Hebrews*, International Critical Commentary (New York: Scribner's, 1924), p. 132.

[90]Jerome Smith, *A Priest for Ever* (London: Sheed and Ward, 1969), p. 124, reminds us that it is not heaven *itself*, but the heavenly *things* (presumably cultic vessels) that are purified, in parallel to the inauguration of the Old Covenant. But this seems to miss the point of the Day of Atonement altogether, and ultimately it is a distinction that does not lead in any helpful directions.

[91]Lane, *Hebrews*, vol. 2, p. 247.

[92]Westcott, *Hebrews*, p. 269.

[93]Lane, *Hebrews*, vol. 2, p. 247.

demonic) force that attacks the sanctuary."[94] Its origin is in human sin, and the cultic response is to purify the sanctuary. The graver the offense, the farther geographically the defilement penetrates into the sanctuary. At the level of presumptuous sins the defilement reaches even to the ark of the covenant within the holy of holies.[95]

It may be that the author of Hebrews applies this conceptual framework to the heavenly sanctuary simply because it is where his exposition leads him, but the possibility that he truly believed that the effects of sin could extend even to the heavenly world must not be so quickly discounted. We have already seen that, in Jewish thought, the sanctuary is the transition point between heaven and earth. One may further say that what appears on earth is a reflection of heavenly realities (8:5). Levine reminds us that

> in the ancient Near Eastern tradition of inverting reality, *earth was perceived as a replica of heaven*, yet poets and writers depicted heaven according to what they knew on earth--an inversion seemingly endemic to the human imagination.[96] (emphasis added)

It is clear that the author of Hebrews believed that "the cultus on earth is inseparably linked to the situation in heaven" (8:5; 9:7,11-12, 23; 12:18-24).[97] One must also remember the prevalent Jewish speculation on the temple/tent as a cosmic institution, either the center of the universe from which the world was created or itself the world depicted in microcosm.[98] In this light it is not a great leap to postulate that the author conceived of the earthly and heavenly realms in a state of intimate solidarity. To suggest then that Christ's sacrifice purifies the heavenlies connects Hebrews with the Old Testament eschatological tradition that links the renewal of the sanctuary with the renewal of the world (for example, Isa. 2:2-4; 60-62, Mic. 4:1-5; Ezek. 40-48).

---

[94]Jacob Milgrom, "Sacrifices and Offerings, OT," *IDBSupp*, p. 766.

[95]Ibid., p. 767.

[96]Levine, "Biblical Temple," p. 211.

[97]Lane, *Hebrews*, vol. 2, p. 247.

[98]Levenson, "Jerusalem Temple," p. 51. For Josephus and Philo on this issue, see Westcott, *Hebrews*, pp. 238-239.

Such an interpretation is in keeping with the phenomenology of defilement and purgation that Johnsson demonstrate.[99] Cody approaches this explanation in his contention that the cleansing of the sanctuary has to do with the removal of (1) some objective impediment to access to heaven and (2) of some hindrance from God conferring the full benefits of his love on human beings.[100] He explains that "when the sanctuary was cleansed, the sins of the people were objectively expiated, and contact between God and the people was re-established."[101] Though he considers the cleansing to be merely an inauguration, the last of a series of necessities before the real salvific work of Christ begins, Cody is to be commended for realizing that

> it seems that for Hebrews the very term of the entire process of the mysteries of salvation is the cleansing of the sanctuary, further specified, as we shall see, by the appearance of Christ before the face of God at the moment of his arrival in heaven in His glorified humanity.[102]

Throughout Hebrews there is little description of the heavenly sanctuary itself. There is mention of God's presence therein (9:24), the throne of grace (4:16), and Jesus enthroned as High Priest (8:1; 10:12). After 9:11-12, it seems that the heavenly sanctuary is not compartmentalized like its earthly counterpart, which is reasonable considering the author's emphasis on direct access to the divine presence. The concept of the holy of holies in fact seems to be "the keystone to the structure of Hebrews' idea of heavenly sanctuary and liturgy."[103] The simplicity of the heavenly architecture is emphasized in 9:24, where alone in the sermon one finds the singular οὐρανός. This is the highest heaven, the dwelling place of

---

[99]William G. Johnsson, "Defilement and Purgation in the Book of Hebrews" (Ph.D. dissertation, Vanderbilt University, 1973).

[100]Cody, *Heavenly Sanctuary*, p. 186.

[101]Ibid., p. 188.

[102]Ibid., p. 183.

[103]Ibid., p. 165.

God, which corresponds to the holy of holies in the earthly sanctuary.[104] Thus the most significant aspect of the heavenly sanctuary is its connection with the presence of God. In the heavenly sanctuary Jesus gains access to the divine presence not only for himself (8:1) but for all believers (10:19-22).[105]

Cultic Performance: The Liturgy

Since God's presence is associated with sacred space in the religion of Israel, such a space is the fitting milieu for Israel's cultic activity. The temple cultus included sacrifices, prayers, songs, and probably dance; but the primary mode of worship in the temple was through the offering of sacrifices. The priestly code of the Pentateuch ultimately codifies the various offerings in fully detailed regulations.[106]

The temple service in the first century held a particular fascination for the Jews. Sirach 50 describes the early stages of the highly impressive service of the Greco-Roman period. Many in fact came to the temple not because of ritual obligations, but to watch the liturgy.[107] The custom of gathering in the temple for prayer at the times of the public sacrifices is attested in Luke 1:10, Acts 3:1, and *m.Tamid* 7:3.

Throughout Hebrews the cultic activity of the Old Covenant Cultus is described in all its variety. This tendency is especially clear in chapter nine, where the author makes reference to many kinds of ritual performances. In 9:6 he refers to the priests going "continually" into the outer compartment of the sanctuary to accomplish their liturgical duties. This may suggest the Tamid or daily sacrifice which was considered the heart of the entire sacrificial system. The continuous offering in the outer tent is contrasted with the once per year entrance of the high priest into the inner sanctum on the Day of Atonement (9:7). The reference to the blood of goats and bulls in 9:13 indicates the two animals sacrificed on that solemn

---

[104]Lane, *Hebrews*, vol. ?, p. 248.

[105]Sharkey, "Heavenly Jerusalem," p. 240. The end result is that the author creates what Isaacs (*Sacred Space*, p. 67) calls "a new and powerful theology of access."

[106]Kraus, *Worship in Israel*, p. 116.

[107]Yehoshua M. Grintz, et al., "Temple," *Encyclopaedia Judaica*, vol. 15 (New York: Macmillan, 1971), p. 972.

occasion, which for the author represents the culmination of the whole sacrificial system.[108]

The mention of rules concerning food and washings (9:10) may apply to the generally held purity rules of Judaism, but the mention of regulations about drink is more specific. These may be connected to the Nazirite vow, or to the injunction against priests taking strong drink before ministering in the sanctuary.[109] The cultic picture takes on further complication in 9:13 with the mention of the "ashes of a heifer," which form an important element in removing corpse-impurity. The author notes the sacrifice associated with the inauguration of a covenant in 9:18.[110] In the very next verse, mention is made of "scarlet wool and hyssop," which can be linked to the rite for purifying a leper (Lev. 14:5-7, 49-52) or to the sin offering described in Numbers 19:6.[111] The ministrations of the Old Covenant Cultus may well be described as taking place "at many times and in many ways" (1:1). In contrast, the author makes a particular emphasis of the singularity of Christ's priestly work (9:12,25-26; 10:10,12,14). Westcott observes that "in proportion as this truth was felt, the weakness of the Levitical offerings, shewn by their repetition, became evident."[112] We must hope no longer in the day by day (9:6) and year by year (10:1) rituals of the old covenant for cleansing, but in the heavenly ritual that Jesus accomplished once for all.

The author's assessment of the Old Covenant Cultus becomes explicit at several points in Hebrews. Perfection is not attainable through its priesthood (7:11), nor can its sacrifices perfect the worshipers (10:1) or cleanse their

---

[108]Here the author is in agreement with Second Temple Judaism as a whole, which considered the Day of Atonement the greatest of the festivals. See Moshe David Herr and Jacob Milgrom, "Day of Atonement," *Encyclopaedia Judaica*, vol. 5 (New York: Macmillan, 1971), p. 1377.

[109]Westcott, *Hebrews*, p. 254.

[110]See Johnsson, "Defilement," pp. 308-318, who demonstrates the likelihood that the puzzling verses 9:16-17 also refer to the ratification of a covenant through the symbolic death of the covenant partners.

[111]Smith, *Priest*, p. 122.

[112]Westcott, *Hebrews*, p. 275.

consciences (9:9; 10:2-3). The reason for these deficiencies is best spelled out in in 9:10: the rites of the old covenant, dealing with bodily matters such as food and drink and washings, avail only for external purity. They have a symbolic, disciplinary value; but in the end they look forward to a more perfect system.[113] On this basis, the author can make the shocking claim in 9:8 that "there was no way to God opened by the Law."[114] Hebrews makes this claim most forcefully in its depiction of the Sinai experience in 12:18-21. A major emphasis of these verses is God's unapproachability under the old covenant. In fact, Casey has noted the seeming *absence* of God in the whole description.[115] Through the Old Covenant Cultus one may not approach "God the judge of all" (9:23), but only fire, darkness, gloom, tempest, trumpet, and a fearsome, impersonal "voice" that offers only the prospect of death. Such a reading of the Sinai experience subverts its importance in Jewish thought as the place where God revealed himself to Israel. The way is not yet opened.

In contrast to the ineffectiveness of the Old Covenant Cultus, the author portrays Christ's cultic role as universally and conclusively effective. Cody has described the ritual performance of Christ as comprising three stages following the typology of the Day of Atonement ritual under the old covenant.[116] He notes two "prior stages" which, though occurring in history and on earth, are heavenly "in their own way."[117] These stages are the passion and death of Christ, which corresponds to the immolation of the victim on the Day of Atonement; and the ascension of Christ, corresponding to the high priest's entrance into the holy of

---

[113]Ibid., p. 251.

[114]Ibid.

[115]Juliana M. Casey, "Christian Assembly in Hebrews: A Fantasy Island?" *Theology Digest*, 30 (1982), 327.

[116]Cody, *Heavenly Sanctuary*, pp. 170-202.

[117]Ibid., p. 180.

holies. The final stage of the ritual, "the heavenly liturgy itself,"[118] takes place in the heavenly sanctuary, where Christ purifies the sanctuary and atones for the sins of the people. This stage corresponds to the sprinkling of the sacrificial blood in the holy of holies. These three movements in Christ's liturgical activity will be taken up in turn.

The passion and death of Christ. Some preliminary words about Jesus' cultic performance are suggested by 4:15-5:10, where it has already been noted that Jesus' prayers take on the characteristics of cultic action. In parallel with the high priests of old who offer gifts and sacrifices for sins (5:1), Jesus offers up prayers and supplications (5:7). The cultic activity of Jesus thus begins even before his death as such, embracing the piety of his entire life. Attridge has noted the connection between the description of Jesus' prayer in 5:7 and common Hellenistic Jewish ideas of piety as found, for example, in Philo.[119] There is no need to link this prayer to specific episodes in the Gospel traditions such as the prayer in Gethsemane or the cry from the cross. As Lane observes, "Jesus' passion is described in its entirety as priestly prayer."[120]

Christ's sacrifice of prayer and supplication is heard because of his εὐλάβεια. This term denoting "careful and watchful reverence"[121] has been taken both negatively and positively in 5:7. The negative sense of anxiety does not fit in this context, and the suggestion that εἰσακουσθεὶς ἀπὸ τῆς εὐλαβείας means "he was rescued from the source of his fear" does even more violence to the author's argument. Rather, εὐλάβεια must be seen here positively as "reverent and thoughtful shrinking from over-boldness"[122] which is a keystone of Jewish piety. The author of Hebrews presents the passion of Christ as necessary instruction leading to obedience and finally to perfection (5:8-9). Despite his status

---

[118]Ibid.

[119]Harold Attridge, "Heard Because of His Reverence," *JBL*, 98 (1979), 90-93.

[120]Lane, *Hebrews*, vol. 1, p. 120.

[121]Westcott, *Hebrews*, p. 127.

[122]Ibid.

as Son (5:8), Jesus "suffered, was tortured, and had to learn the painful lesson of obedience and the acceptance of a sorrowful death"[123] before he could appear before God for the sake of those who obey him.

Brief mention is made in chapter nine of Jesus offering "himself" (e.g., 9:14,25). Verses 15-17 describe the necessity of death for the confirming of a covenant. In previous covenants, this would have been the symbolic death of the covenant-maker through the sacrifice of an animal; in the new covenant, however, Christ himself has died not in symbol but in truth.

The shamefulness of Jesus' death is noted in 12:2. The author graphically conveys the same thought in 13:11-13. There Jesus' suffering outside the walls of Jerusalem is compared to the disposal of the carcases of sacrificial animals.[124] One might expect Jesus' death compared to the slaughter of animals on the altar within the temple complex, but the author pushes the imagery to an even cruder and more shocking level by linking the death of Jesus to the burning of the corpses after their blood has already been applied.

Despite the graphic depiction of Jesus' suffering and death, the author clearly sees it as an integral part of Christ's ritual accomplishment.[125] Jesus experienced death "for the sake of everyone" (ὑπὲρ παντός, 2:9). In 5:8-9 Jesus' saving work is conceived as a unity that includes his suffering, glorification, and establishment as the source of eternal salvation. The work of salvation begins on earth, but in terms of its eternal value it is heavenly through and through.[126]

The ascension of Christ. The resurrection of Christ is curiously missing from Hebrews' depiction of his salvific work, occurring explicitly only in the benediction at 13:20-21. Cody is certainly correct in stating that the rationale for

---

[123]Leonardo Boff, *Passion of Christ, Passion of the World*, trans. Robert R. Barr (Maryknoll: Orbis, 1987), p. 85.

[124]The flesh of most sacrificial victims was divided among the priests and the offerer(s). With the sin offering (חַטָּאת), however, if any blood was brought into the tent of assembly the animal became a source of impurity and its body was burned outside the altar area. See Milgrom, "Sacrifices," p. 767.

[125]Cody, *Heavenly Sanctuary*, p. 170.

[126]Ibid., pp. 171-172.

this omission is that the ascension better fits the Day of Atonement typology of entering the holy of holies. The resurrection "is implicitly included" in the author's discussion of ascension even though it never occupies a central place of its own. [127] The spatial imagery of Jesus moving from one realm to another occurs at several important points in Hebrews.

Barrett discusses three major themes in the eschatology of Hebrews: the saints' everlasting rest, the pilgrim's progress from the city of destruction to the celestial city, and the holy place above.[128] The last of these is central to our understanding of Christ's heavenly liturgy. We have already seen how the heavenly sanctuary is charged with eschatological meaning. From one point of view, the heavenly tent and its ministrations are eternal archetypes, but they can also be understood as eschatological events, a fact of cardinal importance for the interpretation of Hebrews.[129] As will be seen below, the language of 9:26 strongly suggests an eschatological event which has taken place, which is reinforced in the next verse by reference to another eschatological event: the return of Christ.

Given this background, it becomes apparent that Christ's entrance into heaven is itself an eschatological experience. A key verse in this regard is 1:6, which is in fact the first clear reference to Jesus' transition to the heavenly world. What exactly does the author mean by εἰς τὴν οἰκουμένην? The phrase has been taken as a reference to the birth of Christ, the parousia, and the enthronement in heaven. Οἰκουμένη occurs only fifteen times in the New Testament and usually can be translated simply "world" or "inhabited world." This occurrence in Hebrews is more problematic. In apocalyptic language, the οἰκουμένη often carries the idea of judgment and testing that mark the end of the age (e.g., Lk. 21:26; Rev. 3:10; 12:9; 16:14). The phrase οἰκουμένη μέλλουσα is the most common translation of the Hebrew הבא עוֹלם, "the world to come." Since this exact phraseology is found in a similar context in 2:5, a strong case can be

---

[127]Ibid., p. 174.

[128]C. K. Barrett, "The Eschatology of the Epistle to the Hebrews," in *The Background of the New Testament and Its Eschatology*, ed. D. Daube and W. D. Davies (Cambridge: University Press, 1956).

[129]Ibid., p. 385.

made that this is the meaning of 1:6, that is, that here as well οἰκουμένη refers to the heavenly world, the "world of salvation."[130]

Christ's entrance into the inner sanctum is not, of course, the final consummation of his liturgy. It is, however, a necessary transition from the earthly world to the heavenly. The importance of this *transitus* may be seen in the attention it receives in Hebrews. In 4:14 believers have a great high priest who has passed through the heavens. This image is clarified in 6:19-20 where the author speaks of a hope "that enters the inner sanctum behind the veil," whither Jesus the forerunner has himself already entered. The full meaning of Jesus' entrance into heaven comes out in 9:11-12 in the author's exposition about the heavenly and earthly sanctuaries, and finally in 9:24-25 where it becomes clear that he has entered heaven itself to appear before God on our behalf.[131] Christ's movement into the heavenly realm thus closely parallels the movement of the high priest on the Day of Atonement as he passes beyond the curtain into the holy of holies. Like the high priest of old, Christ's entrance is accomplished through blood which attains access, but unlike the levitical high priest the blood he offers is his own.

Cody suggests that it is in the ascension that Jesus is "perfected" as a priest, which perfection is necessary for him to be able to complete his work of salvation.[132] But Cody is not entirely consistent at this point, arguing one page earlier for the session of Christ at the right hand of God as the perfecting of his

---

[130]This is in fact the conclusion of George Johnston, "οἰκουμένη and κόσμος in the New Testament," *NTS*, 10 (1964), 354. It is further supported by the parallelism between 1:6, where God leads the first-born εἰς τὴν οἰκουμένην and 2:10, where he leads many sons and daughters εἰς δόξαν, with reference to Jesus as the ἀρχηγός.

[131]The possibility of a Platonic influence on the heavenly vs. earthly imagery in Hebrews has long been suggested. As Isaacs notes, however, the author uses Platonic words (e.g., σκία and εἰκών in 10:1) but not the metaphysical sense of second- and first-order worlds (*Sacred Space*, p. 116). Isaacs correctly states that the author's preoccupation is with the categories of sacred and profane rather than ideal and perceptual (Ibid., p. 61). Much of the author's imagery is in fact drawn from the Old Testament depiction of a heavenly temple and "there is nothing distinctly 'Platonic,' 'philosophical,' or 'noumenal'" in the author's presentation according to L. D. Hurst, *The Epistle to the Hebrews*, SNTSMS 65 (Cambridge: University Press, 1990), p. 42. See also Juliana Casey, "Eschatology in Hebrews 12:14-29: An Exegetical Study" (S.T.D. dissertation, Catholic University of Louvain, 1976), pp. 616-621.

[132]Cody, *Heavenly Sanctuary*, p. 177.

priesthood.[133] The matter of Jesus' "perfection" (5:9) in his priesthood will be addressed below.

The appearance of Christ in the inner sanctum. The leading motif in the author's use of cultic terminology "is that access to God is only possible through the medium of blood."[134] The use of the motif of blood in Hebrews should not be simplistically equated with violent death, as does Gordon.[135] It may in fact be argued that the scriptural idea of blood is essentially that of life, not death.[136] In the end, the ideas of life and death cannot be too easily distinguished when talking about blood, but the motif of life through blood seems to predominate in Hebrews nine. It must first of all be noted that the author's concern here is not so much with the death of Christ as a victim, but with the use of his blood as a source of purification (9:12-14).[137] This accords well with the typology of the Day of Atonement ritual, where the high priest would accomplish the actual rite of expiation not at the outdoor altar but within the holy of holies, where he sprinkled the blood on the Ark of the Covenant. Here Johnsson's explanation of the neologism αἱματεκχυσία in 9:22 is to be preferred over the common translation of the term as "shedding of blood" (KJV, NAS, NRSV, etc.). In the overall context of the passage, the term is much more likely to refer to the "application" of

---

[133]Ibid., p. 176.

[134]Lane, *Hebrews*, vol. 2, p. 218.

[135]Victor Reese Gordon, "Studies in the Covenantal Theology of the Epistle to the Hebrews in Light of Its Setting," (Ph.D. dissertation, Fuller Theological Seminary, 1979), pp. 257-261, who favorably quotes Johannes Behm, *TDNT*, vol. 1, p. 174 to the effect that "blood of Christ" is "simply" (?) another, even more graphic phrase than "cross" for the death of Christ. See also Leon Morris, *The Apostolic Preaching of the Cross* (Grand Rapids: Eerdmans, 1955), pp. 108-117.

[136]See Westcott, *Hebrews*, pp. 293-295, for whom the blood of Christ has both quickening power and the power of consecration.

[137]Ibid., p. 261. See also Christopher Crocker, "Ritual and the Development of Social Structure: Liminality and Inversion," in *The Roots of Ritual*, ed. James Shaughnessy (Grand Rapids: Eerdmans, 1973), p. 71, on the mystical potency of blood in ritual.

blood than to its provision,[138] although obviously a provision of blood must be made (9:25,28; 10:10).

For both Christ and the levitical high priest, the blood of the sacrifice gains entrance into the divine presence in the holy of holies. Christ enters the inner sanctum through his own blood (διά, 9:12, RSV "taking"). One might expect a description of Jesus somehow applying his blood in heaven, but such is not the case. Gordon goes so far as to claim that in Hebrews there is no indication "that Jesus presents or offers his blood in heaven."[139] This is true in terms of the explicit description of the Christ Cultus in Hebrews, but on the other hand the author leaves no doubt that Jesus' blood is in fact in heaven, speaking a better word than the blood of Abel (12:24). Omanson argues that the statements in 9:23 do in fact describe Christ taking his own blood into the heavenly sanctuary to cleanse it.[140] Many interpreters shrink away from such an interpretation because of a theological concern that the atonement be made to depend on some event subsequent to the cross.[141] The author's interest, however, is not to denigrate the redemptive power of the death of Jesus. Rather, it is to express fully the redemptive power of the resurrection and exaltation of Jesus. It is, after all, because of the neverending life of Jesus that he is the Great High Priest (7:3,16,23-25).[142] Gordon claims too much by suggesting that the idea of Jesus presenting his blood in heaven represents "a misunderstanding of the writer of Hebrews' use

---

[138]Johnsson, "Defilement," pp. 322-323.

[139]Gordon, "Covenantal Theology," p. 298.

[140]Roger L. Omanson, "A Superior Covenant: Hebrews 8:1-10:18," *RevExp*, 82 (1985), 368.

[141]For such a view, see Bruce, *Hebrews*, pp. 213-214; Philip Edgcumbe Hughes, "The Blood of Jesus and His Heavenly Priesthood in Hebrews," *Bibliotheca Sacra*, 130 (1973), pp. 207-212; Young, "Gospel," pp. 207-209.

[142]See also Romans 4:25, where Jesus "was handed over to death for our trespasses and *was raised* for our justification" (NRSV); and Romans 5:10: "For if while we were enemies, we were reconciled to God through the death of his Son, much more surely, having been reconciled, will we be saved by his *life*" (NRSV).

of typology."[143]

Gordon himself seems to misunderstand the unconventional use of προσφέρω in Hebrews. The use of this verb in 9:7 for the application of blood in the holy of holies is without precedent in the LXX.[144] The act of aspersion, which is clearly the author's intended meaning in 9:7, was indicated by ραίνω or ἐπιτίθημι. Προσφέρω referred to the actual sacrifice, and it is in fact used of the death of Christ in 9:14,25,28; and 10:12. The author's unconventional usage "prepares the way" for his upcoming exposition on the heavenly liturgy of Christ, [145] and it also creates a close connection between the provision and the application of the blood of the sacrificial victim.

Through the medium of his blood, Christ has entered heaven itself, "now to be shown before God on our behalf" (9:24). The passive infinitive ἐμφανισθῆναι is often overlooked. Christ is made "a clear object of sight" in the presence of God.[146] Thus it is not so much that Jesus has been granted a vision of God, but that God now looks upon Jesus.[147] This appearance before God is "once for all" (9:26), and points to eschatological realities in that it occurs "at the consummation (συντελεία) of the age," and issues in the promise of Christ's future appearance to save believers (9:28). This completes the author's typological exposition of the Day of Atonement liturgy, in which the high priest returns from the inner compartment of the sanctuary after atonement has been made.

The idea of Jesus' presence before God is the key to understanding the author's concept of Jesus' function as High Priest.[148] It is in God's presence behind the curtain that Jesus fully performs his priestly duties of purifying the sanctuary (9:23), appearing before God on our behalf (9:24), and forever

---

[143]Gordon, "Covenantal Theology," p. 298, n. 199.

[144]Lane, *Hebrews*, vol. 2, p. 223.

[145]Ibid., p. 223.

[146]Westcott, *Hebrews*, p. 272.

[147]Ibid.

[148]Cody, *Heavenly Sanctuary*, p. 193.

interceding for us (7:25).[149] The results of Christ's liturgy may be seen both positively and negatively. Negatively, Christ's sacrifice removes sin as a barrier to union with God. Positively, it makes direct access to God available.[150]

Hebrews devotes a considerable amount of attention to the motif of enthronement beginning at 1:3. The author's main point is in fact that we have a high priest "seated at the right hand of the throne of the Majesty in the heavens" (8:1). Cody remarks that the author seems even more concerned with the session of Christ than with his ascension.[151] This emphasis is a natural outgrowth of the author's insistence on the once-for-all nature of Christ's liturgical performance, as becomes clear in 10:11-14. The earthly priest stands day after day; but Christ offered a single, definitive sacrifice and then sat down, having perfected the people for all time.

Toward an Understanding of the Christ Cultus

Before examining the relevance of Hebrews' depiction of the Christ Cultus and the Old Covenant Cultus for Christian spirituality there remains the question of a broad conceptual framework. How is one to understand the author's central assumptions and declarations regarding the liturgical activity of Jesus as High Priest in the heavenly sanctuary? In this section we suggest that the typology of rites of passage is a helpful framework in which to interpret the author's cultic exposition.

We begin with Radcliffe's observation of "cultic irony" in Hebrews' interpretation of Jesus' saving work.[152] Radcliffe notes three aspects of this irony, namely

1. that Jesus is called a priest even though the Gospels consistently depict him

---

[149]Ibid., p. 193.

[150]Ibid., p. 168.

[151]Ibid., p. 175.

[152]Timothy Radcliffe, "Christ in Hebrews: Cultic Irony," *New Blackfriars*, 68 (1987), 494.

as a layperson who ignores the rules of cultic purity,[153]

2. that God's supreme creative act, closely connected with ritual activity, is not the cosmic distinctions of Genesis 1 (e.g., between light and darkness, sea and dry land, etc.) but the death and resurrection of Christ,[154] and

3. that Jesus' priesthood is based not on separation from but solidarity with others, thus transforming God's relationship to suffering and death.[155]

One notes that the ironic elements that Radcliffe isolates all have to do with the preliminary phases of the Christ Cultus and, except for the mention of resurrection under number two, all are specifically tied to the initial movement of Christ's liturgy in his passion and death. In terms of our tripartite division of the Christ Cultus we might remark that the depiction of the death of Jesus as ritual action involves ironic cultic personnel (Jesus, who does not belong to the priestly class, 7:13-14), place (outside the city gate rather than within the temple complex, 13:12), and performance (not formally cultic at all but a shameful death with great suffering, 5:7; 12:2). The one cultic connection the author could have made with the death of Jesus was the time of its occurrence, at Passover (1 Cor. 5:7; 10:15), but this avenue of interpretation is never addressed in Hebrews. With the transition to the heavenly realm the ironic fades away and Jesus becomes an exalted heavenly figure.

The description of the Christ Cultus in Hebrews bears some affinities with van Gennep's discussion of rites of passage that are worthy of exploration.[156] As is well known, van Gennep suggests that a rite of passage has three distinct phases. First is the phase of *separation* that clearly demarcates sacred space and time. After this comes the phase of *transition*, often called the liminal or "threshold" phase, in which the subject of the rite passes through a period of ambiguity. Finally, the rite concludes with an aggregation or *incorporation* phase in which the subject returns

---

[153]Ibid., see also Heb. 7:13-14. For this reason Jesus constantly raises the ire of the Pharisees, who were in fact laypeople who observed strict cultic purity.

[154]Ibid., p. 497.

[155]Ibid., p. 499. Radcliffe's argument at this point needs to have included reference to the contradictory statment that Jesus is separated from sinners in 7:26.

[156]Arnold van Gennep, *The Rites of Passage*, trans. Monika B. Vizedom and Gabrielle L. Caffee (Chicago: University Press, 1960).

to a new, relatively stable and well-defined position in the total society.[157] At first sight, it would seem that the transition phase in this typology would correspond most closely to Christ's ascension. In his passion and death he is separated from his previous earthly status, ultimately to be exalted to a heavenly status after "passing through the heavens" (4:14). In actuality, it is the death of Christ that most partakes of the quality of "liminality." Turner has developed the idea of liminality primarily by reference to the rituals of the Ndembu people of Zambia. Of particular interest here, he describes how a chief-elect must be abased by his future subjects as part of his installation rite. In this and other rites of passage "the passage from lower to higher status is through a limbo of statuslessness."[158] In this light, is it possible that the irony that Radcliffe notes in the cultic imagery of Hebrews is due not to irony as such but rather to the liminal character of the sufferings of Jesus? This would seem plausible as a way of understanding the statement in 2:10 that Jesus is made perfect through his sufferings. Radcliffe sees this statement as an ironic depiction of priestly ordination through suffering,[159] but phenomenologically one would expect a priest-elect (assuming that is the role Jesus here plays) to undergo trials before the ultimate consummation of his office.

Another hint toward the nature of the Christ Cultus as a rite of passage comes from attention to Hebrews' use of the word τελειόω. While many have sought in this word a technical term for priestly ordination,[160] many others remain unconvinced. As Peterson has demonstrated, τελειόω is used in the LXX in many different contexts. Though its usage is formal, religious, and cultic, the word need not be a technical term for the consecration of priests.[161] Although some contend

[157]Ibid., pp. 10-11.

[158]Turner, *The Ritual Process*, p. 97.

[159]Radcliffe, "Cultic Irony," p. 500.

[160]Martin Dibelius, "Der himmlische Kultus nach dem Hebräerbrief," in *Botschaft und Geschichte*, vol. 2 (Tübingen: Mohr, 1956), p. 166; Vanhoye, *Old Testament Priests*, p. 83.

[161]David Peterson, *Hebrews and Perfection* (Cambridge: University Press, 1982), pp. 23-30.

that the word can be rendered "consecrate" in LXX texts that involve ritual activity,[162] Loader has analyzed every occurrence in Hebrews and refutes any claim that it there describes priestly consecration.[163] Similarly, Scholer surveys the evidence for moral/ethical, consecratory, and "paideutic" interpretations of "perfection" in Hebrews and finds all three to be inadequate.[164]

Johnsson's observation that since the author of Hebrews distinguishes between τελειόω and ἁγιάζω it is highly unlikely that τελειόω means "to consecrate" is well taken.[165] His own conclusion is that ἁγιάζω and τελειόω are related to each other as the initiation and culmination of the general cultic activity of καθαρίζω or "purgation."[166] As he describes it, ἁγιάζω "marks the point of transition, of separation from the profane, in the approach to the Sacred,"[167] while τελειόω comprises the *summum bonum* of believers: access to the divine presence and participation in the heavenly cultus made possible by definitive cleansing.[168] In this light Johnsson suggests "incorporation" as a more fitting translation for τελειόω than "perfection," "consecration," or "initiation."[169]

One immediately notes the rite-of-passage terminology that Johnsson uses to describe ἁγιάζω and τελειόω in Hebrews: "transition," "separation," and "incorporation." The connection becomes even clearer in Johnsson's diagram on

---

[162]John M. Scholer, *Proleptic Priests*, JSNTSS 49 (Sheffield: Academic Press, 1991), p. 190.

[163]William G. Loader, *Sohn und Hoherpriester* (Neukirchen-Vluyn: Neukirchen, 1981), pp. 40-47.

[164]Scholer, *Proleptic*, pp. 187-195. He finally concludes that τελειόω is equivalent to προσέρχομαι and εἰσέρχομαι, and that all three words have to do with access to the heavenly holy of holies, pp. 198-199.

[165]Johnsson, "Defilement," p. 262.

[166]Ibid., p. 265.

[167]Ibid., p. 264.

[168]Ibid., pp. 260-266.

[169]Ibid., p. 261.

page 265:

ἁγιάζειν - - - - - - - - - - - - - - - -> τελειοῦν
separation   incorporation

Johnsson contends that what we are calling the Old Covenant Cultus provides consecration (separation) but no incorporation; but that both consecration and incorporation are to be found in the Christ Cultus and the New Covenant Cultus.[170] Remarkably, Johnsson only once makes mention of the affinities of his conceptualization of defilement and purgation with rites of passage, and there only in passing.[171] Thus, while he is able to describe incorporation as a state of being fit for cultic participation, the fuller implications of this incorporation are left to be developed.

It is left for us to determine more precisely the "passages" that are implied in the author's cultic exposition. Most obviously, the Christ Cultus effects passage of a corporate nature for believers. The question also remains as to whether this typology can be pressed to describe Jesus' own experience of death, ascension, and entrance into heaven.

Corporate Rites of Passage

Although most scholars today make particular note of individual rites of passage at times of personal crisis such as birth, puberty, marriage, and death, van Gennep also suggests that whole societies can undergo such rites. Corporate rites of passage are often tied to the calendar and coincide with transition points in the agricultural year. Such ceremonies do not conclude with an elevation of status as is most often the case with individual rites but rather tend to sustain the overall functioning of the whole group. As Turner states of the incorporation phase of such corporate rites,

> for those taking part in a calendrical or seasonal ritual, no change in status may be involved, but they have been ritually prepared for a whole series of changes in the nature of the cultural and ecological activities to be undertaken and of the relationships they will then have with others--all these holding good for a

---

[170]Ibid., p. 264.

[171]Ibid., p. 270.

specific quadrant of the annual production cycle.[172]

Such corporate rites of passage were indisputably part of Israel's cultic heritage. Our question at this point is which of the many corporate rite paradigms the author employs to describe the Christ Cultus and how in fact he did so.

One corporate rite of great importance in Hebrews is the rite of covenant inauguration. The question of whether or not an annual covenant renewal ritual was a part of ancient Israel's cultic experience is beyond the scope of our concern. For the author of Hebrews the important thing was that Israel was indeed brought into a special covenantal relationship with Yahweh at Mount Sinai.

The author of Hebrews postulates that Christ is the guarantor or mediator of a better covenant (7:22; 8:6). This proposition is most fully explored in chapter 8, where the author quotes an extensive section of Jeremiah's prophecy of a new covenant between God and his people. The epitome of this new covenant is the cleansing of the συνείδησις (9:14; 10:2).

Although this new covenant is described in chapter 8 the full explanation of its connection with the first covenant appears only in 9:15-22. Here the author makes obvious reference to the covenant inauguration rite depicted in Exodus 24. The author does, however, merge his presentation of the event with the scene of the initiation of the tent and its worship in Numbers 7.[173] In Hebrews, the blood of the covenant is no longer divided nor dashed against the altar as Exodus describes. Instead there is a sprinkling of the scroll, the people, the tent, and the sacra. Lehne has commented that this act of sprinkling "bears more resemblance to an expiatory cleansing rite than to a covenant sacrifice."[174] In fact, the text itself leads one to that conclusion with the mention of purification in 9:22.

For the author of Hebrews, the inauguration of the old covenant was essentially a blood ritual with its own internal logic regarding the meaning of sacrifice and blood. This logic becomes apparent in 9:15-17 and again at 9:22. First one must deal with the *crux interpretum* in 9:16-17 regarding the meaning of

---

[172]Turner, *Process, Performance and Pilgrimage*, pp. 16-17.

[173]Susanne Lehne, *The New Covenant in Hebrews*, JSNTSS 44 (Sheffield: Academic Press, 1990), p. 23.

[174]Ibid.

διαθήκη: is it a "covenant" or a "will" in these verses? Here Johnsson must be correct in his discussion of the logical and syntactical reasons for taking διαθήκη as covenant here.[175] The issue would appear to be settled by the phrasing of verse 18 which makes reference to ἡ πρώτη. This must mean ἡ πρώτη διαθήκη, picking up the subject from verse 17, and in context can only be translated "the first *covenant.*"

What, then, of the death of the διαθέμενος in 9:16? In the ancient world covenants were made with a sacrifice that might be understood to represent the death of some party to the transaction.[176] Thus the διαθέμενος can be the "mediator" of a covenant as well as the "testator" of a will.[177] In this light, Nairne suggests that several words or phrases in 9:16-17 might be taken as expressing such a theory of covenant sacrifice.[178] If Nairne is correct, these two verses would be translated as follows:

> For where there is a covenant, it is necessary for the death of the covenanter to be represented (φερέσθαι), for a covenant is made secure over dead bodies (ἐπὶ νεκροῖς), since it is not then (μὴ τότε)[179] in force when the covenanter lives.

For the author of Hebrews the new covenant, like any covenant, is inaugurated by a blood rite that involves the death of the one who inaugurates it. Unlike previous covenants, in the new covenant this death is not merely symbolic but actual. As the author conceives it, the purpose of the covenant blood is purificatory (9:22). Here, as elsewhere in Hebrews, the author has let his presumption about the role of Christ color his interpretation of religion in general.

---

[175]Johnsson, "Defilement," pp. 306-311. Attridge, *Hebrews*, p.255, argues, however, that διαθήκη must mean "testament" here. Bruce, *Hebrews*, p. 221 prefers the comprehensive term "settlement."

[176]Alexander Nairne, *Epistle of Priesthood* (Edinburgh: Clark, 1913) p. 365; Johnsson, "Defilement," p. 314; *contra* Bruce, *Hebrews*, p. 223.

[177]Nairne, "Priesthood," p. 365. Johnsson, "Defilement," p. 310 suggests the translation "covenanter."

[178]Nairne, "Priesthood," p. 365.

[179]Nairne prefers this variant to the μήποτε, "otherwise" in the Nestle-Aland text. This point is not crucial to the overall interpretation he suggests.

Just as earlier he depicted the requirements of the high priestly office in terms of what he wanted to say about the character of Christ (4:15-5:10), here he describes the efficacy of covenant blood in terms of what he is getting ready to discuss in terms of the efficacy of Jesus' blood (9:23-26).

This then is the first rite of passage paradigm the author uses to describe the Christ Cultus. Through this paradigm the author depicts Christ's role in effecting believers' transition from a status of having no special covenant relationship with God to the status of covenant partners. The moment of incorporation is properly found in the rite of sprinkling of the blood of the covenant. The preeminent corporate rites of passage in the Jewish calendar would be the three pilgrimage festivals of Booths, Passover, and Pentecost. The Day of Atonement also partakes of some of the same features. As the climax of the ancient Hebrew New Year's Festival, the Day of Atonement is also a cyclical rite of passage for the entire community as it moves from the impurity of past sins to a renewed state of holiness.[180]

That the imagery of the Day of Atonement ritual is a primary paradigm in Hebrews' cultic exposition is beyond dispute, and much of this imagery has already been discussed above. It is appropriate, however, to devote some time to a discussion of the Day of Atonement as a rite of passage.

Hebrews' treatment of the Day of Atonement answers to the typology of a rite of passage in two distinct ways. First, as already mentioned, the Old Testament rite from which the author draws his imagery is a rite of passage of the cyclical, corporate type described by van Gennep. It was and is a time of repentance for the sins of the past year in preparation for the coming year. The day was regarded as a festive day (*b.Sabb.* 119), yet Israel was enjoined to "afflict the soul" thereon (Lev. 16:29). This phrase has been taken to mean that the people are obliged to keep a

---

[180]Victor Turner, "Liminality, Kabbalah, and the Media," *Religion*, 15 (1985), 207-208 suggests that, in addition to individual and calendrical rituals there is a distinct third category: rituals of affliction. These are rites that have to do with remedying misfortune, illness, and the like, and may be either corporate or individual. The Day of Atonement would undoubtedly qualify as a corporate ritual of affliction, but here our concern is more generally with individual versus corporate rituals.

strict fast on this particular day.[181] As the people experienced self-denial, so also the high priest was in a sense brought low on this day.[182] Milgrom has noted certain correspondences between the Day of Atonement and the Babylonian New Year celebration.[183] In particular he notes one aspect of the Babylonian king's duties at the new year which approximates the cleansing of the sanctuary on the Day of Atonement. Before the king may enter the sanctuary to purge it with sacrificial blood, he is stripped of his clothing and subjected to "rites of humiliation."[184] It may be a similar mark of liminality that on the Day of Atonement the high priest is divested of his princely garments and dressed in "simple linen vestments."[185]

What is a rite of passage for the people of Israel as their sins are atoned in the repurification of the sanctuary is equally a rite of passage for the high priest himself. In a very literal sense the high priest crosses the threshold into the very presence of God. Then, after completing his ritual tasks, he is reincorporated into the congregation as he appears to bless the people.

The author's use of Day of Atonement imagery also provides a a unique reinterpretation of the traditional Hebrew understanding of expiation. As it stands in the Old Testament and in contemporary Jewish thought, defilement and purgation follow one another in a never ending oscillatory cycle. Whatever cleansing is

---

[181]According to *m.Yoma* 8:1 eating, drinking, washing, anointing, putting on sandals, and marital intercourse were forbidden. Neither could people engage in work (*m.Yoma* 8:3): the same kinds of work forbidden on the sabbath were forbidden on the Day of Atonement (*m.Meg.* 1:5). According to *Jubilees* 5:17-18 the day was established on the day that Jacob heard of Joseph's death, and thus one should perform rites of mourning. Philo considered the day an experience of true joy derived from abstinence and devotion to prayer morning to night (*Spec.* I, 186-188; II, 193-203; *Mos.* II, 23-24).

[182]He was adjured to perform the liturgy correctly to the extent that both he and his assistants wept (*m.Yoma* 1:5). On the eve of the day he was kept awake all night long (*m.Yoma* 1:4,7). Before he entered the inner sanctum he made a public rite of confession of sins (*m.Yoma* 4:2).

[183]Jacob Milgrom, *Leviticus*, vol. 1, The Anchor Bible (New York: Doubleday, 1991), pp. 568-569.

[184]Ibid., p. 568.

[185]Ibid., p. 569. While this may have been the original intent of the vestments, in the first century they were, in fact, quite costly garments (*m.Yoma* 3:7).

experienced in the high priest's ministrations on the Day of Atonement is a temporary arrangement. For this reason the high priest must year after year offer the same sacrifices (10:1). The particularity of Hebrews' cultic thought is, however, that in the cultic work of Christ, this cycle can be broken by a conclusive, never to be repeated sacrifice (10:10).[186] The Christ Cultus is then a rite of passage that removes believers from the cycle of defilement and purgation and establishes them in a new kind of relationship with God where their status as cleansed persons is permanent. In both corporate paradigms, in fact, the whole group of believers experience a definite elevation of status. These corporate rites are not cyclical but linear. The establishment of covenant relations with God and the cleansing from sins are both unique, never to be repeated events.

An Individual Rite?

We have seen how the cultic activity of Christ may fit the typology of a rite of passage with respect to its effect on believers. Can the model also shed light on the meaning of Jesus' cultus for Jesus himself? Here we address the question as to how and when Jesus became our Great High Priest.

It must first be frankly acknowledged that the author of Hebrews gives no straightforward answer to the question of precisely when Jesus became High Priest.[187] Hebrews nevertheless asserts that Jesus was not a priest from all eternity: he became a priest (2:17; 5:5; 6:20), was constituted a priest (5:1; 7:11,15,28; 8:3), and, like Aaron, received the priestly honor from God (5:4-6).[188] Roman Catholic scholars have widely held that Christ became high priest in the incarnation.[189] Others see Jesus' incarnation, particularly his life of obedience (5:8), as preparatory to attaining this office.[190] In any event, all are agreed that the consummation of Christ's eternal priesthood is to be found in his entrance into the

---

[186]Johnsson, "Defilement," p. 376.

[187]Peterson, *Hebrews and Perfection*, p. 193.

[188]Cody, *Heavenly Sanctuary*, p. 93.

[189]Ibid., pp. 94-98, is typical of this view.

[190]Peterson, *Hebrews and Perfection*, p. 194.

heavenly sanctuary and enthronement at the right hand of God.[191]

We have already seen how the sufferings of Christ may point to the quality of liminality in the Christ Cultus. It is yet to be seen whether or not we are justified in thinking of the Christ's "perfection" in Hebrews as any sort of priestly ordination.

According to de Vaux, priests in ancient Israel were not ordained but began their work "without any religious rite conferring on them grace, or special powers."[192] While this view is nearly unthinkable in light of current understandings of the importance of ritual in traditional cultures, it need not be refuted here. The author had at his disposal the model for such an ordination in the consecration of Aaron and his sons in Leviticus eight.

It must be stated at the outset that τελειόω cannot be pressed to mean "to ordain" in Hebrews for reasons which have already been set forth.[193] If Hebrews depicts the process of Jesus becoming priest at all, then his "perfection" is not the process as a whole, but the final, culminative stage.[194] This stage involves the exaltation of Christ in heaven. Its central emphasis is not consecratory but eschatological. More properly, the author conceives of cultic consecration through eschatological exaltation.[195]

There is, however, one aspect of the consecration rite described in Leviticus eight that commands our attention. This is the fact that the consecration of Aaron

---

[191]Ibid., pp. 192-193; Cody, *Heavenly Sanctuary*, pp. 176-177.

[192]de Vaux, *Ancient Israel*, p. 347.

[193]The only real evidence for this usage is the septuagintal expression τελειόω τὰς χείρας ("to fill the hands"), a literal translation of the Hebrew expression for installing a priest in his office. Peterson's argument that the verb by itself cannot be pressed into such a precise meaning is quite convincing.

[194]Scholer, *Proleptic*, pp. 196-197; see also Ernst Käsemann, *The Wandering People of God*, trans. Roy A. Harrisville and Irving L. Sandberg (Minneapolis: Augsburg, 1984), p. 144; Moisés Silva, "Perfection and Eschatology in Hebrews," *Westminster Theological Journal*, 39 (1976), 65; Michel, p. 146;

[195]Silva, "Perfection," p. 67.

and his sons was completed with a rite of blood sprinkling (Lev. 8:30).[196] The presence of such a blood rite is a common strand in the ceremonies of covenant inauguration, sanctuary purgation, and priestly consecration. The similarities between the rites in Leviticus 8 and 16 point to a similar function.[197] Both the priests and the sacred furniture must be prepared with blood as sacred vessels. Likewise, Levine has noted that the dashing of blood against the altar in the consecration of priests is reminiscent of the scene at the inauguration of the Sinaitic covenant (Exod. 24:6-8).[198] In fact, the only two instances of people being sprinkled with blood in the Old Testament are at the covenant inauguration in Exodus 24 and the consecration of priests in Exodus 29 and Leviticus 8.[199]

Hebrews' use of the title "High Priest" is closely connected to the use of the designation "Son" (3:1-6; 5:5-6). Both titles seem to reach their consummation in the eschatological enthronement of Jesus, whatever may be said for when it first becomes appropriate to bestow these titles on him. The pre-incarnate Christ is indeed called "Son" in 1:2. But, as we have seen, the divine proclamation "you are my Son" (1:5) occurs in the context of Christ's heavenly exaltation, which resembles here a royal enthronement liturgy.[200] Peterson makes the point that the proclamation of Jesus' eternal high priesthood in the exaltation must not be divorced from his previous high priestly work.[201] It is thus not quite correct to

---

[196]"This ritual effectuated the consecration of the priests" according to Nahum Sarna, *Exodus*, The Jewish Publication Society Torah Commentary (Philadelphia: Jewish Publication Society, 1991), p. 189. See also Baruch A. Levine, *Leviticus*, The Jewish Publication Society Torah Commentary (Philadelphia: Jewish Publication Society, 1989), p. 54.

[197]Milgrom, *Leviticus*, p. 522, in fact notes a pattern of two blood rites in each case: blood is first daubed at the extremities (either the horns of the altar or the ear, thumb, and toe of the priests), and then sprinkled (Lev. 8:23,30 and Exod. 29:20-21 for priests; Lev. 16:18-19 for Day of Atonement).

[198]Levine, *Leviticus*, p. 53.

[199]Westcott, *Hebrews*, p. 267.

[200]Lehne, *New Covenant*, p. 28.

[201]Peterson, *Hebrews and Perfection*, p. 193.

speak of Christ's τελείωσις as his "attaining to his heavenly office"[202]: he already held it while on earth. Nevertheless, the Christ Cultus does by its very nature describe a rite of passage in which Christ himself departs the earthly realm by passing through a liminal stage of status reversal (5:7-8) and finally enters into the heavenly realm where he serves before God as High Priest (5:9-10).[203]

We conclude then that the Christ Cultus has affinities with a rite of priestly consecration, and that it culminates in the "perfection" of Jesus' priesthood (2:10; 5:9). These affinities, though, have more to do with the nature of both the Christ Cultus and the levitical consecration ceremony as rites of passage than with any specific attempt to depict the ordination of Jesus as a priest. The imagery of priestly consecration is the best cultic model available to the author to describe what the Christ Cultus meant to Jesus himself, but it is not a perfect fit. In the Christ Cultus, particularly in the final phase of heavenly exaltation, Jesus' priesthood is proclaimed and consummated. This is not to suggest, however, that it was only in the heavenly sanctuary that Jesus "became" a priest. One must draw a distinction between the beginning and end of the process, and the most that can be said here is that in his heavenly exaltation Jesus is openly proclaimed Son and High Priest.

In any event, interpreters should not stumble over the seemingly logical conclusion that the author of Hebrews must have intended to depict Jesus as a full-fledged priest before performing his expiatory ritual. Such is the inclination of Cody,[204] and Scholer explicitly warns that "the consecratory meaning [of τελειόω] logically asserts that Jesus was not a high priest until his 'perfection' in the heavenly realm."[205]. Here the author's strong emphasis on the singularity of the Christ Cultus exerts itself. The author of Hebrews manifests "a sovereign

---

[202]Johnsson, "Defilement," p. 374.

[203]This pattern answers generally to the "setting apart" of priests as even de Vaux is willing to describe it: "The priest, therefore, had quitted [sic] the profane world, and entered into a sacred realm," de Vaux, *Ancient Israel*, p. 348.

[204]Cody, *Heavenly Sanctuary*, p. 176.

[205]Scholer, *Proleptic*, p. 192. Peterson, *Hebrews and Perfection*, p. 193 also falls into this logic.

disdain for the niceties of the old cult"[206] which involve scores of discrete regulations and activities. In contrast, the Christ Cultus is one and "once for all." There is simply no room in the author's conceptualization for another rite involving Jesus: his cultus is simultaneously a rite of passage for both himself and his people.

We conclude that the Christ Cultus is fruitfully explained in terms of three interlocking paradigms, all of which may be conceived as rites of passage. Two of these paradigms, covenant inauguration and the Day of Atonement, reflect the benefits of Christ's ritual performance for human beings. A third paradigm, that of priestly consecration, partially describes Christ's own experience of suffering and exaltation. We may summarize these paradigms as follows:

previous status   passage   new status

corporate rites:

no relationship-------------->(blood)-------->covenant partner
defiled---------------------->(blood)---->definitively cleansed

individual rite:

considered as laity---------->(blood)-------->exalted as priest

The bond that links these rites together is the central rite of blood aspersion involved in each of them in their Old Testament setting. In his primary assumption of passage through blood (9:7,12), the author produces a creative synthesis of three strands of Old Testament ritual through which he tells the story of Jesus.

The Cultic Foundation and the
Spirituality of Hebrews

The true flowering of Hebrews' spirituality is to be found in the author's depiction of the cultic activity of believers both on earth and as participants in the heavenly liturgy. Nevertheless, some preliminary remarks are appropriate at this time. Primarily, some assessment may now be made of the author's understanding of authentic and inauthentic religion. Something may also be said about the practice

---

[206]Robert J. Daly, *Christian Sacrifice*, CUASCA 18 (Washington: Catholic University of America, 1978), p. 282.

of spirituality.

*Expressions of Authentic
and Inauthentic*

The study of the cultic foundation of Hebrews indicates the author's preoccupation with a cluster of closely related themes. Paramount among these is that of direct access to God.[207] Everything, it seems, hinges on whether or not such access is available. Access to the divine presence is the consummate expression of authentic spirituality in Hebrews. The author denies that such access is possible under the Old Covenant Cultus, indeed he interprets Old Testament tradition in such a way that even in the Sinai theophany and Ark of the Covenant access to God is severely restricted, if possible at all. In contrast, Jesus has appeared before God on our behalf, and has won for us access to the inner sanctum.

In the most basic terms, the author of Hebrews is concerned with (1) sin, which restricts access to God and (2) blood, which permits it. This contrast holds true in both the Old Covenant Cultus and the Christ Cultus. In both systems the culprit is sin, an almost physical defilement that requires cleansing;[208] and in both systems the definitive cleansing agent is sacrificial blood. Furthermore, in describing both systems the author asserts the need for a qualified intermediary to offer the blood and thus put away sin.

Although blood is efficacious in both cultuses, the extent of its effectiveness varies. In the Old Covenant Cultus, sacrificial blood is capable of external cleansing (9:9-10), but it cannot purge the inner self ($\sigma\upsilon\nu\epsilon\acute{\iota}\delta\eta\sigma\iota\varsigma$, 9:9; 10:2). In contrast, the Christ Cultus effects definitive and eternal cleansing. As a corollary to this understanding of purgation and defilement, the author asserts that the ministrations of the Old Covenant must be continuously repeated, while Christ's sacrifice was once for all.

Finally, the author makes a strong distinction between the heavenly and the earthly *vis-à-vis* the two cultuses. The old covenant priests minister in a sanctuary

---

[207]Louis Bouyer, *History of Christian Spirituality*, vol. 1 (London: Burns and Oates, 1960), p. 144.

[208]Crocker, "Ritual and the Development," p. 70-71, notes that dirt is often a liminal symbol in that it speaks of things "out of place," that is, no longer ordered in the proper categories. The result is "pollution" that must be removed through ritual means.

which is a mere "sketch" or "shadow" of the true sanctuary in heaven (8:2,5). This is an earthly tent (9:1), but Christ has passed through the greater and more perfect tent not made with hands (9:11). Ultimately, the author dismisses the whole Old Covenant Cultus as "that which can be touched" (ψηλαφώμενος, 12:18). In so doing, he locates the only sacred space worth having in heaven itself.[209] It must be remembered, however, that the author is dealing with axiological realities more than with cosmological ones.[210] By uniting the earthbound, temporal death of Jesus so closely with the remainder of the Christ Cultus, Hebrews makes it too a part of a heavenly liturgy. The author thus opens the door for the possibility that something of the heavenly may be experienced on earth.

In summary, the author of Hebrews notes two aspects of the authentic which obtain in both the Old Covenant Cultus and the Christ Cultus: the need for a mediator and the effectiveness of blood for cleansing from sin. Of these the latter is the central concern of his cultic exposition in 9:1-28.

Additionally, there are three aspects in which the Old Covenant Cultus exemplifies the inauthentic and the Christ Cultus the authentic. First and most important, the Christ Cultus provides direct access to the divine while the Old Covenant Cultus knows only a severely restricted access which in practical terms is no access at all. Second, the sacrifice of Christ brings conclusive, eternal purgation and is able to cleanse even the conscience of the worshipers while the levitical system can cleanse only superficially and temporarily. Finally, Jesus' priesthood, sanctuary, and liturgy are of heavenly value while the cultic elements of the Law are earthly in nature.

The Practice of Spirituality

At this point strong conclusions regarding the practice of spirituality in Hebrews are premature. Two observations are offered, however, in the expectation of further development at a later time.

The first observation has to do with the role of Jesus as High Priest. No spirituality would be true to the message of Hebrews that did not make much of the central role of Jesus himself in obtaining salvation for those who believe in him.

---

[209]Isaacs, *Sacred Space*, p. 67.

[210]Cody, *Heavenly Sanctuary*, pp. 78-84.

Jesus is the center of spirituality in Hebrews, as indeed he must be in any genuinely Christian spirituality.[211] In this light, we have already seen the use of terms like "forerunner" (πρόδρομος, 6:20) and "leader" (ἀρχηγός, 2:10; 12:2) as titles for Christ. Whatever Christians do to live out their Christian faith, Jesus is their empowerer.

The second observation is a corollary of the first. It is that Christ's piety described in 5:7-8 contains definite echoes of traditional Hellenistic Jewish teachings about the spiritual life. This is particularly seen in the description of Jesus' prayer in verse 7, which shows affinities with the opening paragraphs of Philo's *Quis rerum divinarum heres sit* and his teachings about how a pious person ought to pray. The idea of learning through suffering is also a common theme in the Hellenistic world, no doubt encouraged by the verbal similarity between μαθ– and παθ–. The author of Hebrews thus looked upon Jesus as an example of true piety; and therefore it is not unreasonable to suggest that he saw Jesus not only as a Priest to be obeyed and trusted, but as an example to be followed.

---

[211]Rea McDonnell, *The Catholic Epistles and Hebrews* , Message of Biblical Spirituality 14 (Wilmington: Glazier, 1986), p. 89.

Chapter 4

THE HEAVENLY CULTUS

The ritual activity of Christ may justifiably be called a heavenly as well as a new covenant cultus, but for ease of reference, these two terms have a specific meaning in this study. By Heavenly Cultus we mean those acts of worship performed by angels. Similarly, the term New Covenant Cultus implies the activities of believers on earth which are cultic in their conceptualization.

The Heavenly Cultus is overall a minor concern in Hebrews, but it does figure prominently in two important passages. The first of these is 1:5-14, where the angels are called on to worship the exalted Son. The second passage to be considered is 12:18-24, where worshiping angels are present in the heavenly Jerusalem. After a survey of thought on the subject in relevant literature outside of Hebrews we shall examine these passages with particular reference to the author's depiction of the Heavenly Cultus.

The Heavenly Cultus in Judaism and
Early Christianity

Thought about angels is most fully developed in religions such as Judaism that emphasize the distance between God and humanity and thus have the greatest need for intermediary beings.[1] After the Exile a profound change occurred in Jewish speculations about angels. This change is expressed most articulately in the Dead Sea Scrolls and the Pseudepigrapha, and it is in the direction of greater

---

[1]Allison Coudert, "Angels," *The Encyclopedia of Religion*, vol. 1, ed. Mircea Eliade (New York: Macmillan, 1987), pp. 282-283.

speculation as to the nature and role of angels. For the first time angels are called "spirits" (*1 Enoch* 39:2) and joined with cosmic powers or principalities (*1 Enoch* 41:9; 61:10). It is at this time that a definite hierarchy of angels appears and individual angels with names come to prominence (e.g., Michael, Gabriel).

In postexilic Judaism the role of angels as intercessors becomes highly developed. The angels carry prayers into the divine presence (Tob. 12:15; 1QH 6:13) and act as intercessors for the righteous (*2 Apoc. Bar.* 6:7; *1 Enoch* 9:10; 15:2; *T. Levi* 3:5; 5:6-7; Dan. 6:2; 10:13,21). Thus, special emphasis is given to their role as guardians of God's people (Dan. 11:1; 12:1; 2 Macc. 11:6; 3 Macc. 6:18; see also Matt. 4:6; 18:10).

It was only natural in such a climate for Jews to wonder about the role of angels in heavenly worship. The raw material for such speculations was to be found in the scriptures in familiar passages such as the sixth chapter of Isaiah. In the Old Testament the Heavenly Cultus is always one of praise (Pss. 29:1-2; 103; 148; Isa. 6:2-3) or intercession (Job 33:23-24; Zech. 1:12). Heavenly worship is always performed by angels[2] and it never involves expiation.[3] Although the notion of a heavenly sanctuary became a relatively developed idea in Second Temple Judaism, the Heavenly Cultus remained largely undeveloped outside of apocalyptic writings and even there it was the sanctuary itself rather than the rituals therein performed that captured people's attention.[4]

In extracanonical Jewish literature the idea of a Heavenly Cultus became more developed. From the perspective of apocalyptic, it is in fact the principal function of angels to render homage to God.[5] In *1 Enoch* 9:3 four archangels intercede in heaven, while in the (Christian?) *Ascension of Isaiah* 9:23 it is Michael

---

[2]The role of the righteous dead in the Heavenly Cultus does not arise until the Hellenistic era.

[3]Aelred Cody, *Heavenly Sanctuary and Liturgy in the Epistle to the Hebrews* (St. Meinrad, IN: Grail, 1960), p. 48.

[4]Ibid., p. 47. On the role of heavenly sanctuary speculation on the formation of apocalyptic traditions, see Allan J. McNicol, "The Heavenly Sanctuary in Judaism: A Model for Tracing the Origin of an Apocalypse," *Journal of Religious Studies*, 13 (1987), 66-95.

[5]Kurt Hruby, "Les anges dans le culte synagogal et la piété juive," in *Saints et sainteté dans la liturgie*, ed. A. M. Triacca and A. Pistola (Rome: Edizioni Liturgiche, 1987), p. 152.

who performs this duty. An angelic liturgy is also described in *Testament of Levi* 3:4-8 which in one textual tradition seems to be expiatory and in some sense sacrificial:

> In the uppermost heaven of all dwells the Great Glory in the Holy of Holies superior to all holiness. There with him are the archangels, who serve and offer propitiatorysacrifices (οἱ λειτουργοῦντες καὶ ἐξιλασκόμενοι) to the Lord in behalf of all the sins of ignorance of the righteous ones. They present (προσφέρουσι) to the Lord a pleasing odor, a rational and bloodless oblation. In the heaven below them are the messengers who carry the responses to the angels of the Lord's presence. There with him are thrones and authorities; there praises to God are offered (προσφέρονται) eternally.[6]

Cody argues that the phrases describing an expiatory sacrifice are likely interpolations from a Christian source. If they are eliminated, the passage falls back into the normal Old Testament tradition.[7] It would, however, be a strange brand of Christianity indeed that predicated of angels the role of offering sacrifices for sins. In any event, the thought in this passage is not really that different from what appears in rabbinic thought about the Heavenly Cultus.

The Heavenly Cultus played a significant role in the thought of the Qumran sectarians. Strugnell's publication of the first excerpts of 4QShirShabb indicated a deep interest in the nature of angelic worship on the part of the Dead Sea community.[8] This series of thirteen songs for the Sabbath depict an angelic priesthood, complete with hierarchy and vestments, engaged in worshiping God.[9] Each of these songs begins with a call for the angels to praise God. In fact, the songs focus on the fact of the praise itself to the extent that the content of the praise

---

[6]The Greek text is from M. de Jonge, ed., *The Testaments of the Twelve Patriarchs: A Critical Edition of the Greek Text* (Leiden: Brill, 1978).

[7]Cody, *Heavenly Sanctuary*, pp. 52-55.

[8]John Strugnell, "The Angelic Liturgy at Qumran, 4Q Serek Sirôt ʿOlat Hassabat," *Supplements to Vetus Testamentum* 7 (1960), 318-345. The entire text is available in Carol A. Newsom, *Songs of the Sabbath Sacrifice* (Atlanta: Scholars, 1985).

[9]For a summary of the content of the songs, see Carol A. Newsom, "He Has Established for Himself Priests': Human and Angelic Priesthood in the Qumran Sabbath *Shirot*," in *Archaeology and History in the Dead Sea Scrolls*, ed. Lawrence E. Schiffmann (Sheffield: Academic Press, 1990), pp. 104-113.

nowhere appears.[10] Like earthly priests, the heavenly priests of 4QShirShabb perform expiatory functions: "they propitiate His good will for all who repent of sin."[11]

Only in Revelation and Hebrews does the New Testament canon develop the idea of the Heavenly Cultus. Throughout Revelation this cultus is again a liturgy of praise and intercession performed by angels. On occasion the righteous dead also participate in these celestial acts of worship (Rev. 4:9-10; 5:9-10,14).

In Philo there are no allusions to a Heavenly Cultus, despite the wealth of material in the Alexandrian's writings regarding the heavenly temple.[12]

Rabbinic literature adds relatively little to the picture of angelic worship so far ascertained.[13] Perhaps in reaction against the extravagances of apocalyptic literature, the rabbinic corpus tends to downplay the importance of angels. The Mishnah does not mention angels at all.[14] *Exodus Rabbah* 33:4 articulates the principle that there is a correspondence between what God has created in heaven and on earth, a principle applied even to the existence of a heavenly temple and altar. This correspondence involves a Heavenly Cultus parallel to the earthly:

> When the Holy One, blessed be He, told Israel to set up the Tabernacle He intimated to the ministering angels that they also should make a Tabernacle, and when the one below was erected the other was erected on high. The latter was the Tabernacle of the youth [or 'servant'] whose name is Metatron, and therein he offers up the souls of the righteous to atone for Israel in the days of their exile (*Num. Rab.* 12:12).[15]

Similarly, the archangel Michael offers sacrifices on a heavenly altar in *b.Hagigah* 12b. In the same passage is a reference to ministering angels who sing God's

---

[10]Ibid., pp. 105, 108.

[11]Ibid., p. 105, quoting 4Q400 1 i 16.

[12]Cody, *Heavenly Sanctuary*, p. 55.

[13]For a brief but informative synthesis of rabbinic teachings about angels, see David E. Fass, "How the Angels Do Serve," *Judaism*, 40 (1991), 281-285.

[14]Hruby, "Les anges," p. 153.

[15]All quotations from Midrash Rabbah are from H. Reedman and Maurice Simon, eds., *Midrash Rabbah*, 10 vols. (London: Soncino, 1951).

praises by night but keep silent during the day so that Israel may praise God.

The Heavenly Cultus in Hebrews

In comparison with other Jewish and Christian sources, the depiction of the Christ Cultus in Hebrews as a ritual of expiation stands out in its originality. When the subject of Jesus' cultic action is addressed, we approach the genius of the author to the Hebrews. But the author does not entirely neglect the more traditional conception of the Heavenly Cultus as the worship performed by angels. To this topic we now turn.

The Heavenly Cultus in Hebrews 1:5-14

Many suppose a polemic purpose behind the catena of scriptural quotations in Hebrews 1:5-14.[16] Nevertheless, the exact target of such a polemic remains elusive. Suggestions have included the practice of angel-worship (cf. Col. 2:16), some sort of doctrine regarding worshiping *with* the angels that compromised the unique mediatorial role of Christ, and a form of christology that spoke of Christ himself as an angel. All of these suggestions are problematic in that none of them finds specific refutation in the course of the passage.[17]

Angels played a role in the giving of the law in Josephus (*Ant.* 15:136), *Jubilees* 1:29, and the rabbinic corpus (*Mek.* on Exod. 20:18; *Sipre* on Num. 12:5). For many Jews the angels would have been intimately associated with the cultus in terms of its divine origin.[18] The concept appears in the New Testament in

---

[16]Harold W. Attridge, *The Epistle to the Hebrews*, Hermeneia (Philadelphia: Fortress, 1989), pp. 51-52; J. Daryl Charles, "The Angels, Sonship and Birthright in the Letter to the Hebrews," *Journal of the Evangelical Theological Society*, 33 (1990), 171-178; Charles Duey Taylor, "A Comparative Study of the Concept of Worship in Colossians and Hebrews," (Th.D. dissertation, The Southern Baptist Theological Seminary, 1957), pp. 68-71.

[17]The view of Lou H. Silberman, "Prophets/Angels: LXX and Qumran Psalm 151 and the Epistle to the Hebrews," in *Standing before God*, ed. Asher Finkel and Lawrence Frizzell (New York: Ktav, 1981), that the author here is comparing Jesus to human messengers, while intriguing, is unlikely.

[18]Although F. F. Bruce, *The Epistle to the Hebrews*, rev. ed., New International Commentary on the New Testament (Grand Rapids: Eerdmans, 1990), p. 67, n. 3, doubts that

Acts 7:53 and Galatians 3:19. Hebrews assumes the validity of this tradition (2:2), but uses it to buttress its own argument that Jesus is a superior messenger from God whose words must be taken even more seriously. The inferiority of the angels points to the absolute superiority of Christ, and thus to the superiority of the cultic order which he inaugurated. The connection between angels and the giving of the law suggests the logic behind the author's opening words. He first asserts that Jesus is the God's best and final word to his people. He then asserts that Jesus, having dealt with human sin, has been exalted far above the angels, that is, above those beings who were God's attendants at the inauguration of the Mosaic ritual system.

Although the author takes great pains to demonstrate Jesus' superiority over the angels in 1:5-14,[19] the evidence for any kind of polemical intent behind his exposition is weak. It is preferable here to agree with Thompson that the purpose of the catena is not to combat a definite heresy but to present a scriptural meditation on the exaltation of Christ.[20] The author's interest in angels is primarily that they are where Jesus is: in heaven.[21]

The Old Testament quotations the author chooses aptly demonstrate the focus of his interest: of the seven scriptural quotations in the passage, only two deal with angels at all. The remainder serve to demonstrate the greatness of the exalted Son.[22] Nevertheless, three times in this passage the author uses an

---

angels can truly be called mediators of the law on the basis of these texts. On this view see especially Silberman, "Prophets/Angels."

[19]Attridge, *Hebrews*, p. 50, views this as the "explicit purpose" of the catena.

[20]James W. Thompson, *The Beginnings of Christian Philosophy*, CBQMS 13 (Washington: Catholic Biblical Association of America, 1982), p. 140. Neither is it necessary to see in the passage successive stages of exaltation, as do Otto Michel, *Der Brief an die Hebräer*, Kritisch-Exegetischer Kommentar über das Neue Testament (Göttingen: Vandenhoeck & Ruprecht, 1966), p. 109, and Ernst Käsemann, *The Wandering People of God*, trans. Roy A. Harrisville and Irving L. Sandberg (Minneapolis: Augsburg, 1984), pp. 99-101.

[21]Marie E. Isaacs, *Sacred Space*, JSNTSS 73 (Sheffield: Academic Press, 1992), p. 177.

[22]Susanne Lehne, *The New Covenant in Hebrews*, JSNTSS 44 (Sheffield: Academic Press, 1990), p. 28, remarks that the string of quotations "is modelled after a royal enthronement

introductory formula to highlight the difference between the Son and the angels (1:5,7,13).[23]

Attridge notes two important factors for assessing the significance of this passage: (1) the theme, common in early Christian thought, of Christ as superior to the angels (cf. Phil. 2:9; Eph. 1:20; 1 Pet. 3:22), and (2) the function of the passage in establishing on scriptural grounds the most significant elements of the exaltation schema as it is stated in 1:1-4.[24]

This passage exhibits a formal similarity with catenae and florilegia found at Qumran (4QFlor; 4QTestim).[25] The possibility exists that the author had at his disposal a scriptural florilegium derived from Christian or Jewish tradition.[26] As to the literary structure, it must first be noted that Psalm 110:1, quoted at the end of 1:3 and again in 1:13, serves as an inclusion that announces the theme of the passage: Christ has sat down at God's right hand.[27] To this the author adds in 1:14 some concluding remarks about the function of angels.

The catena expands upon the confession of Christ's session in 1:3d-4. Within the catena, 1:5-6 deals with relationships in the heavenly order: the Son enjoys a unique filial relationship with God while the angels remain subordinate. In 1:7-12, the essence of the Son as immutable is contrasted with the angels' changeable and transitory nature. Finally, in 1:13-14 the position of the Son as enthroned at the right hand of God is contrasted with the subservient role assigned

---

liturgy."

[23]William G. Lane, *Hebrews*, vol. 1, Word Biblical Commentary (Dallas: Word, 1991), p. 22.

[24]Attridge, *Hebrews*, pp. 52-53. See also Lane, *Hebrews*, vol. 1, p. 17; Thompson, *Beginnings*, p. 130.

[25]Attridge, *Hebrews*, p. 50.

[26]Käsemann, *Wandering*, pp. 170-171; David M. Hay, *Glory at the Right Hand*, SBLMS 18 (Nashville: Abingdon, 1973), p. 38-39.

[27]Thompson, *Beginnings*, p. 130.

to angels.[28] Similarly, one may think of 1:5-6 as affirming the status of the Son, while in 1:7-12 the status of the Son is proved from scriptural evidence.[29] The structure of the passage may be represented as follows:

A   1:5-6   Affirmation of the Son's superior status
B   1:7-12   Evidence of the Son's superior status
A' 1:13-14 Reaffirmation of the Son's superior status

Angels thus figure in the passage at key junctures: in the center and at both ends of the parallelism. Hebrews' key assertion about the role of angels is that God calls upon them to worship the Son (1:6). While it is unwise to suggest here that the angels have here a primarily literary function,[30] it is true that the angels form a bridge between the exordium (1:1-4) and the author's first expositional section (2:1ff.). Our interest at this time, however, is merely to evaluate the author's depiction of angelic worship in the catena.

The author asserts Jesus' superiority over the angels. He establishes this superior status through two Old Testament quotations which confer upon Jesus the title "Son" (1:5), introduced by a formula that draws attention to the fact that no angel has ever received such a title. In contrast to the Hebrew Bible the LXX never unambiguously applies the term "sons of God" to angelic beings.[31] The author's assertion, however, is based on more than mere ignorance of the original text. As Westcott observes, although angels as a group are sometimes called "sons of God" in the Hebrew Bible, to no one angel is the title "Son of God" given individually.[32] Furthermore, when the term is applied to angels it is never in the context of proclaiming their glorification.[33] In contrast, the exalted Christ is given the title "Son" and in both quoted passages this sonship is the result of divine decree and

---

[28]Albert Vanhoye, *Situation du Christ* (Paris: Cerf, 1969), pp. 121-123.

[29]Thompson, *Beginnings*, pp. 130-131.

[30]Attridge, *Hebrews*, p. 53.

[31]Vanhoye, *Situation*, p. 128. See LXX Job 1:6; 2:1; 38:7; Deut. 32:43.

[32]B. F. Westcott, *The Epistle to the Hebrews*, 2nd ed. (Grand Rapids: Eerdmans, 1955), p. 20.

[33]Vanhoye, *Situation*, p. 131.

favor and points to the special, unique relationship between the Son and his heavenly Father.[34]

It is in the context of this exaltation theme that the Heavenly Cultus is first described in Hebrews. The introductory formula of 1:6 is fraught with exegetical difficulties which in one way or another have to do with the setting in which the proclamation of Christ's divine sonship occurs. The phrase ὅταν δὲ πάλιν εἰσαγάγῃ τὸν πρωτότοκον εἰς τὴν οἰκουμένην ("but again when he brings the Firstborn into the world") has been interpreted as a reference to the incarnation, the exaltation, or the parousia.

Our conclusion is that 1:6 describes the time of Christ's heavenly exaltation. Πρωτότοκος occurs in connection with the resurrection of Christ in Colossians 1:18 and Revelation 1:5. Here as well a post-resurrection usage is justified. That Jesus is the "Firstborn" speaks of his relationship to humankind in his own glorified humanity.[35]

The key to interpreting 1:6 as a reference to the exaltation is the difficult word οἰκουμένη. While it may often be translated in the New Testament simply as "world" or "inhabited world," the word does allow for a more technical meaning. The appearance of οἰκουμένη here is parallel with its only other occurrence in Hebrews, at 2:5, where the author specifically spells out that he is dealing with the "world to come" (τὴν οἰκουμένην τὴν μέλλουσαν), i.e., the world of eschatological fulfillment. In both verses the subordinate role of angels is the topic of discussion. Furthermore, in 2:5 the author states that the "world to come" has been his concern all along (περὶ ἧς λαλοῦμεν). Also it must be noted that the immediate context of 1:5-6 is in fact the sacrificial death of Jesus followed by his exaltation (1:3-4).[36] In the LXX, οἰκουμένη can describe the world with particular reference to God as its Creator (Isa. 62:4) and the world

---

[34]Ibid., p. 130.

[35]Westcott, Hebrews, p. 23.

[36]Lane, Hebrews, vol. 1, p. 27; Thompson, Beginnings, p. 129; Käsemann, Wandering, p. 99.

which God will one day set straight (Ps. 95:10).[37]

Finally, to see this verse in reference to Christ's heavenly exaltation conforms to what has already been demonstrated about the Christ Cultus as a rite of passage. In accordance with 2:9, Christ's incarnation, with its sufferings and death, represent a time of statuslessness in which Jesus is made inferior to the angels.[38] For Jesus to receive angelic adoration at this time would be incongruous.[39] A similar passage, 10:5, describes another entrance of Jesus. Hebrews 10:5 does not describe the same event as 1:6, as is clear when the respective depictions of Christ's status are considered. In 10:5 the realm Jesus enters is the κόσμος, a word with clear negative connotations in Hebrews (see 9:1). Christ's entrance into the κόσμος is described in terms of his death; but his entrance into the οἰκουμένη in 1:6 is a time of angelic rejoicing, as befits the culmination of the Christ Cultus with the Son's re-incorporation into the heavenly realm. As Peterson notes, "[Jesus'] enthronement marks the consummation of his messianic work, the proclamation of his sonship to all and the moment when the Son begins to enter into his inheritance."[40] This time in the career of the Son best describes the setting of Hebrews 1:6. Such is also in keeping with the traditional motif of the angels paying homage to the heavenly Messiah (Rev. 5:8-10).

The stage for the Heavenly Cultus in this passage is thus the heavenly realm itself and its occasion is the entrance of the Risen Lord into that region as the culmination of his own High Priestly activity. Since for the author of Hebrews that

---

[37]George Wesley Buchanan, *To the Hebrews*, The Anchor Bible (Garden City: Doubleday, 1972), p. 17. See also Albert Vanhoye, "L'οἰκουμένη dans l'épître aux Hébreux," *Biblica*, 45 (1964), 248-253.

[38]Vanhoye, *Situation*, p. 155.

[39]In fact, a second century A.D. source, the *Ascension of Isaiah*, describes how the Messiah is unrecognized by the angels when he descends into the world, but receives their homage when he ascends back to heaven (*Asc. Isa.* 10:7-15; 11:23-32).

[40]David Peterson, *Hebrews and Perfection* (Cambridge: University Press, 1982), pp. 192-193.

which is inferior renders homage to that which is superior (cf. 7:4-8),[41] the worship given Jesus by the angels demonstrates his exalted position over them. The angels are, in fact, completely overshadowed by the Son. In contrast to the intimate address to Jesus as "Son," God does not speak to the angels at all; instead he voices a command in the third person: προσκυνησάτωσαν, "let them worship."[42] The angelic liturgy thus takes a back seat to the exaltation of Christ itself. According to Vanhoye, "the angels are not at the center of God's attention; he is not interested in them except secondarily . . . ."[43] The quotation itself (from Deut. 32:43) was widely used liturgically in late antiquity in temple, synagogue, and church.[44]

The following quotation in 1:7 reemphasizes the subordinate role of angels: "He who makes his angels winds and his ministers flames of fire." The reference to wind and fire may be intended to call to the reader's mind the physical accompaniments at the giving of the Law (see 2:2; 12:18-21).[45] In rabbinic literature the quoted verse, Psalm 104:4, is interpreted to demonstrate either the transcendence of God who executes his will through the angels (*Exod. Rab.* 25) or the superior power of the angels themselves (*Tg.* Ps. 104:4). In contrast, the author of Hebrews uses the verse to show the inferiority of angels: they are changeable and they do not stand above the created order.[46] Unlike the Son who is sovereign and unchanging (1:8-12), the angelic hosts are mutable, material, and

---

[41]Thompson, *Beginnings*, p. 132.

[42]Vanhoye, *Situation*, p. 151.

[43]Ibid.

[44]Lane, *Hebrews*, vol. 1, p. 28, notes Rev. 15:3; *Det.*, 114; *LA. III*, 105; *Plant.*, 59; 4 Macc. 18:6,9,18,19; and Justin, *Dialogue*, 130.

[45]Westcott, *Hebrews*, p. 25.

[46]Thompson, *Beginnings*, p. 133; Michel, *Hebräer*, p. 117; Lane, *Hebrews*, vol. 1, p. 29.

transitory.[47]

The cherubim, as Yahweh's heavenly steeds, are identified with the wind in the parallel lines of Psalm 18:10: "He rode on a cherub, and flew; he came swiftly upon the wings of the wind" (NRSV). Similarly, seraphim are depicted as fiery serpents in Numbers 21:6-8 (שָׂרַף, "to burn") and are associated with scorpions in Deuteronomy 8:15 and Isaiah 30:6. To associate the nondescript angels in 1:7 with cherubim and seraphim is unwarranted, but such Old Testament depictions underline the role of angels as God's servants and the executors of his will. In this verse angels are called λειτουργοί, a word with possible cultic connections which will be explored below.

One connection which may be drawn is that of "fire" in 1:7 and in the description of the Sinai event in 12:18. Fire in the latter verse has a definite negative connotation contrasted with the heavenly, nonmaterial world which believers have attained.[48] It may be that the author intends for his readers to understand angels as possessing some kind of materiality which places them outside the highest heavenly realm where Christ sits enthroned.[49]

The middle term of the catena (1:7-12) indicates the exalted nature of Christ in two lengthy quotations from the Old Testament. Angels are then mentioned for the last time in 1:13-14 in a manner which parallels their appearance at the beginning of the catena. Once again the author uses a rhetorical question to draw a distinction between the superiority of Christ and the subordinate status of the angels: "but to which of the angels has he ever said . . . ?" This formula introduces the first direct quotation of Psalm 110:1 in Hebrews,[50] describing Jesus' session at the right hand of God and the subjection of his enemies. Angels are often pictured around God (1 Kgs. 22:19; Isa. 6:1; Tob. 12:15) but never seated at his right hand. Conversely, the Old Testament does witness to God "seated" upon angels as upon a throne or a chariot (Exod. 25:22; 1 Sam. 4:4; Pss. 80:2; 99:1;

---

[47]Westcott, *Hebrews*, p. 25.

[48]Thompson, *Beginnings*, p. 133.

[49]Ibid., p. 134.

[50]The verse is clearly alluded to in 1:3.

Ezek. 10:1,4).[51] The citation reiterates the main points of the author's argument regarding Christ and the angels: the angels do not share in the Son's exaltation and they are cosmologically subordinate to him.[52]

This section of Hebrews ends with a remark about the nature and function of angels: "are they not all ministering spirits (λειτουργικὰ πνεύματα) sent for service on behalf of those who are about to inherit salvation?" (1:14). One must ask whether it can be said that the angels "minister" in the cultic sense. The answer to this question can only be found through an investigation of the terms involved.

Originally, λειτουργέω and its associated noun λειτουργία were wholly secular in meaning, although in the LXX there is an "almost uniform cultic and priestly use of the words."[53] The words were used cultically in nonbiblical Greek; and though the LXX does not use them for non-cultic forms of service, it can use them even for worship in pagan contexts.[54] In fact, of the hundred-plus occurrences of the words in the LXX, most are in Exodus 28-39, Numbers, Chronicles, and Ezekiel 40-46: writings where the cultus predominates.[55] Λειτουργέω is often the translation of שׁרת (pi 'el), but with only a few exceptions it is only where שׁרת has a cultic reference. In other contexts translators preferred παρίστημι, λατρεύω, δουλεύω, or some other verb.[56] Josephus uses the words exclusively of the priestly cultus.[57] Thus there is ample evidence for interpreting the verbal root from which λειτουργός and λειτουργικός derive in a cultic sense, and in fact the word is used throughout

---

[51]Vanhoye, *Situation*, p. 211.

[52]Thompson, *Beginnings*, p. 139.

[53]H. Strathmann and R. Meyer, "λειτουργέω, κ.τ.λ.," *TDNT*, vol. 4, p. 215.

[54]Ibid., pp. 218-220.

[55]Ibid., p. 219.

[56]Ibid.

[57]Ibid., p. 222.

Hebrews with just such a connotation. With regard to the noun and the adjective themselves, however, the picture is not as clear.

The noun λειτουργός is rarely used in secular Greek for a liturgical official. Most often it denotes one who performs manual work.[58] It is not common in the LXX, but in the fourteen times that it occurs it almost always translates מְשָׁרֵת. Λειτουργός is used in a cultic sense only in Isaiah 61:6, 2 Esdras 20:40 (= Nehemiah 10:40), and Sirach 7:30. Normally the term simply indicates the servant of another. Angels are called λειτουργοί in Psalms 102:21 and 103:4. The term is used only twice in Hebrews. In 8:2 Jesus is the λειτουργός of the true tent in a statement that is obviously cultic. In other New Testament uses (including Hebrews 1:7), Strathmann argues that there is no need to find a priestly or cultic sense to the word.[59]

Finally, there is the adjective λειτουργικός. The word occurs six times in the LXX and always in the sacral sense of "belonging to the cultus."[60] Its only occurrence in the New Testament is at Hebrews 1:14, where, according to Vanhoye, a cultic meaning is not likely, since angels are here sent for service on behalf of believers on earth.[61] Strathmann emphatically denies a cultic sense here.[62]

A further possibility of finding a cultic connotation to λειτουργικός is suggested, however, by attention to the usage of the Hebrew term מלאכי השרת in the Dead Sea Scrolls and in the rabbinic corpus. This phrase, which may be rendered "messengers of ministration" or "ministering messengers," is

---

[58]Ibid., p. 229.

[59]Ibid., p. 230; contra Ceslaus Spicq, "La Panégyrie de Hebr. XII,22," Studia Theologica, 6 (1952), 36.

[60]Strathmann and Meyer, "λειτουργέω," p. 231.

[61]Vanhoye, Situation, p. 221. See also Attridge, Hebrews, p. 62.

[62]Strathmann and Meyer, "λειτουργέω," p. 231.

often used of angels; and its liturgical connotation predominates.[63] Caquot notes that the use of שׁרת for liturgical service directed towards someone other than God is not without precedent. For example, in Numbers 3:6 and 18:2, the levites "serve" Aaron in his cultic ministrations. Similarly, in 4Q511 35 human worshipers on earth are said to "serve" the angels as they perform their Heavenly Cultus:

> the adepts are not directly the officiants of the cultus worthy of God; they are only the intermediaries of the angels and they are *vis-à-vis* the latter in a relationship analogous to that of the levite with respect to the priest, that of a "servant" rather than of a "celebrant" or a "minister." *God's earthly cultus is nothing other than the service of the angels*; and it belongs to these to render to God, in heaven, the true cultus that is appropriate for him.[64] (emphasis added)

This description of the Heavenly Cultus depicts very nearly the opposite of Hebrews 1:14, where the angels serve as ministering spirits for human believers.

Still, to assert that the author sees the angels here in a cultic role is problematic. Although the author's usage of related terms and the usage of parallel Hebrew terminology in the Qumran literature lean heavily in favor of such an assertion, the immediate context is ambivalent. Broadly speaking, the context is the worship of the exalted Son by the angelic hosts. More immediately, however, 1:14 speaks of angels sent from heaven to earth to render service ($\delta\iota\alpha\kappa\text{ov}\acute{\iota}\alpha$) to humans. In light of 4Q511 such language may imply angelic assistance in earthly worship, but the data for Hebrews is insufficient to prove this hypothesis. We prefer to see in 1:14 the author's assessment of the role of angels with respect to believers, without burdening the point with cultic connotations. The role of angels as God's agents who carry messages to his people and accomplish his will is well attested in Judaism. The author of Hebrews posits nothing different here.

In summary, Hebrews 1:5-14 depicts a Heavenly Cultus which is motivated and indeed overwhelmed by the more central cultus involving Christ himself. As Jesus enters the heavenly world, God calls upon all his angels to worship him as the Firstborn. But in contrast to the highly elaborated presentation of the Christ Cultus, the author takes no pains to describe the content of this angelic worship. Angels figure prominently in the passage as a way for the author to speak of the

---

[63] André Caquot, "Le service des anges," *Revue de Qumran*, 13 (1988), 421.

[64] Ibid., p. 425.

incomparable greatness of Christ in his relationship both to God and to creation. Furthermore, contemporary angelic speculation provided the author a means of introducing the theme of the superiority of the cultic realities that Jesus brings into being. The Heavenly Cultus here is thus a vivid demonstration of the angels' subservient status.

The Heavenly Cultus in Hebrews 12:18-24

Properly speaking, this passage is not a description of the Heavenly Cultus but a comparison of the Old and New Covenant Cultuses. The author's focus is clearly not on angels but on the believers he addresses (προσεληλύθατε, 12:18,22). Nevertheless, the passage does describe angels at worship and introduces the idea of the righteous dead as partners in the cultus. The fuller implications of 12:18-24 for believers is deferred until chapter five. Our concern here is with the angelic aspects of the passage.

As it sets forth in vivid terms the contrast between the old and the new covenants, the text is a kind of summary of the entire sermon.[65] It consists of two Greek sentences, each focusing on the verb προσεληλύθατε, "you have approached." In this framework the author's description of Mount Zion is "loosely balanced" with that of Mount Sinai.[66] Hebrews 12:18-19 lists seven elements of the Sinai experience, with an extended description of Israel's fear at these phenomena in 12:20-21. This is followed by an eight-part description of the believers' arrival at the heavenly Mount Zion.

The panorama presents a further basis for the author's call to pursue peace and sanctification (12:14). The vision of heavenly worship provides a more positive ground for action than the negative example of Esau in 12:15-17.[67] The festive atmosphere of the author's images of Mount Zion encourage bold approach

---

[65]Juliana Casey, *Hebrews*, New Testament Message 18 (Wilmington: Glazier, 1980), p. 88.

[66]Attridge, *Hebrews*, p. 372, n. 16.

[67]Ibid., p. 372.

to the presence of God,[68] and the terrifying aspects of the Sinai experience seem to underscore this attitude of joy.[69]

The author has clearly sculpted the Old Testament traditions of the Sinai theophany to meet his polemic needs. For example, he omits significant elements from the pentateuchal accounts such as the divine name (Deut. 5:23-27 LXX) while presenting only those external elements that depict an atmosphere of dread and confusion. In the end "the impression is conveyed that God was not unambiguously present at Sinai."[70]

In contrast, believers who have approached Zion have boldly drawn near to the divine presence (4:16, 10:19), where they are welcomed by angels, departed saints, and God himself together with Jesus, the mediator of the new covenant. Dumbrell has suggested that the nature of the occasion may be described as "covenant conclusion."[71] This is an apt description of this event, rich with apocalyptic images, in which the people of God ultimately realize their eschatological hopes.[72]

The setting of this celebration is "Mount Zion, and the city of the living God, heavenly Jerusalem" (12:22). The idea of a heavenly Jerusalem appears frequently in Jewish writings, and in visionary literature its temple could be a present reality (*1 Enoch* 14:15-20; 71:5-7; *T. Levi* 5:1-2).[73] In the first century, Jewish literature gave increasing attention to Jerusalem as a transcendent reality (*4 Ezra* 10:25-27; *2 Apoc. Bar.* 4:2-7) despite the fact that the anticipated ideal

---

[68]Lane, *Hebrews*, vol. 2, p. 464.

[69]Ibid., pp. 445, 449.

[70]Ibid., p. 460.

[71]W. J. Dumbrell, "'The Spirits of Just Men Made Perfect,'" *Evangelical Quarterly*, 48 (1976), 156.

[72]Lane, *Hebrews*, vol. 2, p. 465.

[73]Sarah Ann Sharkey, "The Background of the Imagery of the Heavenly Jerusalem in the New Testament" (Ph.D. dissertation, Catholic University of America, 1986), pp. 128-129.

Jerusalem remained for the most part earth-centered.[74] The key element in understanding the importance of Jerusalem in this period, in continuity with the Old Testament tradition, is the ideal of the presence of God among his people.[75] Thus we see the culmination of the development of Jerusalem from a royal capital city into "a symbol describing an ideal reality with spiritual significance."[76] The first Christians adapted this symbolic view of Jerusalem to give expression to their own religious sensitivities (Gal. 4:26; Rev. 3:12; 21:2,10).

An underlying motif in the depiction of faith in Hebrews is that the stability of a city is exclusively an aspiration for the future (11:10; 13:14). In the present world, the paradigm for the faithful is life in tents (11:9) or even caves (11:38). "City" thus becomes an eschatologically charged image for Hebrews.

We now approach the aspects of 12:22-24 that allow us to speak of the scene in terms of a Heavenly Cultus. In 12:22b-23 the author writes that his audience has drawn near "to myriads of angels, a festive gathering, and the assembly of the firstborn who have been enrolled in heaven, and to the Judge, God of all, and to the spirits of righteous ones who have been made perfect." Commentators have variously construed the exact construction of these words.[77] The problem centers around πανηγύρει ("a festive gathering") and whether it is to be taken with what comes before or after it. If it is recognized that the elements in the author's description are all separated from one another by copulative καί's[78] it becomes clear that the word must be in apposition with what comes before and thus gives further description of the angels.[79]

The reference to innumerable angels may be a reminder of the ministrations of heavenly beings at the giving of the law (2:2; Deut. 33:2) or in carrying out

---

[74]Ibid., p. 129.

[75]Ibid., p. 130.

[76]Ibid., p. 72.

[77]See Attridge, *Hebrews*, p. 375.

[78]Lane, *Hebrews*, vol. 2, p. 464.

[79]*Contra* Dumbrell, "Spirits," p. 156.

divine judgment (Dan. 7:10). Whatever the case, the addition of πανηγύρει indicates that in the present context they are no longer messengers of awe but of rejoicing (cf. Job 38:7).[80] Πανήγυρις "has reference to a joyful gathering in order to celebrate a festival."[81] It is an assembly for the purpose of celebration.[82] In the LXX it is occasionally used of set feasts, and is set parallel to ἑορτή (Hos. 2:13; 9:5; Amos 5:21). The verb πανηγυρίζω is used in Isaiah 66:10 in the general sense of "be glad" (NRSV). The word is used in secular Greek of national assemblies and sacred games.[83] Significantly, Philo (*Legat.* 12) uses the word to describe the celebrations throughout the Roman empire upon the accession of emperor Gaius to the throne. The word is found only here in the New Testament, where the author describes another type of "accession": the triumphal culmination of the believers' covenant relationship with God. Revelation 4 may describe a similar festal assembly.[84]

The "assembly of the firstborn" cannot be understood as angelic beings, the determining factor being that they have been enrolled in heaven.[85] The phrase refers to the earthly element in the celebration. Ἐκκλησία occurs in Hebrews only at 12:23 and 2:12, where Jesus says: "I shall proclaim your name to (or 'with') my brothers and sisters (τοῖς ἀδελφοῖς μου), in the midst of the assembly I shall sing hymns to you." The two occurrences of the word are clearly related.[86] In both, the thought is that the people of God have assembled "to

---

[80]Westcott, *Hebrews*, p. 414.

[81]Lane, *Hebrews*, vol. 2, p. 467.

[82]Spicq, "Panégyrie," p. 31.

[83]Ibid., pp. 34-35.

[84]Heinrich Seesemann, "πανήγυρις," *TDNT*, vol. 5, p. 722.

[85]Attridge, *Hebrews*, p. 375; *contra* Spicq, "Panégyrie," p. 36.

[86]Juliana Casey, "Eschatology in Hebrews 12:14-29: An Exegetical Study" (S.T.D. dissertation, Catholic University of Louvain, 1976), p. 360.

exercise their privileges and to enjoy their rights."[87] The celebration is also related to the Heavenly Cultus in chapter 1 by the appearance of the word πρωτότοκος ("firstborn"). In 1:6 Jesus is the Firstborn, while in 12:23 the title is applied to believers as an indication of their association with Christ.[88] In both instances angels are present, worshiping.

In the midst of the celebration is God himself. The presence of the word "Judge" indicates that the author sees this gathering as in some sense one of judgment, but other elements in the description once again temper any sense of dread. The scene implies an approving judgment for those who have drawn near.[89]

Next in the heavenly vision are "the spirits of righteous ones who have been made perfect." The spirits or souls of the righteous is a common idiom for the godly dead (*Jub.* 23:30-31; *1 Enoch* 22:9; 102:4; 103:3-4; *2 Apoc. Bar.* 30:2). Here the phrase refers to those who have died and now inhabit the heavenly city to which the pilgrim people of God on earth must journey.[90]

While the inclusion of the righteous dead in a heavenly liturgy is peculiar to Revelation and Hebrews in the New Testament,[91] speculation about the departed saints is in fact a common motif in apocalyptic writings (Dan. 3:86 LXX; *1 Enoch* 22:3-9; 70:1-4; *4 Ezra* 7:99) and other Jewish literature (Wisd. 3:1; Philo, *LA. III*, 74; *b.Hag.* 12b; *b.Sabb.* 152b). There is a strong tendency in this literature to conceive of both angels and the righteous dead as a single congregation in the presence of God (*1 Enoch* 39:5; 104:6; 4QShirShabb).[92] The motif is explored in depth in the Dead Sea Scrolls. For example, 1QH 3:21-23 states:

Thou hast cleansed a perverse spirit of great sin
  that it may stand with the host of the Holy Ones,

---

[87]Westcott, *Hebrews*, p. 415. See also Dumbrell, "Spirits," p. 157.

[88]As Michel, *Hebräer*, p. 464, notes, the term is probably "an apocalyptic term of honor of the Jesus community." As to the application of such a word to believers, see chapter 5 below.

[89]Lane, *Hebrews*, vol. 2, p. 470.

[90]Ibid.

[91]Cody, *Heavenly Sanctuary*, p. 71.

[92]Gaster, "Angel," p. 133.

and that it may enter into community
    with the congregation of the Sons of Heaven.
Thou hast allotted to man an everlasting destiny
    amidst the spirits of knowledge,
that he may praise Thy Name in a common rejoicing
    and recount Thy marvels before all Thy works.[93]

In the Greek *Apocalypse of Baruch* 10:5, the righteous dead perform their own acts of worship: "And the angel said, 'Listen, Baruch: This plain which surrounds the lake, and in which are other mysteries, is the place where the souls of the righteous come when they assemble, living together choir by choir.'"

The author of Hebrews assumes the validity of this tradition but refrains from elaborating upon it. Like the tradition of angelic worship, the idea of the worshiping spirits of the righteous only appears to add color to his overall theme, the consummation of the new covenant.

Conclusions Regarding the Heavenly Cultus

Despite the wealth of material regarding the Heavenly Cultus in contemporary Jewish literature, the author of Hebrews shows a measured restraint in his treatment of the topic. The Heavenly Cultus never takes center stage in Hebrews, and in both passages where it appears it serves only to further some greater cultic theme. The author's brevity is in itself the best testimony to his conception of the Heavenly Cultus' significance.

Cultic place. The setting for the Heavenly Cultus is the heavenly world (1:6), where Jesus has gone to sit at the right hand of God. Although the author does not locate the Heavenly Cultus specifically within a sanctuary, it is likely he assumed that the angels would perform their worship at a place that was in some sense appropriate for the occasion. The most he asserts is that the angels and the righteous dead are gathered within the heavenly city (12:22).

Nevertheless, angels are the inhabitants of the realm toward which Christians journey (13:14). If for no other reason, this truth generates a certain amount of interest in them and their activities. In their heavenly locale, angels experience something of the intimacy with God that for earthly believers must be

---

[93]Unless otherwise noted, all quotations from the Dead Sea Scrolls are from Geza Vermes, ed., *The Dead Sea Scrolls in English*, 2nd ed. (Baltimore: Penguin, 1975). The column and line designations here are from Eduard Lohse, ed., *Die Texte aus Qumran: Hebräish und Deutsch* (Munich: Kösel, 1971).

deferred until the time of eschatological fulfillment.

Cultic personnel. Great effort is made in 1:5-14 to demonstrate the angels' inferior status in the celestial hierarchy. Unlike Jesus or even the priests of the old covenant, angels are never given a mediatorial role.[94] Hebrews affirms pious Jewish ideas about the distance between humanity and God, but bridges that distance not through any angelic being but through Jesus alone. As mediator figures, angels are made to look particularly unimpressive. They are subject to change (1:7), whereas Jesus remains unchanging (1:8,11-12; 13:8). While Jesus is the exalted and enthroned Son of God, angels are but servants and messengers dispatched to do his will on earth (1:7,14). Even in the world to come angels hold no positions of authority (2:5), and they are excluded from Christ's salvific concern (2:16).

The righteous dead in Hebrews are wholly positive yet two-dimensional figures. They have been "perfected" (12:23, see 11:40) and they are citizens of the heavenly Jerusalem. As such they represent the future state of earthly believers. Beyond this their status and function remain obscure.

Cultic performance. With one possible (but unlikely) exception,[95] no explicitly cultic terminology is applied to angelic worship. Both the verb προσκυνέω (1:6) and the nouns λειτουργός (1:7) and πανήγυρις (12:22) may be used in ritual contexts, but none of these words may properly be called cultic technical terms. Neither the dominant symbol of Hebrews' cultic foundation, blood, nor its central activity, entrance into the divine presence, appear in the author's description of the Heavenly Cultus.

The Heavenly Cultus in Hebrews is thoroughly secondary to other cultic concerns. In 1:5-14 the angelic worship is completely overshadowed by the final stage of the Christ Cultus where the exalted Son enters the heavenly realm, thus consummating his high priesthood. The angels are thus participants in this phase of the Christ Cultus, but in a purely ancillary role.

---

[94]Charles Talbert, "The Myth of a Descending-Ascending Redeemer in Mediterranean Antiquity," *NTS*, 22 (1976), 418-439, catalogues the great extent to which Jewish speculation sought to make angels into mediators of redemption. He finds in Hebrews a "very definite polemic against angels" in this role (p. 438).

[95]i.e., the reference to angels as λειτουργικὰ πνεύματα in 1:14.

Similarly, the author's concern in 12:18-24 is with the New Covenant Cultus performed by earthly believers. Particularly, these verses emphasize the final eschatological fulfillment of the new covenant promises and the exhortation to "draw near" (4:16; 10:22) and "enter" (4:11; 10:19) the divine presence. Once again the angelic hosts are relegated to a secondary position. Thus, even in the Heavenly Cultus itself, angels take the part of "assistants" or even "spectators" of the true cultic participants. It is exactly for such a role that they were created.

The Heavenly Cultus and the Spirituality of Hebrews

The Heavenly Cultus never occupies a central place in the thought of the author of Hebrews. His concern is primarily with the cultic action of Christ himself and, as shall be demonstrated in the next chapter, with Christian existence as a kind of cultic performance. The Heavenly Cultus does, however, make its own contribution to the overall plan of the author's spiritual teaching.

Expressions of Authentic and Inauthentic

The Heavenly Cultus is not inauthentic as such, but neither does it fully express the traits of authenticity described in the author's foundational cultic assumptions. The concern for cleansing from sin and the purgative power of blood is nowhere mentioned with regard to the Heavenly Cultus, which perhaps underscores its secondary and derivative nature. The Heavenly Cultus is not something earthly believers should aspire to: it does not address their deepest spiritual need.

Furthermore, although this cultus is not "earthly," it is in some sense wrapped up in creation and subject to mutability and transitoriness (1:7-8). As such it is not to be compared to the transcendent ritual of Christ which bears the qualities of stability and eternity. Even so, the heavenly city where the angels worship is a legitimate aspiration of the believer on earth. In this sense, and only in this sense, the angels enjoy something that living believers are temporarily denied.

Angels in Hebrews fulfill an apologetic purpose with regard to human believers as well. During the rabbinic period teaching about the inferiority of angels was often a tool of Jewish apologetics.[96] By stressing God's preference for Israel over even the angels, the rabbis spoke a message to a people who were often persecuted and without a homeland.[97] In Hebrews as well teaching about angels serves in fact to exalt the people of God.[98] Hebrews' angelology thus becomes a word of encouragement to a persecuted people who are wondering whether or not to leave the faith. The author exhorts his congregation by reminding them how much more precious they are than angels.

The clearest statement of authenticity in the Heavenly Cultus is in its Christ-centeredness. The angelic hosts, well aware of their subordinate role, pay fitting homage to Christ at his exaltation (1:6). Peterson argues that it is in fact the primary function of angels to render such worship, which serves as an example to believers as well.[99] Because Jesus has completed his cultus and consummated his high priesthood, he alone is worthy of worship.

The Practice of Spirituality

The restraint the author shows in dealing with the traditions available to him about angels and the Heavenly Cultus serves a double purpose. First, it discourages the kind of speculative tendencies evident in contemporary literature on the subject of celestial beings. As examples for ritual activity, angels in Hebrews offer little guidance; as mediator figures, they are a complete washout.

Much more central is the fact that Hebrews' treatment of the Heavenly Cultus reinforces the emphasis on a Christ-centered spirituality most clearly developed in the cultic foundation. By depicting the angelic liturgy as he does, the author encourages believers on earth to honor Christ appropriately.[100] The angels, however, are not our guides as much as our assistants and well-wishers. At the consummation of the new covenant, when believers approach the divine presence

---

[96]As surveyed by Fass, "Angels," pp. 285-289.

[97]Ibid., pp. 288-289

[98]Most clearly at 2:16.

[99]David Peterson, "Towards a New Testament Theology of Worship," *Reformed Theological Review*, 43 (1984), 66.

[100]Ibid., p. 67.

(12:22-24), angels are in attendance but they serve no vital role.

Chapter 5

THE NEW COVENANT CULTUS

Like every other religious tradition originating within the matrix of Early Judaism, primitive Christianity in general and the book of Hebrews in particular bears witness to a crisis of faith related to separation from the Jerusalem cultus. For the author of Hebrews (as for his many contemporaries) this separation produced a crisis not merely for theology but also for spirituality. Theologically, separation from the cultus necessitated a radically new conception of God's presence and activity among his people. Spiritually, it required new answers to the question of how one is to experience God's presence and live out one's faith commitment in all of life. In describing the death and exaltation of Jesus as a cultic performance, the author to the Hebrews addresses the theological question. In describing the Christian life as cultus, he addresses the issue of spirituality. We thus turn our attention now to the author's cultic description of Christian spirituality.

Two extreme answers are often suggested to the question of how Hebrews employs cultic terminology with respect to believers. On the one hand, some see the cultic imagery in strictly metaphorical terms.[1] Others claim several levels of meaning for the cultic language, including a specific cultic or sacramental referent.[2]

---

[1]Among these would be Helmut Koester, "'Outside the Camp': Hebrews 13:9-14," *Harvard Theological Review*, 55 (1962), 299-315; Friedrich Schröger, "Der Gottesdienst der Hebräerbriefgemeinde," *Münchener Theologische Zeitschrift*, 19 (1968), 161-181; and Ronald Williamson, "The Eucharist and the Epistle to the Hebrews," *NTS*, 21 (1975), 300-312.

[2]Such as Paul Andriessen, "L'Eucharistie dans l'Épître aux Hébreux," *Nouvelle Revue*

Lehne surveys both of these interpretations and, quite correctly, finds them both unsatisfactory.[3]

To find an acceptable explanation we shall first briefly survey the various options which Jews in the first century explored in re-interpreting their cultic matrix for religious life separated from the Jerusalem cultus. This will necessitate a discussion of what is meant by the difficult term "spiritualization." With this background, we shall approach the question of how Hebrews reinterprets cultic terms with regard to the activities of believers.

The Spiritualization of Cultus in Antiquity

As has often been noted, the word "spiritualization" is open to many different and opposing meanings. Daly lists as common synonyms the words "dematerializing, sublimating, humanizing, deepening, ethicizing, rationalizing, interiorizing, symbolizing."[4] Schüssler Fiorenza prefers to abandon the term altogether and speak of the "transference" of cultic imagery.[5] In her words this usage "indicates that Jewish and Hellenistic cultic concepts were *shifted* to designate a reality which was not cultic."[6] It is not entirely correct, however, to say that the shift was always away from a material cultus. The early rabbis, for example, thoroughly ritualized the practice of daily prayer in the absence of the temple ritual, but this is not the same thing as moving away from cultus altogether.

We prefer to keep the term "spiritualization," but with the expanded definition that Daly suggests:

Théologique, 94 (1972), 269-277; and James Swetnam, "Christology and the Eucharist in the Epistle to the Hebrews," *Biblica*, 70 (1989), 505-519.

[3]Susanne Lehne, *The New Covenant in Hebrews*, JSNTSS 44 (Sheffield: Academic Press, 1990), p. 109.

[4]Robert J. Daly, *The Origins of the Christian Doctrine of Sacrifice* (Philadelphia: Fortress, 1978), p. 6.

[5]Elizabeth Schüssler Fiorenza, "Cultic Language in Qumran and in the NT," *CBQ*, 38 (1976), 161.

[6]Ibid.

We are using the word spiritualization in a much broader sense than simply antimaterialistic. This sense includes all those movements and tendencies within Judaism and Christianity which attempted to emphasize the true meaning of sacrifice, that is, the inner, spiritual, or ethical significance of the cult over against the merely material or merely external understanding of it.[7]

We acknowledge at the outset that the "true meaning" of the cult will be interpreted differently from tradition to tradition. This definition is wide enough, however, to embrace groups and traditions that never disavowed the external cult (e.g., the Old Testament prophetic tradition). We thus hope to avoid prejudging the question by importing dualistic or anti-cultic biases into our analysis.[8] We begin by turning to the pagan and Jewish spiritualizing traditions that may have informed the process of spiritualization in Hebrews.[9]

Spiritualization in Greek Thought

While the Old Testament and Judaism in general sought to revitalize the cultus through the religious reformation of the offerers, many Greek philosophers believed that true piety ought to lead to a radical abandonment of the sacrifices.[10] Thus when the author of Hebrews declared that it was impossible for animal blood to take away sins (10:4), he would have met little resistance from the philosophers. In fact, objection to external sanctuaries and bloody sacrifices was a common theme

---

[7]Daly, *Origins*, p. 7.

[8]Schüssler-Fiorenza, "Cultic Language," pp. 160-161, observes that spiritualization can denote inner as opposed to the outer realities (for example, in Roman Catholic liturgy), and thus is not necessarily an anti-cultic tendency.

[9]The benchmark study of this issue is that of Hans Wenschkewitz, "Die Spiritualisierung der Kultusbegriffe: Tempel, Priester und Opfer im Neuen Testament," *Αγγελος* 4 (1932), 70-230. Wenschkewitz reflects a slight anti-materialistic bias and depicts spiritualization as a late, Hellenistically influenced phenomenon. Hans-Jürgen Hermisson, *Sprache und Ritus im altisraelitischen Kult* (Neukirchen-Vluyn: Neukirchener, 1965), rejects a negative understanding of the ancient Israelite cult and thus serves as a good corrective to Wenschkewitz. The major spiritualizing traditions from the Old Testament to Eusebius are outlined in English in Everett Ferguson, "Spiritual Sacrifice in Early Christianity and its Environment," in *ANRW*, vol. II.23.2.

[10]Valentin Nikiprowetzky, "La Spiritualisation des sacrifices et le culte sacrificiel au Temple de Jérusalem chez Philon d'Alexandrie," *Semitica*, 17 (1967), 99.

in certain strands of Greek philosophical literature.[11]

Philosophers hostile to a physical cult raised their criticisms on metaphysical grounds: true sacrifice required neither animal blood nor a physical sanctuary.[12] The true cult was the continual praise of God and the true sacrifice was prayer and reason.[13] Greco-Roman moralists commonly applied sacrificial language to the realm of prayer and ethics.[14] Above all, it was the condition of the heart, not the size of the offering, that truly mattered. Seneca in *De Beneficiis* 1.6.3 echoes the common assessment that the wicked find no favor with the gods "although they dye the altars with streams of blood." These arguments later proved especially useful to the Christian apologists in their rejection of the Jewish cult (e.g., Justin, *First Apol.*, 13). The sentiment behind them is to be found in the New Testament itself in expressions such as λογικὴ λατρεία (Rom. 12:1) and πνευματικὰς θυσίας (1 Pet. 2:5), which constitute the formulations of Hellenistic theology in general.[15]

Spiritualization in Judaism

Penitential prayer was made to coincide with the afternoon Tamid, or daily sacrifice, as early as Ezra 9:4-5 and became an increasingly important element of Jewish piety. The coincidence of times of prayer with times of sacrifice occurs in the Maccabean period (Dan. 9:21; Jud. 9:1) as well as the first century (Luke 1:10; Acts 3:1). None of these texts, however, suggested a regulation of liturgy or an obligation to pray. The sacrificial cultus had a fixed form and content, but prayer

---

[11]As noted by Nikiprowetzky, "Spiritualisation," pp. 98-99; Sidney Sowers, *The Hermeneutics of Philo and Hebrews*, Basel Studies of Faculty 1 (Richmond: John Knox, 1965), p. 55.

[12]James W. Thompson, *The Beginnings of Christian Philosophy*, CBQMS 13 (Washington: Catholic Biblical Association of America, 1982), p. 103.

[13]Nikiprowetzky, "Spiritualisation," p. 99.

[14]See Ferguson, "Spiritual Sacrifice," pp. 1151-1156; Thompson, *Beginnings*, pp. 103-115.

[15]Nikiprowetzky, "Spiritualisation," p. 99.

did not.[16] As a part of the temple ritual itself, prayer was not mandated;[17] but the evidence of the Psalms strongly indicates the inclusion of liturgical prayer as part of the ritual, as Isaiah 56:7 also implies. In any event, many Jews did in fact go to the temple to pray. Prayer and sacrifice were thus closely linked in early Jewish thought. When Jews became separated from the sacrificial cult, prayer and other substitute ritual forms received a new emphasis.[18]

Judaism in the Diaspora. It was not feasible for Jews living far from Palestine to make yearly pilgrimages to Jerusalem to participate in the temple cultus. For them the "obvious answer" to their predicament was prayer, which could be offered anywhere (Dan. 6:11).[19] By the third century B.C. Jews in the diaspora had built numerous "prayer houses" ($\pi\rho\sigma\sigma\epsilon\upsilon\chi\alpha\acute{\iota}$) in which to practice their communal piety.[20] They based this practice on the abundant Old Testament evidence to the effect that prayer was superior (e.g., Pss. 40:7-10; 51:19; 69:31-32) or at least equal (e.g., Pss. 119:108; 141:2) to sacrifice. All of these passages seem to be from the Hellenistic period and they should not be regarded as anti-temple polemics but rather "pleas to God to recognize the validity of worship that did not include sacrifices."[21] Diaspora Jews also sought to imitate the cultic meals associated with the temple with their own $\sigma\acute{\upsilon}\nu\delta\epsilon\iota\pi\nu\alpha$, as is attested in Josephus (*Ant.* 14.213-215,260-261). Although it was not practical for Jews in the diaspora to pray at the temple on a regular basis, they might occasionally make a pilgrimage

---

[16]Shaye J. D. Cohen, *From the Maccabees to the Mishnah*, Library of Early Christianity 7 (Philadelphia: Westminster, 1987), p. 68. The Eighteen Benedictions apparently did not attain a comparable fixity of content and form until the second century A.D. See *m.Abot* 2:13.

[17]In the *Letter of Aristeas* 92-95, it is claimed that the act of sacrifice was performed in silence.

[18]Harold Louis Ginsberg, et al., "Cult," *Encyclopaedia Judaica*, vol. 5 (New York: Macmillan, 1971), p. 1155.

[19]Cohen, *Maccabees*, p. 66.

[20]According to Cohen, *Maccabees*, p. 66, Palestinian Jewish "meeting houses" ($\sigma\upsilon\nu\alpha\gamma\omega\gamma\alpha\acute{\iota}$) are not attested before the first century B.C.

[21]Ibid., p. 67.

to Jerusalem.[22] In fact, the *Letter of Aristeas* attests to a very hellenized Judaism which still had a strong emotional attachment to the temple and its cultus.

Philo. The philosophical flowering of Hellenistic Judaism is best represented by Philo of Alexandria. Philo's writings generally indicate a positive assessment of the temple cultus. He himself made pilgrimages to Jerusalem to pray and sacrifice in the temple (*Prov.* 2, 64), and he describes the temple cultus in exalted terms (*Spec.* I, 73,193; *Legat.,* 198). Philo's major concern in *Legatio ad Gaium* is with the profanation of the temple.

Though an apologist for the Jerusalem cultus, Philo also appreciated the assumptions of Middle Platonic philosophy. His understanding of the temple and its worship was influenced by the anti-ritualistic elements of the Bible itself as well as Greek philosophy.[23] Unlike the Greeks, however, Philo never advocated the abolition of the material cultus. He believed that the cultus conveyed symbolically an extrinsic significance and thus recognized the common person's need for ritual sacrifice despite his own desire to move beyond it.[24] Philo reinterprets the outer cultus in terms of an inner one and enlists this reinterpretation in the service of mysticism.[25]

The Jerusalem cultus has value in that it points to a "better sacrifice."[26] It could cleanse the body, but the soul was more important (*Spec.* I, 259-269). That higher part of human existence could only be cleansed by a "spiritual cult" offered

---

[22]Ibid.

[23]Nikiprowetzky, "Spiritualisation," p. 97.

[24]David Winston, "Philo and the Contemplative Life," in *Jewish Spirituality*, vol. 1, ed. Arthur Green, World Spirituality (New York: Crossroad, 1987), pp. 216-217.

[25]Wenschkewitz, "Spiritualisierung," p. 72. Jack N. Lightstone, *The Commerce of the Sacred* (Chico: Scholars, 1984), pp. 171-185, demonstrates that Philo was not the proponent of a Jewish "mystery," but that he does believe in a real ascent of the soul through contemplative exercises.

[26]Thompson, *Beginnings*, p. 114.

by the soul to God (*Fuga*, 117-118; *Spec.* I, 272).[27] For Philo, the true cultus is the spiritual one, in which the human soul is at once victim, temple, and priest:

> Thus, in the perspective of the "spiritual cult," the soul of the offerer is at the same time the sacrificial victim, the temple where this victim is immolated and the priest who celebrates there the sacrificial rites. And, in effect, the essential objective of the "spiritual cult" is that these three realities become indivisibly merged.[28]

Following the Old Testament prophetic tradition, Philo places great emphasis on the ethical prerequisites of cultic participation. What matters is the intentionality of the worshipper. He goes so far as to insist that when the worshiper's heart is pure there is no need for a material sacrifice (*Mos.* II, 107-108; *Plant.*, 108).

The Dead Sea Scrolls. The Qumran covenanters also experienced a separation from the Jerusalem cultus even though they lived nearby in the Judean desert. They separated themselves from the temple, however, because they regarded it as polluted. The Qumranians abandoned the temple not because they denied the validity of the cultus, but because they valued it so highly.[29] Since the Torah did not permit them to build a new temple (Deut. 12:5-6), they interpreted the community itself to be God's eschatological temple. By so separating themselves they intended "to continue in a better and purer way the cultic celebrations of Israel."[30]

Although the immediate occasion for the Qumranians' spiritualization of cultic motifs was their rejection of the polluted temple, Schüssler Fiorenza suggests that the deeper theological reason was their conviction that they were living in the end time with God already in the midst of his people.[31] They thus used cultic language because of their understanding of the covenant community as the locus of God's activity on earth.

Since there could be no actual sacrifice without a temple, the Qumran

---

[27]Ibid., p. 115.

[28]Nikiprowetzky, "Spiritualisation," p. 103.

[29]Schüssler-Fiorenza, "Cultic Language," p. 165.

[30]Ibid., p. 162.

[31]"In the community, the eschatological temple of God is present on earth," Ibid., p. 163.

community declared prayer and right living to be spiritual sacrifices (CD 9:3-5; 1QS 10:3ff.). The function or goal of the community as the eschatological temple was to observe cultic purity and atone for Israel's sins through their spiritual cultus, thus making atonement possible in the last days.[32] Although the Dead Sea Scrolls reinterpret the temple as the community and the sacrifice as prayer and right living, the community maintained the distinction between priests and laity and thus could not transfer the term to the community as a whole (except, perhaps, for CD 3:21).[33]

Rabbinic Judaism. With the fall of Jerusalem and the destruction of the temple in A.D. 70 Judaism utterly lost its sacrificial cultus. Since then the only option for maintaining a cultic piety was to spiritualize the old cultic images. This is what happened in the scribal tradition which eventually became rabbinic Judaism: the rabbis found in the theoretical study of the sacrifices a substitute for the offerings themselves (cf. *b.Ta 'an.* 27b; *b.Menah.* 110a).[34]

Neusner charts the course of the rabbis' treatment of the cultic data by examining the Mishnah's seder *Qodashim*.[35] He argues that by codifying the everyday details about the temple cultus at a time when there was no conceivable way to put that learning into practice, the rabbis had mapped a "fictitious territory" and a "forbidden city."[36] In the absence of the territory itself, such a map was all they could hope for.[37] Studying this map thus filled the same kinds of religious needs that the cultus itself once addressed. The Mishnah "democratizes" the

---

[32]Ibid., p. 166.

[33]Ibid., p. 167.

[34]Anson Rainey, et al., "Sacrifice," *Encyclopaedia Judaica*, vol. 14 (New York: Macmillan, 1971), p. 607.

[35]Jacob Neusner, "Map without Territory: Mishnah's System of Sacrifice and Sanctuary," *History of Religions*, 19 (1979), 103-127.

[36]Ibid., pp. 110, 112.

[37]"Here the form is all we have for meaning," Ibid., p. 117.

cultus.[38] No longer must there be a priest: anyone can study Torah. No longer must there be a temple: one can learn anywhere. "What Mishnah does . . . is to permit Israel . . . to experience anywhere and anytime that cosmic center of the world described by Mishnah: *Cosmic center in words is made utopia.*"[39] The Mishnah therefore does not spiritualize the cultus by positing a new form of cultic performance, but by turning backward to the old, this-worldly situation.

At the same time, rabbinic Judaism tended to formalize the aspects of piety that remained possible without a temple. It is only in the rabbinic period that one finds clear evidence for statutory prayer.[40] Because of its association with the sacrificial cultus (either as a counterpart or an equivalent), Jewish prayer traditions gradually absorbed some of that institution's fixity and regularity. After A.D. 70 many customs and rituals from the Temple were consciously transferred to the synagogue.[41] In *Sipre to Deuteronomy* 41 the rabbis are even able to speak of an "*abodah* [Yom Kippur liturgy] of the heart." The rabbinic injunction to pray twice daily corresponded to the offering of the daily sacrifice[42] and was no less obligatory, although the individual or worship leader was allowed some leeway in the precise language used (*m.Ber.* 4:1-7). The regulation of content and structure of prayer was another step toward assimilating prayer to sacrifice. Furthermore, charitable deeds took on a cultic nuance. *Abot de Rabbi Nathan* 4 relates the occasion when Yohanan ben Zakkai asserted, on the basis of Hosea 6:6, that acts of mercy were just as effective for atonement as the recently destroyed temple.

The New Covenant Cultus in Hebrews

Daly indicates that the three main aspects of the New Testament theology of

---

[38]The word is suggested by Cohen, *Maccabees*, p. 75.

[39]Neusner, "Map," p. 125.

[40]Cohen, *Maccabees*, p. 68.

[41]Louis Isaac Rabinowitz, et al., "Synagogue," *Encyclopaedia Judaica*, vol. 15 (New York: Macmillan, 1971), p. 583.

[42]Cohen, *Maccabees*, p. 67.

sacrifice are (1) the Christian community as the new temple, (2) the sacrifice of Christ, and (3) the sacrifice of the Christian.[43] The first of these is absent in Hebrews except for the passing reference at 3:6.[44] The second aspect, which we have termed the Christ Cultus, dominates Hebrews and has been discussed in detail in chapter three. It is left, therefore, to examine Hebrews' depiction of the Christian life in cultic terms: the New Covenant Cultus.

The author presents the New Covenant Cultus mainly in the final, exhortatory section of Hebrews (10:19-13:21). Within this section, three major texts stand out in reference to the Christian life as a cultus. These will now be considered in turn.

The New Covenant Cultus in Hebrews 10:19-25

Hebrews 10:19-25 forms a high point of the book.[45] In this paragraph the author summarizes what has gone before about Christ as High Priest and appeals to his audience to apply the blessings of Christ's ministry in daily life. In the course of the sermon, 10:19-25 serves the same structural function as Romans 12:1-2: It brings to a close a central expository section and encourages the audience toward "sacrifice," conceived as Christian life lived in community.[46] There are close structural affinities between this section of the letter and its parallel at the beginning of the central exposition in 4:14-16. Both passages begin with reference to Jesus as the High Priest who has passed into the heavenly realm. Because we have such a High Priest (ἔχοντες οὖν, 4:14; 10:19), the author encourages us to approach the divine presence (προσερχώμεθα, 4:16; 10:22) with boldness (παρρησία, 4:16, 10:19). The same message finds expression in 9:11-14, the pivotal center of

---

[43]Robert J. Daly, *Christian Sacrifice*, CUASCA 18 (Washington: Catholic University of America, 1978), p. 262.

[44]Ibid.

[45]William G. Lane, *Hebrews*, vol. 2, Word Biblical Commentary (Dallas: Word, 1991), p. 281; Gaspar Mora, *La Carta a los Hebreos como escrito pastoral* (Barcelona: Herder, 1974), p. 189.

[46]Daly, *Origins*, p. 73.

Hebrews,[47] where believers are encouraged to worship (λατρεύειν, 9:14) the living God because of the definitive cleansing that Jesus accomplished for them by entering the heavenly sanctuary.

The author employs a similar argument with the motif of God's rest in 4:1-11. For the author, God's "rest" is not earthly Canaan but a heavenly reality which God himself entered upon completing the work of creation (4:3b-5). Rest is thus equated with being in the presence of God.[48] Just as believers are exhorted in 10:19-25 to enter the inner sanctum, in 4:9-11 they are encouraged to enter the σαββατισμός of God.[49] The rest and the holy of holies both speak of the believer's right of approach to God, secured by Christ,[50] to perform acts of worship.

The exhortation of 10:19-25 comes in a series of three hortatory subjunctives: let us draw near (10:22), let us hold fast (10:23), and let us care for one another (10:24). Each of these is qualified by a reference to the traditional Christian virtues of faith, hope, and love.[51]

Verses 19-21 summarize the central priestly section in light of which, beginning in verse 22, the audience is urged to draw near. As this priestly section has already received our attention, we may pass through it briefly on our way to the exhortations. By means of the blood of Jesus, believers have παρρησίαν εἰς τὴν εἴσοδον τῶν ἁγίων ("confidence to enter the sanctuary," NRSV). The

---

[47]William G. Johnsson, *Hebrews*, Knox Preaching Guides (Atlanta: John Knox, 1980), p. 65.

[48]Marie Isaacs, *Sacred Space*, JSNTSS 73 (Sheffield: Academic Press, 1992), p. 83.

[49]The term σαββατισμός occurs here for the first time in Greek literature. It is a more comprehensive term for Sabbath observance (Harold W. Attridge, *The Epistle to the Hebrews*, Hermeneia [Philadelphia: Fortress, 1989], p. 131), involving the joy and festivity associated with the Sabbath in traditional Jewish piety (Lane, *Hebrews*, vol. 1, pp. 101-102). Regretably, time does not permit an extended discussion of the cultic dimensions of the motif of rest in Hebrews.

[50]Although Christ is never explicitly described as entering God's rest, the author does contrast his exalted position, seated at God's right hand, with the constant activity of the old covenant priests (7:27; 10:11-12). In any event, Christ's entry into the divine presence does present certain parallels to the entry of Christians into the divine rest (Attridge, *Hebrews*, p. 128).

[51]Attridge, *Hebrews*, p. 283; Lane, *Hebrews*, vol. 2, p. 281.

unusual word εἴσοδος may refer to the act of entering (1 Thess. 1:9; 2:1; Acts 8:24) or to the means (2 Pet. 1:11). Given the parallel term ὁδός in the next verse, 10:19 is probably a reference to the means by which believers enter the sanctuary.[52] Because of their newfound status before God (3:6; 4:16; 10:19,35) Christians have boldness to approach the entryway into the inner sanctum. This expression no doubt is intended to contrast with the "fear" at making approach to God in the Old Covenant.[53] In Leviticus 10:2 those who drew near were consumed with fire, and m. Yoma 5:1 describes how the high priest hurried in the inner sanctum lest the people fear that he had been struck dead in the presence of God (cf. Luke 1:21). In contrast, Christians may enter with boldness, which Attridge defines as "an attitude of confidence that enables a free and unimpeded behavior before God and humankind."[54]

Jesus has inaugurated (ἐνεκαίνισεν) a "fresh and living way" for us through the curtain (καταπέτασμα).[55] With the reference to the curtain (9:3; 10:20), the author's argument has come full circle. Now the barriers are down and believers may make their approach with no more numinous unease in the presence of the Holy.[56] The question arises as to whether the curtain is something negative that prevents access to God or something positive that permits it. Westcott argues

---

[52]B. F. Westcott, *The Epistle to the Hebrews*, 2nd ed. (Grand Rapids: Eerdmans, 1955), p. 318.

[53]George Wesley Buchanan, *To the Hebrews*, The Anchor Bible (Garden City: Doubleday, 1972), p. 167; R. Alan Culpepper, "A Superior Faith: Hebrews 10:19-12:2," *RevExp*, 82 (1985), 375-376.

[54]Attridge, *Hebrews*, p. 284.

[55]Lane, *Hebrews*, vol. 2, p. 284, (following Johannes Behm, "καινός, κ.τ.λ.," *TDNT*, vol. 3, p. 454) sees the primary nuance here that of making a way or making access available, in parallel with 6:19-20. In contrast, N. A. Dahl, "A New and Living Way: The Approach to God according to Hebrews 10:19-25," *Interpretation*, 5 (1951), 403-404 argues that ἐγκαινίζω can be cultic here, and Otto Michel, *Der Brief an die Hebräer*, Kritisch-Exegetischer Kommentar über das Neue Testament (Göttingen: Vandenhoeck & Ruprecht, 1966), admits that both nuances are there. One must wonder, however, how else than by cultic means the author of Hebrews would conceive of a religious good being accomplished. Both 6:19-20 and 10:19-25 have obvious cultic overtones and in both it is ritually-conceived activity that accomplishes the entrance. See also 9:18.

[56]William G. Johnsson, "Defilement and Purgation in the Book of Hebrews" (Ph.D. dissertation, Vanderbilt University, 1973), p. 352.

for a negative sense.[57] Roman Catholic scholars generally argue for a positive sense and go on to equate the curtain with the flesh of Jesus.

Admittedly, the phrase τουτ' ἔστιν τῆς σαρκὸς αὐτοῦ is difficult. We prefer, however, to see it in terms of the parallel structure of 10:19 and 20. Both passages refer to (1) new access, (2) the divine presence as its goal, and (3) the sacrifice of Christ as its ground. In 10:19 these images are predicated on Christians, while in 10:20 Christ himself is the subject.[58] Τῆς σαρκὸς αὐτοῦ should then be taken in an instrumental sense parallel to ἐν τῷ αἵματι Ιησοῦ.[59] The author's reference to the curtain is consistent here with the local and literal sense it has in 6:19 and 9:3. It is the curtain that hangs before the sanctuary. The curtain need not be a negative image but simply the point of entry into the divine presence.[60] Any sacralized space must have borders that delimit the transition from profane to sacred and back.[61] The curtain is neither a means nor a denier of access but a dividing line that, because of Christ's sacrifice, believers may now cross with priestly privilege. The author describes the actual crossing of the boundary between the profane and the sacred in the exhortations of 10:22-25. What was at best partially attainable under the Old Covenant is now a reality: "the freedom and confidence actually to draw near to God in worship and prayer."[62] The fundamental exhortation here is the first, on which the other two depend: "let us draw near" (προσερχώμεθα). In Hebrews the verb προσέρχομαι always

---

[57]Westcott, *Hebrews*, p. 319.

[58]Lane, *Hebrews*, vol. 2, p. 284.

[59]Ibid.; Johnsson, "Defilement," pp. 354-355.

[60]Attridge, *Hebrews*, p. 287; David Peterson, *Hebrews and Perfection* (Cambridge: University Press, 1982), p. 154.

[61]Victor Turner, *Process, Performance and Pilgrimage*, Ranchi Anthropology Series 1 (New Delhi: Concept, 1979), p. 97.

[62]John M. Scholer, *Proleptic Priests*, JSNTSS 49 (Sheffield: Academic Press, 1991), p. 131.

denotes the approach to God.[63] In each of its seven occurrences in the sermon it connotes the awe and reverence with which one approaches God, although twice (10:1; 12:18) it appears in a negative context describing the Old Covenant Cultus.[64] The cultic nuance of the term is widely accepted.[65] In the LXX the term "regularly connotes cultic activity,"[66] either of the people of God in general (e.g., Exod. 3:5; 22:8; Num. 16:5; Deut. 4:11; 5:27) or the priests in particular (Exod. 38:27; Lev. 9:7-8; 10:9; 21:23).

The priestly aspect is clearly part of the author's depiction of Christian existence.[67] Such is indicated in the two participial phrases that describe the believers' act of "drawing near." The conjunction of sprinkling and washing in 10:22 calls to mind a number of Old Testament ritual images. Sprinkling may suggest priestly consecration,[68] although Lane considers the image of covenant inauguration more satisfactory.[69] The sprinkling of humans with blood in fact occurs only in these two contexts in the Old Testament. As we have previously shown, there is no real need to choose between them: the Christ Cultus is able to effect several types of passages simultaneously.[70]

---

[63]Lane, *Hebrews*, vol. 2, p. 460; Michel, *Hebräer*, p. 461.

[64]Juliana Casey, "Eschatology in Hebrews 12:14-29: An Exegetical Study" (S.T.D. dissertation, Catholic University of Louvain, 1976), p. 310.

[65]See Ernst Käsemann, *The Wandering People of God*, trans. Roy A. Harrisville and Irving L. Sandberg (Minneapolis: Augsburg, 1984), p. 54; and Michel, *Hebräer*, p. 461, who compare it to Christian liturgy.

[66]Scholer, *Proleptic*, p. 91.

[67]Buchanan, *Hebrews*, p. 170; Daly, *Origins*, p. 72; Scholer, *Proleptic*, p. 124.

[68]James Moffatt, *A Critical and Exegetical Commentary on the Epistle to the Hebrews*, International Critical Commentary (New York: Scribner's, 1924), p. 144; Michel, *Hebräer*, p. 346; Dahl, "Living Way," pp. 406-407; Olaf Moe, "Der Gedanke des allgemeinen Priestertums im Hebräerbrief," *Theologische Zeitschrift*, 5 (1949), 162-163; *contra* Attridge, *Hebrews*, p. 288.

[69]Lane, *Hebrews*, vol. 2, p. 287.

[70]Since we have discovered that Christ's ritual work makes believers priests, we must

With regard to the believers' admonition to draw near, Scholer asks the right question:

> ... just how do living, breathing, corporeal entities draw near to the throne, or enter into the heavenly holy of holies, or stand in God's very presence-- especially since such access is already a present enjoyment, as seen by the προσεληλύθατε in 12.22?[71]

This question must be always before us in our investigation of the New Covenant Cultus and a final answer must be postponed to the end. Scholars have suggested various interpretations of the admonition to "draw near." Primarily, interpreters see here and elsewhere in Hebrews the exhortation to draw near to God through worship, prayer, or eucharistic celebration. It must first be noted that the admonition is always in the present tense: the believers' approach to God is something they must continue to do rather than something they are to aspire to in some futuristic sense. The drawing near is (or should be) a part of Christian experience "today" (3:13-14; 4:6-7).

This drawing near is to be accomplished with a sincere heart, echoing the new covenant motif in 8:10. It involves full assurance of faith (πληροφορία πίστεως), which has to do with the certainty and stability that Christ's work creates in believers to enable them to remain loyal.[72] The basis of the author's appeal is the existing relationship of the believers with God, made explicit with the two perfect participles ῥεραντισμένοι and λελουσμένοι. Although the latter phrase, "having been washed in body with pure water," is widely acknowledged to be a reference to baptism, attempts to find a eucharistic reference in the former phrase are unconvincing.

---

alter our previous conceptualization of the rites of passage effected by the Christ Cultus to the following:

previous status	passage	new status

corporate rites:

no relationship------------>(blood)----------->covenant partners
defiled---------------------->(blood)-------->definitively cleansed
laypeople------------------>(blood)------------------------->priests

[71]Scholer, *Proleptic*, p. 106.

[72]Lane, *Hebrews*, vol. 2, p. 286.

The two other cohortatives follow on the basis of the call to draw near. The addressees are also to "hold fast the confession of hope unwavering." The accusative adjective ἀκλινῆ qualifies the confession, not the confessors, and parallels earlier exhortations to hold certain things "secure" (cf. 3:6,11; 6:19).[73] They are to remain faithful in their confession because the one they confess, the one in whose promises they share, is himself faithful. This confession may be a technical term for an objective, traditional confession of faith, but such is not a necessary conclusion.[74]

Finally, the author exhorts his audience to consider or care for (κατανοέω) one another for the purpose of stirring up love and good works (10:24-25). The passage here reaches its climax in a pointed reminder of the importance of the Christian gathering. "A community thrives on the participation of its members."[75] Some, however, were failing to attend church meetings. The parenthetical remark to this effect in 10:25 may be the surest indication of the concrete problem the sermon was written to address.[76] The author confronts the problem with a reminder of the need for Christians to care for one another through love, good works, and mutual encouragement.[77] Holding fast the confession of hope would have been difficult work in a time of impending persecution; in these trying times, as they "see the Day drawing near,"[78] the believers needed each other perhaps more than ever before. While individual Christians might practice the virtues of faith and hope alone, love

---

[73]Attridge, *Hebrews*, p. 289, *contra* Lane, *Hebrews*, vol. 2, p. 289.

[74]Lane, *Hebrews*, vol. 1, p. 104, and vol. 2, p. 228, believes that the confession of 4:14 is "clearly" such a technical term, but sees a more general sense in 10:23.

[75]Culpepper, "A Superior Faith," p. 377.

[76]Attridge, *Hebrews*, p. 290.

[77]Lane, *Hebrews*, vol. 2, p. 289.

[78]Alexander Nairne, *Epistle of Priesthood* (Edinburgh: Clark, 1913) p. 383, suggests that it is at least possible that the community here addressed "saw" the day approaching in the political disturbances of the time (cf. Mark 13).

can only be expressed in community.[79] The well-being of each believer is here bound up with the well-being of the whole community.[80]

Why then were these gatherings so important? The nature of public worship in Hebrews has been long debated, with scholars reaching few areas of consensus. Some see a full-blown sacramentalism with a profound meditation on the eucharist,[81] while others doubt that any kind of ritual activity would meet with the approval of the author.[82] Some interpreters advocate a view of communal worship that consists only in what today might be called a "service of the word."[83] Clearly one reason the gatherings were so important was as a communal setting for encouragement and exhortation (cf. 3:13). If Hebrews itself is any indication, preaching would have certainly played an important part.

A key to the community's interpretation of its own assembly may be found in the author's choice of the unusual word ἐπισυναγωγή to describe it. Although Schrage states that the word shows little distinction from the more common συναγωγή, he himself goes on to note the eschatological connotation which it derives from its usage in the LXX.[84] In the LXX, ἐπισυναγωγή can be used in the general sense of people gathering together for any number of reasons. It can also denote a religious gathering (1 Kgs. 18:20; 2 Chr. 5:6; 20:26; Dan. 3:2). Most tantalizing are the uses in the context of the longed-for gathering together of the diaspora. In Isaiah 52:12 (ET 53:12) we learn that "the Lord will go before you, even the Lord God of Israel, who will gather you (ὁ ἐπισυνάγων ὑμᾶς)," and in Psalm 146:2 (ET 147:2), "the Lord builds up Jerusalem; he gathers the outcasts

---

[79]William L. Lane, *Call to Commitment* (Nashville: Nelson, 1985), p. 141.

[80]Westcott, *Hebrews*, p. 324.

[81]For example, Swetnam, "Christology," asserts that the presence of Christ in the eucharist is the author's central concern.

[82]Ronald Williamson, "Eucharist," pp. 300-312, believes that the author is highly anti-sacramental and may in fact be arguing against exactly the position that Swetnam proposes.

[83]Martin Dibelius, "Der himmlische Kultus nach dem Hebräerbrief," in *Botschaft und Geschichte*, vol. 2 (Tübingen: Mohr, 1956), p. 174; Friederich Schröger, "Gottesdienst," p. 174.

[84]Wolfgang Schrage, "συναγωγή, κ.τ.λ.," *TDNT*, vol. 7, pp. 841-842.

of Israel."[85] In the only Septuagintal occurrence of the noun form ἐπισυναγωγή (2 Macc. 2:7), Jeremiah hides the tent of the ark and the altar of incense, and states that the place shall be unknown until God gathers his people together again and shows his mercy. Similarly, the only other occurrence of the noun in the New Testament is 2 Thessalonians 2:1, where once again the eschatological note is evident.

Given that the only other occurrences of ἐπισυναγωγή in the Greek Bible clearly point to an eschatological ingathering, and since the usage of the related verb form also often leans in this direction, it is most likely that the author of Hebrews understands the church to be an eschatological community and its corporate worship some kind of eschatological event. This is confirmed in the text itself by reference to the coming Day as the Christians' motive for assembling for mutual support. Corporate worship for Hebrews is, as Galley describes, a foreshadowing in time of an eschatological salvation event.[86] This conceptualization is coherent with the use of cultic language elsewhere in Hebrews. The call for believers to approach God is predicated upon Jesus' own cultic approach. Believers may only go where Jesus leads; and since Jesus' entrance into the divine presence is heavenly and eschatological in nature, so likewise the experience of believers. The exact nature of this experience, however, is yet to be explored; although we certainly accept the conclusion of Scholer that the priestly activity of believers in Hebrews is still awaiting a final consummation: it is "proleptic" and "penultimate."[87]

The Christian assembly must have seemed insignificant next to the ritualism of the Jewish sacrificial cult.[88] By interpreting the meeting in such rich terms, the author links it to the central religious feelings to which he appeals throughout Hebrews. To return briefly to an earlier question, we conclude that in this particular passage, the priestly approach of believers is to be understood in terms of corporate worship. Support for this view is to be found in references to the

---

[85]See also LXX Ps. 105:47; 2 Macc. 1:26-27; 2:18.

[86]Hans-Detlof Galley, "Der Hebräerbrief und der christliche Gottesdienst," *Jahrbuch für Liturgik und Hymnologie*, 31 (1987-1988), 77.

[87]Scholer, *Proleptic*, p. 207.

[88]Westcott, *Hebrews*, p. 326.

confession and baptism in 10:23 and in the elaborate exhortation to continue gathering for worship in 10:25.[89] We must not, however, conclude that the often repeated call to draw near is to be understood exclusively in this sense. Other possibilities present themselves in other passages.

The New Covenant Cultus in Hebrews 12:18-24

The relationship of this passage to the Heavenly Cultus has already been examined. Here our concern is simply to discern its message with respect to earthly believers. The passage takes the form of a step parallelism with three elements in each part:[90]

A   12:18-19a   The old covenant setting
B   12:19b-20   The old covenant participants
C   12:21   The old covenant mediator
A' 12:22a   The new covenant setting
B' 12:22b-23   The new covenant participants
C' 12:24   The new covenant mediator

Like 10:19-25, this passage provides a summary of Hebrews' christology, eschatology, ecclesiology, and soteriology.[91] It is "a haunting, mystical, and unique apocalyptic depiction of Christian worship."[92]

Following on the sharp warning of 12:14-17, the author here turns to exposition. The imagery may be a portrayal of what the believer stands to lose, and thus serve as a grounds for the warning.[93] It is preferable to see here a word of encouragement that gives way to assurance. This is in fact the author's strategy with other warning passages (6:9-12; 10:32-39). As has been noted previously, the author has carefully added and omitted from the original pentateuchal narratives of the giving of the Law on Sinai to highlight the fearsome elements and thus draw a more graphic contrast with the scene of heavenly glory in 12:22-24. The single

---

[89]Scholer, *Proleptic*, p. 128.

[90]See Juliana M. Casey, "Christian Assembly in Hebrews: A Fantasy Island?" *Theology Digest*, 30 (1982), 325.

[91]Ceslaus Spicq, *L'Épître aux Hébreux*, vol. 2 (Paris: Gabalda, 1952), p. 399.

[92]Peter Rhea Jones, "A Superior Life: Hebrews 12:3-13:25," *RevExp*, 82 (1985), 396.

[93]Casey, "Eschatology," p. 303.

possibly negative element here, the description of God as "judge," need not detract from the overall theme of joyful celebration that marks the passage.[94] Hebrews 12:22-24 describes the privileged position of Christians as a way of encouraging them to live up to their potential and thus guard against apostasy.[95]

The first part of the paragraph describes the approach to God under the old covenant as earthly, temporal, and mediated.[96] The presence of God is itself in question.[97] The divine name, which occurs six times in the narrative of these events in Deuteronomy 5:23-27, is completely absent here. The author's assessment of the Old Covenant Cultus is revealed in the first term he uses to describe it: "that which can be touched." Christians have not come to what may be touched because they seek a world and a city yet to come (2:5; 13:14).[98]

Both halves of the passage begin with the assertion "you have come" (προσεληλύθατε), reflecting the language of Deuteronomy 4:11 (LXX), "you came" (προσήλθετε). Again, we find the verb προσέρχομαι used to describe the present condition of believers. Once again, the term carries a cultic nuance.[99] The vocabulary of this section has a clearly cultic flavor (ἐκκλησία,

---

[94]According to Spicq, *Hébreux*, vol. 2, p. 408, the term κρίτης corresponds to μισθαποδότης in 11:6. God discerns and chooses the inhabitants of the heavenly Jerusalem, but he also punishes their persecutors. See also D. Eduard Riggenbach, *Der Brief an die Hebräer* (Leipzig: Erlangen, 1922), pp. 417-418, who interpretes κρίτης in light of the Old Testament image of judges as benefactors who provide justice for the oppressed (cf. LXX Ps. 67:6).

[95]Lane, *Hebrews*, vol. 2, p. 459.

[96]Scholer, *Proleptic*, p. 140.

[97]*Contra* Scholer, *Proleptic*, p. 140, n. 2, who argues that there is no question of God's absence here, merely of access to God's presence. Scholer, however, fails to see that even Casey, with whom he is arguing, admits that at Sinai God is near yet inaccessible ("Eschatology," p. 331).

[98]Lane, *Hebrews*, vol. 2, p. 461, *contra* Thompson, *Beginnings*, pp. 45-47, who sees here the assumptions of Middle Platonic metaphysics. A heavenly-earthly dualism is certainly at work here, but it is in the service of traditional eschatological categories (cf. 12:27).

[99]*Contra* Hans Kosmala, *Hebräer-Essener-Christen* (Leiden: Brill, 1959), p. 123; and Schröger, "Gottesdienst," p. 178. Michel, pp. 469-470, however, sees behind this passage a tradition about the Christian community as (in a spiritualized sense, to be sure) a cultic community.

πανήγυρις). The image of a new Jerusalem has definite cultic overtones in several Old Testament passages (Isa. 2:2-4; 45:14-15; 49:22-23; 60; Zech. 14:10,11,16,20) that describe the nations coming in pilgrimage to worship at Mount Zion. Finally, reference to the "blood of sprinkling" in 12:24 recalls the Jewish sacrificial cult. In Deuteronomy 4:10-14 the Sinai experience is understood in terms of a solemn covenant ceremony.[100] The change to the perfect tense indicates a continuing result of the believer's encounter with God: "what the OT described as a one-time event becomes a more permanent state which has resulted from the original approach."[101] The moment of this initial encounter is the moment of conversion, however construed.[102]

This approach is an internal one that may be connected to worship and prayer.[103] Scholer specifically denies that the approach can be understood as a futuristic vision apprehended by faith or some sort of fully realized eschatology.[104] Given our interpretation of 10:25, the possibility of some kind of eschatological emphasis here cannot be so easily dismissed. In 12:22-24 the reader encounters a barrage of apocalyptic images. The scene can only be described as a kind of heavenly worship. The setting is heavenly Jerusalem; and the participants are angels, the assembly of the first-born, and the spirits of the righteous dead, with God in their midst. The mention of angels calls attention to the other appearance of angels in chapter one, where they are enlisted by God to praise the exalted Son as he enters the eschatological world and is there enthroned. Nevertheless, the full participation of believers in earthly existence is never doubted. They have not yet

---

[100]Lane, *Hebrews*, vol. 2, p. 459.

[101]Casey, "Eschatology," p. 309.

[102]F. F. Bruce, *The Epistle to the Hebrews*, rev. ed., New International Commentary on the New Testament (Grand Rapids: Eerdmans, 1990), p. 372. Casey's suggestion that it is the moment of baptism ("Eschatology," p. 335) neglects the close connections between faith, baptism, and reception of the Holy Spirit in the broad matrix of Christian conversion and initiation, as discussed in James D. G. Dunn, *Baptism in the Holy Spirit* (Philadelphia: Westminster, 1970), pp. 224-229.

[103]Riggenbach, *Hebräer*, p. 414.

[104]Scholer, *Proleptic*, p. 144.

fully "arrived," but as they remain on earth they take part proleptically in the assembly to which they are destined.[105] As Käsemann notes, "now they finish their course in the immediate presence of this heavenly Jerusalem itself, holding the πανήγυρις in view and in turn being observed from it. They have arrived at that place just as the priest nears the altar to perform the sacrifice."[106] The New Covenant Cultus is heavenly and eschatological in nature precisely because it is true encounter. Christians do not hear trumpets, see storms, or fear for their lives. They meet God.[107]

As participants in this heavenly celebration, Christians on earth join with the angels, firstborn,[108] and righteous dead in a remarkable cultic performance.[109] Thus the common apocalyptic image of participation in the angelic liturgy finds fulfillment.[110] They are able to join in this liturgy because of the mediatorial role of Jesus himself, explicitly mentioned in 12:24 along with his sprinkled blood that effects the believers' elevation of status.

The exalted description of heavenly worship gives way in 12:25-29 to a renewed call for constancy in faith and a warning not to turn back from the incredible benefits which Jesus has made available to his people. The chapter concludes with a reprise of the language of the Sinai event (12:28-29) now directed specifically toward Christian worship.[111] On the basis of the sure foundation upon which their confession stands, the author exhorts his audience to worship God

---

[105]Casey, "Eschatology," p. 365.

[106]Käsemann, *Wandering*, p. 54.

[107]Casey, "Eschatology," p. 89.

[108]The identity of the πρωτότοκοι has generated a good bit of debate. We prefer to interpret the term as a reference to the whole people of God as distinct from the angels, following Bruce, *Hebrews*, p. 359; Attridge, *Hebrews*, p. 375; and Lane, *Hebrews*, vol. 2, p. 472.

[109]Ceslaus Spicq, "La Panégyrie de Hebr. XII,22," *Studia Theologica*, 6 (1952), 36.

[110]See *1 Enoch* 39:4-14; 1QH 3:20-23; 11:10-13. Although, as we have already noted, the angelic liturgy *per se* is secondary in Hebrews.

[111]Lane, *Hebrews*, vol. 2, p. 446.

worthily with reverence and awe. Once again, his language is rich in cultic significance. Λατρεύω is a favorite word of the author for levitical worship (8:5; 9:9; 10:2; 13:10). Here it is applied paraenetically to the cultic order of the new covenant.[112] From this admonition, the author "immediately specifies this cultic 'program' with a series of exhortations to the practice of Christian virtue."[113] The very purpose of Christ's sacrifice, it would seem, is for Christians to attain the capacity to offer their own grateful worship.[114]

The New Covenant Cultus in Hebrews 13:10-16

Hebrews 13:10-16 forms a cohesive unit framed by mention of the community's past and present leaders and related catechetical instructions in 13:7-9 and 13:17-19.[115] These seven verses close the sermon with yet another exhortation to authentic Christian living couched in cultic terminology. The passage supports and develops the author's point in 13:9 about the strengthening of the heart by grace, not by foods (χάριτι . . . , οὐ βρώμασιν).[116] With the triumphant declaration "we have an altar" (13:10) the author specifies the source of the grace by which hearts are strengthened. Although the whole of chapter 13 takes up the subject announced at the end of chapter 12, namely, the appropriate worship of God, 13:10-16 poses the issue in a carefully structured argument.[117] The argument flows from the intial declaration. Verses 10-12 are an exposition of the central assertion (ἔχομεν θυσιαστήριον, 13:10). Finally, in 13:13-16 the author applies this exposition to his audience's situation with two hortatory subjunctives:

---

[112]Susanne Lehne, *The New Covenant in Hebrews*, JSNTSS 44 (Sheffield: Academic Press, 1990), p. 110.

[113]Daly, *Origins*, p. 74.

[114]Daly, *Christian Sacrifice*, p. 280.

[115]Attridge, *Hebrews*, pp. 390-391.

[116]Lane, *Hebrews*, vol. 2, p. 537. See also Helmut Koester, "'Outside the Camp': Hebrews 13:9-14," *Harvard Theological Review*, 55 (1962), 305-308; and Thompson, *Beginnings*, pp. 144-145.

[117]See Lane, *Hebrews*, vol. 2, p. 503.

"let us go out to him" (ἐξερχώμεθα πρὸς αὐτόν, 13:13) and "let us offer up a sacrifice of praise" (ἀναφέρωμεν θυσίαν αἰνέσεως, 13:15). Beginning with the inadequacy of the Old Covenant Cultus, the author here moves on to describe the kinds of sacrifices that truly please God.

The impetus behind this passage was no doubt the desire of some in the community to recapture the splendor of the temple cult through ritual meals.[118] Such meals were a major aspect of the sacrificial system and, as already noted, were imitated in the Jewish diaspora. In the Old Testament, Dead Sea Scrolls, and rabbinic corpus cultic meals were associated with being supported by God's grace, especially in the Second Temple period.[119] The liturgy of such a meal may be discerned only through allusions in contemporary literature (*m.Pesah.* 10:6; *Jub.* 22:3-9). The author's assessment of such sacrificial meals is entirely negative: those who occupy themselves with such practices never attain the desired goal of communion with God.[120]

In contrast to cultic meals, the author asserts that Christians have an altar from which those who serve the tent have no right to eat (13:10). This simple statement dominates the entire pericope. The assertion is at bottom confessional, as evidenced by the use of ἔχω throughout the sermon (cf. 4:14; 8:1; 10:19-21); and probably an elaboration of the term "grace" in 13:9.[121] Nevertheless, in light of 13:9 it is difficult not to see at least an indirect polemic against the idea of achieving fellowship with God through cultic meals.[122] The questions surrounding this declaration have been the cause of no small scholarly debate. Does the author refer

---

[118]Westcott, *Hebrews*, p. 436; Lane, *Hebrews*, vol. 2, p. 532.

[119]Jukka Thurén, *Das Lobopfer der Hebräer*, Acta Academiae Åboensis, Series A: Humaniora 47, 1 (Åbo, Finland: Åbo Akademi, 1973), pp. 188-196.

[120]Westcott, *Hebrews*, p. 437. In this light, a eucharistic reference here is untenable. Like the mention of "tasting" in 6:4-5, "eating" in 13:10 points to the proleptic enjoyment of salvation (Ronald Williamson, "The Eucharist and the Epistle to the Hebrews," *NTS*, 21 [1975], 309). See also Lane, *Hebrews*, vol. 2, p. 538.

[121]Lane, *Hebrews*, vol. 2, p. 537.

[122]Attridge, *Hebrews*, p. 397.

here to the eucharistic table?[123] To the cross?[124] Does he have in mind some ideal, heavenly reality?[125] At 13:10 we reach the true center of gravity of the cultic motif in the spirituality of Hebrews. We must ask in what the Christian "altar" consists. How does it relate to the sacrificial work of Jesus? How do believers experience in their everyday lives the benefits of being cultically related to Jesus and to each other?

Although 13:10 speaks in the imagery of a cultic meal, the image shifts abruptly to that of the sin offering on the Day of Atonement in verse eleven. The author of Hebrews may have shared the growing Jewish perception that all sacrifices had atoning significance. More likely this is another instance of the phenomenon noted in Hebrews 9 of intentionally blurring and confusing the details of the Old Covenant Cultus to contrast their great variety with the singularity of Christ's sacrifice.[126] In any event, with 13:11 all reference to eating disappears to be replaced by a comparison of the death of Jesus with the disposal of animal carcasses "outside the camp."

Attridge is correct to see in these verses a clarification of the nature of the Christians' altar as the place where Jesus' sacrifice took place.[127] There is, however, another nuance to the assertion that "we have an altar." The leading images for Christ's salvific work in Hebrews are those of covenant inauguration and the Day of Atonement, both of which were concerned with providing a fit means of access for God's people to use.[128] That Christians have an altar at which to sacrifice is the whole point, a fact which comes out clearly in the author's

---

[123]Paul Andriessen, "L'Eucharistie dans l'Épître aux Hébreux," *Nouvelle Revue Théologique*, 94 (1972), 275-276.

[124]Bruce, *Hebrews*, pp. 399-401; Schröger, "Gottesdienst," pp. 161-181; Thurén, *Lobopfer*, pp. 75-79.

[125]Williamson, "Eucharist," pp. 307-308; Thompson, *Beginnings*, p. 146.

[126]Daly, *Christian Sacrifice*, p. 282.

[127]Attridge, *Hebrews*, p. 391.

[128]In light of the above discussion of believers as priests, the close connection in Lev. 8:10-13 between the consecration of priests and of altar and sanctuary is also a relevant analogy.

concluding exhortation to offer God pleasing sacrifices (13:15-16). The mention of the altar thus not only draws the contrast between the Old Covenant Cultus and the New: it also lays the groundwork for the idea that Christians have their own fitting sacrifices to bring.[129] The altar must be "*at least* the spiritualized equivalent of a sacrificial ritual."[130] (emphasis added)

The assertion "we have" (ἔχομεν) is immediately contrasted with another reality: "they do not have" (οὐκ ἔχουσιν). Here is yet another reference to the liturgy of the Day of Atonement, where not even the priests were permitted to eat from the sacrifice.[131] The contrast must be that believers, as "partakers of Christ" (3:14), do have the right to eat from their altar. To the charge that Christianity is deficient because it has no sacrificial cult, the author replies by taking the offensive. In Christ believers have more, not less, in terms of the experience of worship they perhaps longed for under the old covenant.[132]

In 13:11-12 the author elaborates upon his premise with an interpretation of the meaning of the death of Jesus. His exposition is essentially twofold.[133] First, the death of Jesus fulfilled the necessary condition for the sin offering on the Day of Atonement. Here once again is the author's central typology for understanding the death of Jesus. He draws here on the requirement of Leviticus 16:27 about the disposal of the victims' bodies.[134] As the bodies of the bull and goat were incinerated outside the camp, so Jesus suffered and died outside the walls of

---

[129]Thurén, *Lobopfer*, pp. 74-75.

[130]Daly, *Origins*, p. 75.

[131]Westcott, *Hebrews*, p. 439.

[132]Ibid., p. 439.

[133]Lane, *Hebrews*, vol. 2, p. 542.

[134]Attridge, *Hebrews*, p. 397, finds here the explanation of why these animals cannot be eaten: they are destroyed instead. The primary detail on which the author wishes to focus, however, is the phrase "outside the camp," as Attridge also notes (p. 398).

Jerusalem.[135] The analogy is not perfect. The disposal of the animals' bodies occurred after the sacrifice was accomplished, yet Jesus' suffering outside the gate is the substance of his sacrifice. Nevertheless, the author sees in the levitical regulations yet another means of speaking about the significance of Jesus.

According to the author's second expositional emphasis, the death of Jesus implied the shame of exclusion from the sacred precincts. Jesus is treated like the blasphemer or sabbath breaker who was to be executed outside the camp (Lev. 24:10-16,23; Num. 15:32-36). He died as one rejected: "it was as an outcast that he offered his sacrifice to God."[136]

The key element linking the two interpretations is the phrase "outside the camp" (ἔξω τῆς παρεμβολῆς, 13:11,13; cf. ἔξω τῆς πύλης, 13:12). It was here, outside the bounds of sacred space, that the carcasses were destroyed lest they continue to be a source of uncleanness in the community.[137] Here beyond the borders Jesus died.

The exposition in 13:10-12 resolves into three paraenetic applications.[138] The author issues calls to discipleship (13:13), to worship (13:15), and to ethical conduct (13:16). The focus of this exhortation is on the first element, the call to go out to Jesus and bear his reproach. This point in strongly emphasized by the repetition of the word ἔξω ("outside") in verses 11-13:

13:11   ἔξω τῆς παρεμβολῆς
13:12   ἔξω τῆς πύλης
13:13   ἐξερχώμεθα πρὸς αὐτὸν ἔξω τῆς παρεμβολῆς

Here we find the final resolution of Hebrews' continuing theme of entering the divine presence. The author has worked with the motif of "entering" or

---

135For the equation of Jerusalem with the camp in the wilderness, see *Num. Rab.* 5:3; *b.Zebah.* 116b; *b.Yoma* 65ab.

136Lane, *Hebrews*, vol. 2, p. 542.

137Jacob Milgrom, "Sacrifices and Offerings, OT," *IDBSupp*, p. 767.

138Attridge, *Hebrews*, p. 391.

"approaching" since the beginning as a central metaphor for encounter with God.[139] Here the imagery shifts to movement *in the opposite direction*.[140] The substance of such an encounter now becomes clear: to approach God is to abandon the "camp" and accept Christ's shame. With a stroke of the pen the old, comfortable boundaries fall. The sacred realm is suddenly beyond the pale.

The author laid the groundwork for this startling conclusion beginning in 10:32-34 with a reminder of the audience's admirable behavior in a previous time of persecution. They were "sometimes publicly exposed to reproach and affliction, at other times being comrades (κοινωνοί) with those so treated" (10:33). With their eyes and hearts turned to their greater inheritance, they willingly suffered the loss of their material wealth (10:34). The cost of discipleship becomes clear in the presentation of the many heroes of faith in chapter eleven. The first named example is Abel, who became the first martyr because he offered to God a fitting sacrifice (11:4). The largest section of the chapter is devoted to the patriarchs, especially Abraham, who "went out" (ἐξῆλθεν, 11:8) in obedience to Gods call to live in tents with his family. Moses then receives commendation for leaving Egypt for the promised land, willingly bearing affliction all the while (11:24-27). In a rhetorical flourish the author concludes the chapter with a survey of the kinds of mistreatment the faithful have suffered in the past (35b-38), culminating finally in Jesus himself, "who for the joy set before him endured the cross, disregarding its shame" (12:2). Believers, the author continues, are to consider "the one who has endured such hostility against himself from sinners" in their own struggle against sin (12:3-4). They are furthermore to endure trials for the sake of discipline (12:7-11) and continue to express solidarity with those who are being tortured (13:3).

Clearly, to associate with Jesus in the divine glory of his priesthood is also

---

[139]Compounds with εἰς signifying divine encounter occur at 1:6; 2:10; 3:11,18,19; 4:1,3,5,6,10,11; 6:19,20; 9:6,12,24. Compounds with πρός occur at 4:16; 7:25; 10:1,22; 11:6, 12:18,22. The verb ἐγγίζω, a synonym of προσέρχομαι, occurs at 7:19. The verb ἐξέρχομαι as a description of divine encounter occurs only in 11:8, with reference to Abraham's call, and in 13:13.

[140]Attridge, *Hebrews*, p. 398.

and equally to associate with him in his earthly humiliation.[141] The first duty of Christians is to go out to Jesus beyond the limits of traditional sanctity. As Lane notes, "the writer has perceived that there is a form of intimate sharing that unites Jesus and his followers in the common experience of repudiation and disgrace."[142] Such is in fact to be expected given the status-negating character of Jesus' own sacrifice. Although it was heavenly in its value and its efficacy, the first phase of the Christ Cultus occurred on earth. This also corresponds to the Day of Atonement typology. In the Old Covenant Cultus the altar is *outside* the inner sanctum. The high priest slaughters the animals outside and then brings the blood into the holy of holies. Likewise in the Christ Cultus, Jesus offered himself *outside* the heavenly sanctuary, then went in to present himself before God.[143] In the case of Christians, to assert that "we have an altar" implies a necessary cultic prerequisite to the divine approach itself. The Christians' altar involves earthly existence itself, in which they must identify fully with their self-giving, shame-bearing High Priest. We find in 13:13 the author's own unique appropriation of the Synoptic tradition that Christians must take up their own cross to follow Jesus (Mark 8:34-38 and par.; Mat. 10:37-38; Luke 14:26-27).[144]

In this light we find it unnecessary to see in the "camp" a specific reference to Judaism.[145] Although the author has presented in these verses a masterful argument for severing one's emotional ties with the Jerusalem sacrificial cult,[146] in actuality he aims at an even higher goal. To abandon the camp is to abandon

---

[141]Westcott, *Hebrews*, p. 441.

[142]Lane, *Hebrews*, vol. 2, p. 544.

[143]This observation about the placement of the altar is also made by Isaacs, *Sacred Space*, p. 211.

[144]Ibid., vol. 2, p. 543; Attridge, *Hebrews*, p. 399.

[145]*Contra* Westcott, *Hebrews*, p. 442; Spicq, *Hébreux*, vol. 2, p. 427, and others. Schröger, "Gottesdienst," p. 179 notes the positions of several commentators.

[146]The attack is two-pronged: (1) Jerusalem has lost all redemptive significance because of Jesus' sacrifice outside the gate (13:12-13), and (2) it has lost all eschatological significance because it is not the "lasting city" for which believers seek (13:14). See James Calvin De Young, *Jerusalem in the New Testament* (Amsterdam: Kok & Kampen, 1960), pp. 108-109.

respectability, security, and conventional holiness, however they may be understood.[147] There is thus grace to be found at the Christian altar (13:9), but there is also a personal cost.

In exchange for the fleeting security of earthly existence the author offers a city yet to come (13:14). Although they do not yet possess it (οὐ γὰρ ἔχομεν), the present expectation is "the driving force of the disciples' life."[148] Their current experience of the city and its liturgy (12:22-24) is but a proleptic enjoyment of a promise not yet fully consummated. Thus the readers must remember not just what they have (13:10), but also what they do not have (13:14). In the world Christians must accept the status of aliens as did those who came before them (11:8,15,26-27,38).[149] On this basis the author offers two further words about living the Christian life. There is no longer need for sacrifices of expiation (10:18), but the grateful response of celebratory offerings must continue.[150] These offerings take the form of praise and good works (13:15-16) and thus clarify once more the motif of the Christian altar. The application of sacrificial language to prayer and ethics was widespread in the Hellenistic period not only among Jews critical of cultic formalism (Sir. 34:18-35:11; 2 Enoch 45:3; T. Levi 3:5-6; 1QS 9:4-5) but also among Greco-Roman moralists (cf. Seneca, Benef. 1.6.3). This conceptualization of the Christian life as worship and charity augments the preceding exhortation to discipleship.[151] Our religious duty is not just to suffer for Christ's sake but to

---

[147]Attridge, *Hebrews*, p. 399.

[148]Lane, *Hebrews*, vol. 2, p. 547. According to Robert Jewett, *Letter to Pilgrims* (New York: Pilgrim, 1981), p. 235, Hebrews 13:14 is the central thesis of the book.

[149]Attridge, *Hebrews*, p. 399.

[150]Thurén, *Lobopfer*, pp. 178-182; Lane, *Hebrews*, vol. 2, p. 549; Frances M. Young, *The Use of Sacrificial Ideas in Greek Christian Writers from the New Testament to John Chrysostom*, Patristic Monograph Series 5 (Philadelphia: Philadelphia Patristic Foundation, 1979), p. 129.

[151]Lane, *Hebrews*, vol. 2, p. 548.

express praise and thanksgiving and to perform acts of mercy.[152]

The phrase "sacrifice of praise" (θυσία αἰνέσεως) is commonly used of prayer as opposed to animal sacrifice (LXX Ps. 49:14,23; 106:22). The verb ἀναφέρω is used of Jesus' self-sacrifice in 7:27 and 9:28, thus maintaining the close connection between Jesus and his disciples. Jesus' own praise is recorded in 2:12. Now believers are encouraged to perform their own acts of praise.[153] We must offer these sacrifices through Christ, as is abundantly clear from the emphatic position of δι' αὐτοῦ ("through him"). The call for Christians to offer sacrifice thus remains consistent with the centrality of Christ's own sacrifice in Hebrews' spirituality. The sacrifice of praise is clarified to be the "fruit of lips that confess his [i.e., Jesus'] name" (cf. LXX Hos. 14:3).

In 13:16 the author suggests another sacrificial expression available to believers. Acts of kindness (εὐποιΐα), particularly generosity (κοινωνία), are also cultic acts acceptable before God. The value of these sacrifices is rooted in the theological affirmation that God takes pleasure in them, recalling the account of Enoch in 11:6 and the call in 12:28 to offer pleasing worship.[154]

In these two verses the author adds another layer of significance to the assertion that "we have an altar." The new covenant community does indeed participate in cultic observances. This New Covenant Cultus, however, is something "quite outside the realm of the cultic."[155]

The New Covenant Cultus: Some Conclusions

The author of Hebrews depicts not only the saving work of Jesus as a cultus, but the activities of Christians. Here he finds the solution to the crisis of spirituality precipitated by his audience's separation from the traditional forms of religion. This spiritualized interpretation of Christian existence is a key emphasis in Hebrews' final paraenetic section (10:19-13:21). It reinforces the sermon's central

---

[152]Westcott, *Hebrews*, p. 443.

[153]Lane, *Hebrews*, vol. 2, pp. 551-552.

[154]Attridge, *Hebrews*, p. 401.

[155]Ibid.

cultic exposition through repeated references to the Christ Cultus, but moves strongly in the direction of personal appropriation of the ultimate cultic realities associated with Christ.

Cultic personnel. In two key passages, 4:16 and 10:22, the author uses the cultic term προσέρχομαι with reference to believers and in the context of Jesus' own high priestly function. Since Jesus the High Priest has approached God's presence, those who believe in him may do likewise.[156] Do Christians then comprise a sort of levitical priesthood under their High Priest? Best argues for such an assertion and describes the double strain of thought in Hebrews concerning the cultus: first, the levitical priesthood passes into the priesthood of Christ, then through Christ it passes into the priesthood of Christians.[157] The description in 10:22 of believers as "sprinkled" and "washed" certainly evokes the imagery of the levitical priest's consecration through sprinkling with blood and washing in water. Some fail to see a priesthood of Christians here, arguing that believers do not have their own sacrifices by virtue of which they gain divine access.[158] This, however, is to over-interpret the metaphor. Certainly Christians are only consecrated because of Jesus himself, but they do have an altar and a sacrificial cult to perform (13:10-16). The church in Hebrews is a priestly people making their cultic approach to the living God.

Cultic place. Two streams of thought converge in the author's description of the sacred space in which believers perform their acts of worship. From one perspective, believers are made participants in the worship of the heavenly sanctuary. And yet in other instances the author acknowledges the entirely earthly situation of Christians in troublingly graphic terms.

The clearest reference to believers as participants in the Heavenly Cultus is

---

[156]Durward Veazey Cason, " Ἱερεύς and Ἀρχιερεύς and Related Contexts in Hebrews" (Ph.D. dissertation, The Southern Baptist Theological Seminary, 1931), p. 96. It is, however, too much to claim with Westcott (p. 318) that in virtue of fellowship with Christ each Christian is a "high priest." This honor belongs only to Jesus in Hebrews, even though believers are granted full access to the inner sanctum.

[157]Ernest Best, "Spiritual Sacrifice: General Priesthood in the New Testament," *Interpretation*, 14 (1960), 286.

[158]Moffatt, *Hebrews*, p. 144; Michel, *Hebräer*, p. 209; Attridge, *Hebrews*, p. 288.

12:22-24. There the place of cultic activity is the heavenly city. The image of a city occurs five times in Hebrews. It is the unattained goal of the Old Testament patriarchs (11:10,16) and the promise opened to Christians (13:14).[159] Here as well as in chapter twelve the heavenly and eschatological nuance is unavoidable. The believers' approach to the heavenly city is more specifically an approach to the heavenly sanctuary where God himself sits (10:19).[160] The curtain before the sanctuary remains unmoved, but by the blood of Jesus Christians may pass through it into the divine presence.[161]

Nevertheless, the author never permits his audience to forget their earthbound existence. He holds up their past experience of courageous suffering as an example to emulate (10:32-35). He reminds them of the shameful treatment Jesus himself received and exhorts them to claim it as their own as they go out to meet him "outside the camp" (13:13). In chapter thirteen the author redefines sacred space. He does so not by retreating to heaven, but by relocating the place of divine encounter in the experience of shame and persecution on earth. The daily pilgrimage of believers through a threatening world has become their approach to the holy of holies.[162] The heavenly city they seek is essentially futuristic. On earth they have no such source of security (13:14).

One likely explanation of this dual conceptualization of cultic place is the tension between "already" and "not yet" in the eschatology of Hebrews and of the New Testament generally.[163] This tension occurs in the author's usage of προσέρχομαι. The act of "drawing near" is usually something enjoined upon

---

[159]Casey, "Eschatology," pp. 338-339.

[160]To draw near (10:22) "is to render acceptable worship in the heavenly sanctuary," Lane, *Call to Commitment*, p. 140.

[161]Westcott, *Hebrews*, p. 319.

[162]Jewett, *Pilgrims*, p. 234.

[163]See C. K. Barrett, "The Eschatology of the Epistle to the Hebrews," in *The Background of the New Testament and Its Eschatology*, ed. D. Daube and W. D. Davies (Cambridge: University Press, 1956). See also Bertold Klappert, *Die Eschatologie des Hebräerbriefs*, Theologische Existenz heute 16 (München: Kaiser, 1969); Thompson, *Beginnings*, pp. 41-52; and James Graydon Dukes, "Eschatology in the Epistle to the Hebrews," (Th.D. dissertation, The Southern Baptist Theological Seminary, 1956).

believers, but in 12:22 the term describes a completed action. The same thing happens with God's rest in chapter four. The faithful enter God's rest (present indicative in 4:3, aorist participle in 4:10) and yet the author urges them to strive (σπουδάσωμεν, 4:11) to enter it. While this explanation is basically valid, it does not really advance the discussion.

Cultic performance. The religious activity of the people of God is cultic, but it is never expiatory. Throughout the author's discussion of the Christian life the only sacrifice for sins is that of Christ himself (10:19; 12:24; 13:12). In the one place where the author most clearly discusses the sacrifice of Christians (13:15-16), he first recalls the atoning significance of Jesus' own blood and then encourages his audience to offer their own sacrifices "through him."

Lane sees in the New Covenant Cultus traces of the levitical peace or fellowship offerings (שְׁלָמִים).[164] The peace offering was always the last in a series of sacrifices. Its observance is described in Leviticus 3:1-17 and 7:11-34. This sacrifice could not be offered until atonement was effected. In it the victim's blood was sprinkled on the altar, but its body was cooked and shared in a fellowship meal. These cultic feasts became the occasion for public recital of God's covenant faithfulness (Pss. 26:4-7; 116:11,12,15) or the dedication of worshipers to God's service (Lev. 7:16-17; 22:21). It also played a part in the consecration of priests (Lev. 8:31). The rabbis considered the peace offering a means of bringing peace into the world. It was to be marked by rejoicing on the part of the offerer (*Sipra* 28:1). As an occasion for reflecting on God's past faithfulness and for commitment and recommitment to God's service, the fellowship offering was "particularly suited to stress the reality of consecration to God."[165] In Hebrews 10:19-25 the cultic approach of believers is described in terms reminiscent of this type of sacrifice. They gather for mutual exhortation, which affords an opportunity to remember God's faithfulness (the "confession" of 10:23). Finally, it is an

---

[164]Lane, *Call to Commitment*, pp. 139-141.

[165]Ibid., p. 140.

observance that cannot be made alone (10:24-25).[166]

A similar pattern is visible in 13:10-16. The double admonition to praise God and do good works reflects this typology.[167] In particular, the phrase θυσία αἰνέσεως was used in the LXX as a term for the highest form of fellowship offering, that is, one offered not to fulfill a vow or generally acknowledge God's goodness, but in thanks for some divine favor (Lev. 7:12; cf. 7:16).[168] While Attridge also notes this connection, he prefers to understand "sacrifice of praise" as a metaphor for prayer itself.[169] Ruager suggests that the community did not conceive of the eucharist as a highly sacramentalized event, but as just such a fellowship meal.[170] While certainly true in terms of the actual practice of Christians, the rooting of the term in the sacrificial cult should not be overlooked. The prayer of thanksgiving is considered an offering in *Leviticus Rabbah* 9:27 that will continue though all other sacrifices cease.

The New Covenant Cultus and the Spirituality of Hebrews

With the exposition on the New Testament Cultus we encounter at last the essence of Hebrews' cultically-conceived spirituality. It is with this theme that the author binds together his conceptions of cultus as performed by the levitical priests, the angels, and Christ himself and brings all three into the service of his

---

166According to *Sipra* 28:3, the peace offering should derive from the community as a freewill offering.

167Moffatt, *Hebrews*, pp. 237-238; Thurén, *Lobopfer*, pp. 176-178; Lane, *Hebrews*, vol. 2, pl. 552.

168Westcott, *Hebrews*, p. 443.

169Attridge, *Hebrews*, p. 400. See LXX Pss. 49:14,23; 106:22.

170Søren Ruager, "'Wir haben einen Altar' (Heb 13:10): Einige Überlegungen zum Thema: Gottesdienst/Abendmahl im Hebräerbrief," *Kerygma und Dogma*, 36 (1990), 72-77. The interpretation of the "altar" as the eucharistic table will not stand for reasons ennumerated above, but it is inconceivable that the community would not have observed the Lord's Supper in some fashion. For the interpretation of the eucharist as a sacrifice, see also Young, *Sacrificial Ideas*, pp. 239-284.

overarching pastoral concerns.[171] The result is a fully developed expression of the Christian life in terms drawn from cultic religion.

Expressions of Authentic
and Inauthentic

The same expressions of authentic and inauthentic that first appeared in the author's cultic foundation vigorously assert themselves here. The problem of access to the divine presence is clearly in focus, and once again blood is the sole medium of approach (10:19; 13:11-12).[172] The author never diverts from the centrality of Christ in his pastoral exhortations. For the author the Cross is the center of history that sheds light on humanity's relationships with God.[173] The blood of Jesus qualifies believers to approach God in worship.[174] It is the only basis for their empowerment to enter the heavenly sanctuary (10:22), participate in the celestial liturgy (12:24), and live out their faith commitment on earth (13:13-16).

Neither ritual meals (13:9) nor any other element of the Old Covenant Cultus can accomplish what Jesus has. In response to the felt loss of ritual moorings within the community, the author elaborates not a new ritual system but a theology of praise enveloped in cultic motifs.[175] Nevertheless, Jesus' work and human responsibility are "exactly balanced."[176] Through Jesus believers have gained great privileges, but these must be used as Christians personally and

---

[171]See Otto Kuss, "Der Verfasser des Hebräerbriefes als Seelsorger," in *Auslegung und Verkündigung*, vol. 1 (Regensburg: Pustet, 1963); and Mora, *Hebreos*.

[172]Attridge, *Hebrews*, p. 285; Johnsson, "Defilement," pp. 364-365.

[173]Gaspar Mora, "Ley y Sacrificio en la carta a los Hebreos," *Revista Catalana de Teología*, 1 (1976), 30.

[174]This is the meaning of ἁγιάζω in 13:12 according to Lane, *Hebrews*, vol. 2, p. 541. See LXX Exod. 19:10; 1 Sam. 16:5.

[175]Lane, *Hebrews*, vol. 2, p. 548. Daly, *Origins*, p. 73, is incorrect to state that "living the Christian life has taken over the atoning function of the sacrificial cult." This function was taken over by Christ alone in his death and exaltation. The *celebratory* function of the old cultus, however, is certainly the realm of Christian activity.

[176]Johnsson, "Defilement," p. 352.

corporately exercise their right of access.[177] This they must do with "boldness" (παρρησία, 4:16, 10:19). Παρρησία, in the sense of open and candid speech, is commonly connected to prayer in the LXX (Job. 22:26-27; 27:9-10) and in Hellenistic Jewish piety generally.[178]. It is the quality of "free and joyful standing before God"[179] possible because God himself has granted παρρησία to his people (Lev. 26:13).

Another image of authentic religion arises in chapter 13, where the author reverses his previous image of drawing near to God in order to call his audience to go out to him beyond the camp. The image of leaving the camp suggests severing emotional ties with the familiar trappings of religious expression in favor of true encounter with the divine. As such Hebrews locates God outside the sacred precincts where people of faith have always faced suffering, insecurity, and shame. The image is of a God rejected by his people (cf. Exod. 33:7-8) and living beyond the borders.[180] By holding up such an image as an example for Christian piety the author firmly grounds his spirituality in the real world. Just as Jesus' own sacrifice was physically real and anti-docetic, so must be the sacrifice of Christians.[181] It is only partially true, however, to say with Radcliffe that "our rituals should enact the paradox of gathering a holy assembly around the image of a corpse."[182] The application of cultic motifs to thoroughly non-cultic situations indeed moves us into the realm of liminality in which conventional structures are commonly subverted; but as we shall see in the next chapter, such an assessment misses the deep positive symbolism of blood and imposes a modern misunderstanding of the nature of

---

[177]Westcott, *Hebrews*, p. 321.

[178]Harold W. Attridge, "Heard because of His Reverence," *JBL*, 98 (1979), 90-93. See Josephus, *Ant.* 2:52; 5:38; Philo, *Heres* 5.

[179]Heinrich Schlier, "παρρησία, παρρησιάζομαι," *TDNT*, vol. 5, p. 876.

[180]Michel, *Hebräer*, pp. 510-515; Thurén, *Lobopfer*, pp. 100-104; Lane, *Hebrews*, vol. 2, p. 543-544.

[181]Daly, *Christian Sacrifice*, p. 282.

[182]Timothy Radcliffe, "Christ in Hebrews: Cultic Irony," *New Blackfriars*, 68 (1987), 502.

152

sacrifice.

The Practice of Spirituality

Wenschkewitz lists three types of piety that often spiritualize cultic imagery: prayer, ethical performance, and mystical contemplation.[183] Innocent suffering, particularly through persecution, also acquired strong cultic associations in early Judaism.[184] Hebrews applies cultic terms to nearly all of these to create a well-rounded conceptualization of the Christian life as cultic approach to God.[185] We thus agree with Scholer in seeing in προσέρχομαι a reference to prayer and corporate worship,[186] but would wish to extend the metaphor even farther to include acts of mercy (13:16) and possibly even martyrdom (13:13).[187] Thüsing is undoubtedly correct in seeing in the metaphor of "drawing near" a wide range of activities encompassing the whole of Christian life. He states, "The evidence does not lead to an 'either-or,' but rather to a 'both-and': both eucharistic celebration and the whole Christian life including faith, prayer, worship and suffering."[188] One might even say that the author does not existentialize the ritual as much as he ritualizes existence.[189] Furthermore, Scholer raises the issue of worship in Hebrews without resolving it. What theology or practice of corporate worship

---

[183]Wenschkewitz, "Spiritualisierung," p. 72.

[184]Young, *Sacrificial Ideas*, pp. 66-69.

[185]The author of Hebrews seems not to have had any great mystical leanings if mysticism is to mean anything more than approach to God through spiritual practices. See, however, Ronald Williamson, "The Background of the Epistle to the Hebrews," *Expository Times*, 87 (1975-1976), 232-237, who puts forth the evidence for placing Hebrews within the same Jewish matrix that would eventually give rise to Merkavah mysticism.

[186]Scholer, *Proleptic*, p. 145.

[187]Schussler Fiorenza is then not entirely accurate to claim that "in all the NT writings cultic terminology is consciously avoided to characterize the *worship*, the institutions or the leaders of the Christian community" ("Cultic Language," p. 168, emphasis added). Cultic motifs do figure in Hebrews' concept of Christian corporate worship, albeit in a highly spiritualized sense.

[188]Thüsing, "Laßt uns hinzutreten," p. 12.

[189]Mora, "Ley y sacrificio," p. 30.

would fit into the overall religious matrix of the author or his audience?

It seems quite likely that the author of Hebrews had in mind disaffected Christians who craved a more tangible element in their worship, but this is only half the story. One need not conclude that this community's corporate worship was bland, drab, or experientially bankrupt. The author's "elevated conception of worship"[190] would not permit this. The liturgy of the ancient synagogue involved nothing but a confession of faith, prayers, and the reading of Scripture, but in the first century it was the central worship assembly of Jews in the diaspora.[191] Worship for the recipients of Hebrews would surely have included at least these elements,[192] along with ceremonial washings (6:2; 10:22) and the observance of the Lord's Supper.[193] Given the profound interest in ritual observance apparent throughout Hebrews, one must conclude as a bare minimum that the readers would have gathered for worship fully aware of how important these assemblies were in the task of mutual encouragement and growth in grace (10:24-25).

But corporate worship is only part of the wisdom of Hebrews. The author in fact takes great pains to help his audience see all of life as a cultic approach to God. His exhortation, even in passages such as 10:19-25 where concern for corporate worship is clearly present, looks upon the whole of Christian existence as "a continual approach to the living God."[194] Such an approach, involving the

---

[190]Jones, "A Superior Life," p. 397.

[191]For an excellent introduction to the synagogue liturgy, see Abraham Millgram, *Jewish Worship* (Philadelphia: Jewish Publication Society, 1971), pp. 90-113.

[192]For the confession (ὁμολογία), see 4:14; 10:23; 13:15. As to prayer, see 13:15,18 and the commonly repeated call to "draw near," particularly when linked with the quality of boldness (4:16; 10:19). As to the reading of Scripture, the sermonic character of Hebrews itself must be remembered (13:22).

[193]Lehne, *New Covenant*, p. 112-117, observes that none of the key "eucharistic" passages in Hebrews (6:1-6; 9:20; 10:19-31; 13:9-16) makes a clear reference to the Lord's Supper. This does not make Hebrews anti-eucharistic. Of 13:10-16 Attridge (*Hebrews*, p. 391) rightly states that the passage "is neither an exaltation nor a critique of the eucharist or of a particular sacramental theology. It is a forceful synthesis of the doctrine and paraenesis of the whole text."

[194]Lane, *Call to Commitment*, p. 139.

whole person, is the only cultus in which he truly takes pleasure.[195] As Jesus offered himself in his approach to God, so do we. Our offerings are ourselves.[196]

There is also a strong emphasis on finding outward expression of spiritual sacrifice through good works. Praise to God is service to humanity.[197] In the end Christians may find that the content of their sacrifices is in fact only what is required of followers of Jesus Christ: good works, acts of kindness, generosity, ministry to prisoners, hospitality to strangers, sexual purity, faith, hope, love.

There is one final way in which believers approach God, and that is through the discipline of letting go. The author never suggests that Christians go out of their way to find persecution, but he is aware that a genuine commitment to Jesus often meets with society's resistance. He therefore urges his audience to make the first move, to sever ties with the world that keep them from following Jesus authentically (12:1; 13:13). He can thus applaud the community for once cheerfully submitting to plunder of property (10:34). With no unnecessary worldly entanglements, the pilgrim people of God are free to seek the lasting city which is to come (11:15-16; 13:14). Such an attitude guarantees that believers will live lives at a distance from the world, moving toward God who is to be found outside of human restrictions, creating sacred space where there was none before.

---

[195]Mora, "Ley y sacrificio," p. 46. Mora bases his understanding of Christ's sacrifice in Hebrews a bit too strongly on 10:5-10. He is nevertheless to be lauded for seeing here a paradigm for the Christian life in imitation of Jesus (p. 43).

[196]Cason, "Ἱερεύς," p. 108.

[197]Westcott, *Hebrews*, p. 444.

Chapter 6

CONCLUSION

Although most (if not all) of the strands of tradition which have come together in the New Testament employ cultic concepts, none can match the "consistency and intensity"[1] of the sustained argument the reader encounters in Hebrews. The book has proven itself thoroughly cultic in its spiritual vision. This cultic predisposition arises not only in expressions of authentic and inauthentic religion but in the author's exhortations to live out one's Christian commitment. We now conclude our investigation with some final thoughts on the major issues that have arisen. We shall first summarize the major conclusions of this study regarding cultic imagery and the spirituality of Hebrews. A general discussion of the usage of cultic language in spirituality will follow. Finally, we shall synthesize some conclusions about the spirituality of Hebrews in particular with an eye toward modern relevance.

The Cultic Spirituality of Hebrews

As we have seen, the author of Hebrews communicates his spirituality largely through cultic terminology. At the risk of redundancy, we shall at this time review the major emphases that have emerged in the spirituality of Hebrews.

Expressions of Authentic and Inauthentic

The primary theme of Hebrews may be stated as a predicament and a

---

[1]Robert J. Daly, *The Origins of the Christian Doctrine of Sacrifice* (Philadelphia: Fortress, 1978), p. 285.

solution, both expressed in cultic terms. The predicament is humanity's experience of separation from God because of sin. In Hebrews, sin is generally perceived as uncleanness that extends to the deepest parts of the human self and prevents any meaningful communion between humans and God. Hebrews' solution to the problem of sin and the numinous unease that accompanies it is blood sacrifice. Blood is seen in Hebrews as the definitive cleansing agent and medium of divine access. While the author admits that the blood of sacrificial animals is capable of producing a superficial level of purgation (9:9-10), only the blood of Christ effects total cleansing (9:14). This broad theme is explored in terms of several cultic systems which appear in the development of the sermon.

In the cultic foundation. The central movements of Hebrews (4:15-10:18) make a powerful argument for the superiority of Christ's saving work over the ministrations of the Old Covenant Cultus. Throughout, Jesus' person and actions become cultic in their own right. The centrality and efficacy of Christ have to do with the cultic ideals that he embodies.

Central to the author's argument is the powerful symbolism of blood. In sharp contrast to the old covenant sacrifices, only the blood of Jesus is able to cleanse the conscience of believers (9:14). Furthermore, only Jesus' blood cleanses eternally, decisively, and with no need for repeated applications (9:25; 10:14).

As a result of the application of Jesus' blood, believers have been granted what was once denied them: bold and unrestricted access to the divine presence (4:16; 6:19-20; 10:19-22). The believers' new relationship with God, typified by free access to the heavenly inner sanctum, rests upon and derives from Jesus' cultic performance. This new relationship itself is described in terms derived from the Old Testament's ritual system. Taking a cue from the anthropological study of rites of passage, we described believers in Christ as undergoing a status transition in three distinct but interrelated aspects.

First, the author describes the objective benefits of salvation as a covenant inauguration (9:15-22). Through Christ, and particularly through the power of his blood, a new covenant (and thus a new cultic order) has been inaugurated in which believers are full partners and beneficiaries. They have thus moved from the realm of dead works to the worship of the living God (6:1; 9:14; 12:28) Second, the work of Christ becomes a replacement for the Day of Atonement liturgy, effecting a definitive cleansing from sins. In this aspect, believers move from a state of defilement to one of complete and permanent cleansing from sins. Finally, the Christ Cultus takes the form of a priestly ordination that elevates believers to a status with God where they no longer need a human mediator to assist them in the divine encounter; now they are priests in their own right with full access to the throne of grace (4:16).

In the Heavenly Cultus. The author does not emphasize angelic worship to the extent of some of his contemporaries. He is nevertheless aware of traditions regarding a Heavenly Cultus and employs them in two strategic places in his sermon.

In the worship offered in heaven by the angels and the righteous dead, the cultic accomplishment of Christ is celebrated but not augmented. The first chapter of Hebrews depicts angels celebrating the heavenly exaltation of Christ, who has accomplished the necessary purgation (1:3) and has now sat down in the heavenly seat of honor at the right hand of God (1:3,13). Hebrews 12 describes the angels and righteous dead attending upon believers as they experience proleptically the benefits of Christ's work (12:22-24).

Although angels enjoy access to the divine presence, they are still creaturely and thus limited beings. They never receive the kinds of honors bestowed upon Christ (1:4,5,13). In fact, their role is clearly one of subservience. It must also be mentioned that Christ's saving work was not for the angels nor motivated by concern for them (2:16). There is no mention of blood in connection with angels anywhere in Hebrews.

In terms of spiritual teaching, angels in Hebrews model singleminded worship of Jesus (1:6). They fulfill no mediatory function; instead, their role is to serve human believers (1:14).

In the New Covenant Cultus. Human believers are the exclusive recipients of the cultic benefits that Christ made possible. It is human beings who are plagued by sin (10:1-3), fear of death (2:15), dead works (6:1), and the inauthentic religion of "the camp" (13:13). For these factors to be overcome human consciences must be purged, and the blood of Jesus is the only adequate cleansing agent. The cultic accomplishment of Christ is the only available means of moving beyond inauthentic responses to God and enjoying a genuine encounter with the Divine (10:19-22;

158

12:18-24; 13:10-16).

What is authentic for Christians, the author insists, is the attitude of drawing near to God through Christ. Paradoxically, this approach to the sacred ultimately involves a repudiation of previous forms of devotion that are now revealed to be inadequate (13:13). God, we learn, is to be found beyond the sacred enclosure. To meet him one must leave behind the comfort and security of conventional religious forms and suffer shame just as Jesus himself did (12:2; 13:12). What is authentic for Christians, in sum, is what was authentic for Christ: suffering, persecution, and abuse, but also entrance into God's presence to offer acceptable worship. Finally, the New Covenant Cultus, mirroring the experience of Jesus himself, involves the offering of the whole self to God (10:5-10).

The Practice of Spirituality

In the terms the author employs, we may think of Hebrews' wisdom as the practical answer to the question of what believers must do in order to enter the heavenly sanctuary opened to us by the work of Jesus. A covenant implies a cultic order, and the author is explicit in asserting that believers have both an altar and sacrifices to offer (13:10-16). What then are those sacrifices?

There is not much explicit teaching about Scripture in Hebrews, but clearly the author found it an important element in the Christian life. His sermon is essentially an exposition of biblical texts for the purpose of fostering a deeper commitment to Christ. Hughes in fact argues that the challenge to make the ancient texts of the Old Testament relevant for believers in Christ was the author's major interest.[2] In the stories of Melchizedek, Moses, the wilderness generation, and the multitude of Old Testament heroes of faith set out in chapter 11, not to mention the levitical regulations of the Pentateuch, the author found foreshadowings of Jesus which he marshalled to the service of his distinctively Christian theology.

The author wishes his audience to go on to maturity so they might consume solid spiritual food (5:11-6:3). This call implies the engagement of the mind with the deeper teachings of the Christian faith. These teachings would certainly have included traditions from past leaders (13:7), but most naturally would be found in the Old Testament texts themselves.

Prayer and worship are the most obvious means by which believers might

---

[2]Graham Hughes, *Hebrews and Hermeneutics*, SNTSMS 36 (London: Cambridge, 1979).

experience the kind of communion with God on which the author places such a premium. Christians are to practice these disciplines both privately and corporately. The example of Jesus' own reverent and effective prayer (5:7) should serve as a model for his followers, who also now enjoy the right of bold approach to the divine presence (4:16; 10:19).

Believers also have the example of angelic praise in celebration of Christ's exalted status (1:6). The author exhorts his audience to be engaged in mutual support and encouragement lest any fall short of the loftiest spiritual goals (3:12-13; 10:24-25; 12:15). Finally, the author speaks explicitly of a sacrifice of praise (13:15) which believers offer to God as acceptable worship.

Generosity and acts of kindness are also acceptable sacrifices that Christians are to offer (13:16). They are to urge each other on to love and good works (10:24). These works would include at a minimum those mentioned at the beginning of chapter 13: mutual love (13:1), hospitality to strangers (13:2), ministry to prisoners (13:3), sexual purity (13:4), and rejection of materialism (13:5).

The author of Hebrews points to previous experiences of persecution that demonstrated the faith of his addressees (10:32-34). As he brings his sermon to a close, he reminds them further of the sufferings that Christ himself had to endure (12:3). They, too, must learn that God disciplines his own; and they must endure trials for the sake of the great spiritual fruit that it can produce (12:5-11). The author understands what many after him have claimed: that genuine spiritual growth is often gained in the "providences" of God, not least among them severe trials and afflictions that often produce righteousness.[3]

Here as well we must mention the pilgrimage motif that surfaces from time to time in Hebrews (3:7-4:11; 11:13-16; 13:14). The heroes of faith that the author seems to appreciate the most are those who lived lives beyond society's boundaries, rejecting earthly pleasures for the hope of a greater heavenly reward (10:34; 11:8,24-25,38).

What Hebrews teaches about spirituality is not particularly unique. He asserts the centrality of Christ and the efficacy of his saving work in setting sinners in right relationship with God. So does Paul. When it comes to the practice of

---

[3]Sinclair B. Ferguson, "The Reformed View," in *Christian Spirituality*, ed. Donald L. Alexander (Downer's Grove: InterVarsity, 1988), p. 71.

spirituality there is nothing he writes about scripture, prayer, or moral action that would not have sounded at home in the teachings of Paul or John or even Jesus himself. To find the particularity of Hebrews' contribution to Christian spirituality we must pay attention to the form in which the author presents his teaching. We thus turn now to the role of cultus in spirituality in general before offering some final observations about the cultic spirituality of Hebrews.

The Use of Cultic Language in Spirituality

In some Protestant circles it is virtually impossible to think of ritual without prefixing the adjective "mere." Such is the rationalistic assessment of external religious expressions, but it is an assessment that grossly misunderstands the role of ritual in traditional, pre-industrial societies. As Frere notes, rituals create the many controversies they do precisely because they signify so much.[4] Mowinckel observes the all-pervading nature of the ancient Israelite cultus in its close connection with all the important phenomena of religion.[5] Within such a cultural matrix, a matrix in which the author of Hebrews would have felt quite at home, the importance of cultic concepts becomes apparent.

The modern disdain for the imagery of sacred enclosures, priestcraft, and blood sacrifice is to be expected since none of these elements is part of our religious world. When we use such language in everyday life it is nearly always in an exclusively metaphorical sense. The unfortunate result, however, is a widespread failure to appreciate such images when they occur in the sacred text. Thus it is extremely difficult for us to grasp the original sense of these terms.[6] In effect, moderns spiritualize cultic motifs too easily; so easily, in fact, that they often do not realize they are doing it.

---

[4]W. H. Frere, *Principles of Religious Ceremonial*, quoted by Evelyn Underhill, *Worship* (San Francisco: Harper, 1937), pp. 23-24.

[5]Sigmund Mowinckel, *Religion und Kultus* (Göttingen: Vandenhoeck & Ruprecht, 1953), p. 9.

[6]Hans Wenschkewitz, "Die Spiritualisierung der Kultusbegriffe: Tempel, Priester und Opfer im Neuen Testament," *Αγγελος,* 4 (1932), 70.

As but one example, one might consider the modern idea of sacrifice.[7] In modern usage, sacrifice implies "renouncing" or "giving up" something and thus being "deprived." It denotes therefore sadness or misfortune. A sacrifice is to be avoided if at all possible or at least kept to a minimum. In contrast the ancients spoke of sacrifice with the stress not on *giving up*, but on simply *giving* something to Deity. The sacrifice thus was not characterized by reluctance or sadness but joy and festivity. Although people might give in order to receive something from their God or gods, the sacrifice might just as easily be an expression of thanksgiving for boons already received or expressions of pure praise. In a word, the positive view of sacrifice in traditional societies is almost the exact opposite of our modern, secular usage.

In contrast to current disparaging attitudes, cultic modes of thought and life have a value which is both social and religious. Durkheim has aptly described the effectiveness of cultic practices in inculcating solidarity with and commitment to a group.[8] The liminality created by ritual activity is "society's subjunctive mood," making room for creativity within society while at the same time fostering commitment to the existing social structures.[9] In this light one might mention the common sociological assessment of the Second Vatican Council's liturgical innovations as a step in the wrong direction; by doing away with so much of the old ritual, the institutional church has appeared to disenfranchise many of the faithful.[10]

Ritual's primary role is not, however, sociological; it is religious and even in a sense mystical.[11] As a corollary to Westerners' inability truly to grasp the significance of ritual, it is often the case that we have somewhere lost the ability to appreciate the symbolic, evocative, and nonrational aspects of religious life. We no

---

[7]See Daly, *Origins*, pp. 2-4.

[8]Émile Durkheim, *The Elementary Forms of the Religious Life*, trans. Joseph Ward Swain (New York: Macmillan, 1915), pp. 226, 370 *et passim*.

[9]Victor Turner, "Liminality, Kabbalah, and the Media," *Religion*, 15 (1985), 210.

[10]This observation is made, for example, by Victor Turner, "Ritual, Tribal and Catholic," *Worship*, 50 (1976), 524.

[11]*Contra* Durkheim, *Elementary Forms*, p. 226, who considers this aspect merely the "apparent function" of ritual.

162

longer think symbolically, "and so we fail to understand either our myths or our dreams."[12] This inclination toward rationalism is evident even in religious settings, where a "promiscuous empiricism" is often the rule.[13] Otto describes this phenomenon as "the view that the essence of deity can be given completely and exhaustively in . . . 'rational' attributions."[14]

Rituals strengthen the bonds between the believer and the numinous. For this reason rituals generally look backward to the mythical time of beginnings, *illud tempus*, or what the Australian aborigines call the "dream time."[15] What occurs in ritual is a re-presentation of the deeds of the gods and heroes, which then becomes a pattern for present acts and attitudes.[16] Such an understanding is not foreign to the cultus of ancient Israel. As Levenson remarks, "Israel draws near to God, in part, by perpetuating the primordial within the world of historical change, and the sacred amidst profanity . . . ."[17] Walker likewise concludes,

in liturgical worship, as the saving acts of Yahweh are proclaimed and often dramatically illustrated, the worshiping community becomes aware of the "immediate" presence and reality of these acts; it "experiences" in the cultus the *Heilsgeschichte* which has constituted, still constitutes, and always will constitute the "true Israel" as the people of Yahweh. As to the exact manner in which this occurs, or the precise relationship between the "original" event and the "experienced" event, there is no indication that Israel is concerned about such matters. She only knows that she experiences the salvation of her God,

---

[12]Morton Kelsey, *Prophetic Ministry* (New York: Crossroad, 1984), p. 21.

[13]Ralph W. Hood, "Mysticism in the Psychology of Religion," *Journal of Psychology and Christianity*, 5 (1986), 46-49.

[14]Rudolf Otto, *The Idea of the Holy*, trans. John W. Harvey (London: Oxford, 1950), pp. 1-2.

[15]Mircea Eliade, *The Sacred and the Profane*, trans. Willard R. Trask (San Diego: Harcourt, 1959), p. 86.

[16]Ibid., pp. 104-113.

[17]Jon D. Levenson, "The Jerusalem Temple in Devotional and Visionary Experience," in *Jewish Spirituality*, vol. 1, ed. Arthur Green, World Spirituality (New York: Crossroad, 1987), pp. 36-37.

and she gives thanks for it.[18]

The true significance of the ritual is thus to be apprehended in the matrix of myth, symbolism, and imagination.

When people and societies lose their rituals, or no longer find them compelling, grave consequences usually follow. Kelsey notes the rise of alcoholism among Native Americans and links it to the loss of meaning with respect to their traditional religions and the absence of anything else to fill the gap.[19] Campbell makes a similar observation with regard to the increase in teenage gang violence. With the absence of established coming-of-age rites many urban youths are left to make up their own destructive rituals.[20]

Turner has noted the current growing sense of need for spaces and times that can answer to what Westerners used to derive from their rituals.[21] In fact, Hine traces the trend toward individuals or small groups creating their own rituals to express the sentiments they feel they could not express in any other way.[22] These factors indicate that a message like the one in Hebrews may not be as irrelevant to the modern world as it may at first seem. We therefore undertake now an experiment in applying the spirituality of Hebrews in a modern context.

The Spirituality of Hebrews: Then and Now

The pastoral thrust of Hebrews has been interpreted along a number of lines. Lindars, for example, sees a deep concern with the question of post-

---

[18]William Oliver Walker, Jr., "Cultus and Tradition: A Contribution to the Problem of Faith and History in the Old Testament" (Ph.D. dissertation, Duke University, 1962), p. 433.

[19]Kelsey, *Prophetic Ministry*, p. 85.

[20]Joseph Campbell with Bill Moyers, *The Power of Myth* (New York: Doubleday, 1988), p. 8.

[21]Turner, "Liminality," p. 216.

[22]Virginia H. Hine, "Self-Generated Ritual: Trend or Fad?" *Worship*, 55 (1981), 404-419. This theme is taken up by growing numbers of scholars. See, for example, Tom F. Driver, *The Magic of Ritual* (San Francisco: Harper, 1991); and Chris Harris, *Creating Relevant Rituals* (Newtown, NSW: Dwyer, 1992).

baptismal sins.[23] Many commentators have noted the author's concern with his audience becoming sluggish and discouraged, particularly in the face of persecution. For some, the overarching concern is that the addressees are in danger of reverting to their previous Jewish faith. While all of these are valid to a certain extent, it is possible to find a synthesis on a higher level. We conclude that the spirituality developed and exhorted in Hebrews is a pastoral response to the absence of cultus.[24] We shall bring the study to a close by sketching in broad strokes the rationale for this conclusion and suggesting certain aspects of the cultic spirituality of Hebrews which may be fruitful avenues of inquiry for spirituality in the modern world.

Hebrews' Cultic View
of Reality

The death of Jesus, in its historical facticity, was in no way a cultic act. Nevertheless, the author of Hebrews imports into this event a fully developed interpretation based almost exclusively on cultic categories: it was the perfect sacrifice of the Great High Priest in the heavenly sanctuary. The historical data did not require such an interpretation. That the author deemed it appropriate tells us much about his own understanding of reality, spiritual reality in particular. The centrality of cultic terminology indicates the author's singleminded dedication to cultic categories.[25] If Pauline theology makes Jesus the τέλος of the law (Rom. 10:4), for Hebrews Jesus is the τέλος of the cultus.[26]

In the first place, the author assumes the necessity for clearly demarcated limits between the sacred and the profane. The sacrifice must be performed in a

---

[23]Barnabas Lindars, *The Theology of the Letter to the Hebrews*, New Testament Theology (Cambridge: University, 1991), pp. 13-14.

[24]Marie E. Isaacs, *Sacred Space*, JSNTSS 73 (Sheffield: Academic Press, 1992), pp. 62-66, argues that the preoccupation with sacred space in Hebrews was precipitated by separation from the Jerusalem temple after A.D. 70 (although she herself admits that there is no compelling reason to date the book before or after that date). Her view is thus essentially in harmony with the interpretation proposed here.

[25]John M. Scholer, *Proleptic Priests*, JSNTSS 49 (Sheffield: Academic Press, 1991), p. 137.

[26]This in intentional distinction from Ernst Käsemann, *The Wandering People of God*, trans. Roy A. Harrisville and Irving L. Sandberg (Minneapolis: Augsburg, 1984), p. 179, who calls Jesus the τέλος of the gnostic redeemer myth.

sacred place by a properly consecrated priest. Sacred objects, even *heavenly* sacred objects, must be ritually cleansed (9:23). Jesus has opened the way for believers to approach the divine presence; but this presence still remains within a sacred enclosure, on the far side of a boundary symbolized as the "curtain" (6:19; 10:20). As in the old covenant, divine access is serious business and not to be taken lightly.

Furthermore, Hebrews' axiomatic approach to the motif of blood demonstrates the author's cultic orientation. His basic presupposition is clearly stated in 9:22: "apart from the application of blood the putting away [of sins] does not occur." In contrast to his modern interpreters, the author never attempts to explain *how* a blood sacrifice can cleanse from sins; he simply takes it for granted that it can.[27] In this sense Hebrews maintains a "strictly cultic line of reasoning" that does not repudiate the blood rites of the old covenant as much as argue that the unique blood rite of the new covenant is superior.[28] The Old Covenant Cultus is not intrinsically bad; in contrast to the Christ Cultus, however, it is superfluous.[29]

The author's cult-oriented world view has met with consternation on the part of many interpreters who would have preferred him not to mean what he says on the matter. Scott, for example, identifies the weakness of the author's argument in that

> while he shows the inadequacy of the old ritual conceptions, he never definitely escapes from them. He cannot rid himself of the belief that the substance must in some manner be of the same nature as the type. The true worship must conform to that of the tabernacle, with the difference that it is offered in heaven instead of on earth, and has therefore a higher validity.[30]

Two observations are to made about Scott's assessment. First, Scott assumes that the "old ritual conceptions" ought to have been transcended. This is a modern, rationalistic judgment. Hebrews' cultic vision of reality is only a weakness in that it makes our own hermeneutical task all the more difficult. Second, it is questionable

---

[27]Fisher Humphreys, *The Death of Christ* (Nashville: Broadman, 1978), p. 28.

[28]William G. Johnsson, *Hebrews*, Knox Preaching Guides (Atlanta: John Knox, 1980), p. 65.

[29]Frances M. Young, *The Use of Sacrificial Ideas in Greek Christian Writers from the New Testament to John Chrysostom*, Patristic Monograph Series 5 (Philadelphia: Philadelphia Patristic Foundation, 1979), p. 82; Humphreys, *Death of Christ*, p. 27.

[30]E. F. Scott, *The Epistle to the Hebrews* (Edinburgh: Clark, 1922), p. 137.

whether the author's interest is to conform the Christ event to the pattern of the tabernacle in a wholly consistent fashion. Through the course of this study we have noted instances where the depiction of the Old Covenant Cultus has been carefully crafted to the interests of the author's theology.[31] In these instances at least the sacrificial cultus has been conformed to the pattern of Christ's person and saving work.

While this interpretation of Christian truths is admittedly difficult for us to appreciate fully, it must have resonated with those in the church who longed for the "good old days" of participation in a sacrificial cult. Then, religious life could be largely understood in terms of performing divinely-mandated rituals that manipulated psychologically evocative symbols. Now, says the author, we must transfer our cultic discourse to a higher order of existence.

The Spiritualization of Cultus

As we have seen, the application of cultic categories to essentially non-cultic realities was widespread in antiquity. Indeed, for Judaism after A.D. 70, the trend became absolutely essential. Within this context Christianity arose as the first movement claiming to be a religion without having a material sacrificial cult.[32] For the New Testament writers, the presence of God and the forgiveness of sins were no longer to be found in cultic institutions but in Jesus Christ himself. As Schüssler Fiorenza notes, the New Testament reinterpretation of cultic categories "signifies not only a fundamental criticism of the Jerusalem cult but a redefinition and metamorphosis of both cultic language and cultic reality through Christology."[33]

With a view to such a redefinition, the author of Hebrews denigrates the Old Covenant Cultus in order to replace it with another of a superior order. His cultic terminology must not then be dismissed as simply another way of doing paraenesis. The author does not present a rationalistic critique of all forms of cultus, as if he were a Greek pagan philosopher. His starting point is his conviction that Jesus

---

[31]Most notably in the depiction of priesthood in 4:15-5:4 and the Sinai event in 12:18-21.

[32]Young, *Sacrificial Ideas*, p. 1.

[33]Elisabeth Schüssler Fiorenza, "Cultic Language in Qumran and in the NT," *CBQ*, 38 (1976), 170-171.

"*fulfilled and replaced* the old covenant by a new one and that the ἐφάπαξ, blameless, complete nature of Christ's heavenly sacrifice rendered all further earthly, material sacrifice obsolete."[34]

Hebrews' transposition of cultic motifs takes place on two fronts. First, and most central to his argument, the author asserts that the life, death, resurrection, and exaltation of Jesus Christ was the cultic performance *par excellence*. It is in this saving work that Christians are to find what Hebrews applauds as most spiritually authentic: cleansing from sins that permits direct access to God through the medium of blood.[35]

Second, Hebrews depicts Christian existence as a cultic performance made possible by the saving work of Christ. This cultic interpretation is by no means limited to prayer and worship but encompasses even the practical deeds of Christian life. Without these, as Daly asserts, the process of spiritualization is not complete.[36] Hebrews bids us therefore to see the spiritual life not as something that can be compartmentalized and separated from everyday existence: everyday existence is itself the context for the New Covenant Cultus.

Since, according to Gyllenberg,[37] the cultus was Israel's principal place of divine revelation, Hebrews' equation of life with cultus has obvious implications for spirituality. It is in the spiritual practices of day to day life, prayer and praise but also suffering and charitable deeds, that Christians participate in their foundational myth: the life and death of Christ.[38] In this framework the author of Hebrews has presented the Christian life from conversion to consummation as a grand cultic drama. This drama, he argues, more than compensates for any perceived loss derived from the absence of a material cultus.

---

[34]Susanne Lehne, *The New Covenant in Hebrews*, JSNTSS 44 (Sheffield: Academic Press, 1990), pp. 111-112.

[35]Louis Bouyer, *History of Christian Spirituality*, vol. 1 (London: Burns and Oates, 1960), pp. 144-148.

[36]Daly, *Origins*, p. 138.

[37]Cited by Walker, "Cultus and Tradition," p. 385.

[38]Here, as elsewhere in this study, the term "myth" is used in a purely positive sense.

*Cultus, Spirituality and
Hermeneutics*

Although we have addressed the spirituality of Hebrews in detail in the preceding chapters, the phenomenological question remains: Why does the author say it *in that way*? That is, what does the author mean to tell us by couching common Christian spiritual teachings in the language of cultus?

Few if any Westerners in the twentieth century share the cultic presuppositions of the author of Hebrews. Even if we agree with him, for example, that blood is necessary for atonement, this is the imposition of a particular Christian context; it is not the general assumption of our culture. Confronted with this gap between our world and the world of the New Testament, Christians have generally adopted one of two coping strategies. The first is to seek to do away with the ancient religious models as outdated, primitive, and unsuitable for modern faith. The second is to deny that the problem exists at all. Neither strategy is satisfactory.[39]

In reality, all theological models are culturally conditioned. As Humphreys notes, even such a well-known image as that of God as shepherd is not universally understood. If someone unacquainted with sheep and shepherds appreciates this image, it is because she made an imaginative leap to do so.[40] How much more then must we "think ourselves back"[41] in order to appreciate fully Hebrews' cultic depiction of spiritual reality.

In bringing this study to a close, we suggest one possibility for applying a thoughtful hermeneutical approach to Hebrews' cultic spirituality. In so doing we assume both distance and continuity between the New Testament world and ours. Our interest is to study the author's response to his contemporary situation as a

---

[39]Humphreys, *Death of Christ*, pp. 43-48, discusses three inadequate options for New Testament models of atonement: to repeat, reject, or reinterpret them. He finally suggests that theology attempt to "re-present" the models by conveying their ancient truth in a modern model.

[40]Ibid., p. 35.

[41]Ibid., p. 36.

model to shape our response to our own world.[42] In particular, our attention turns to the message of Hebrews for modern Christian spirituality. Sheldrake notes the role of both critical exegesis and questions of contemporary relevance for the interpretation of spiritual texts.[43] What is needed, he writes, is "a receptive and at the same time critical dialogue with a spiritual text in order to allow the wisdom contained in it to challenge us and yet to accord our own horizons their proper place."[44] Admitting that "there is no single, true interpretation of a spiritual classic,"[45] the exegetical results of this study do suggest some fruitful avenues for investigation. In what follows there is no attempt to develop any particular theme beyond the level of mere suggestion. To go farther would only serve to produce an unwieldy and ill-focused study.

Liminality as a hermeneutical key. The category of liminality has presented itself before in this study as an important aspect of ritual. Liminality signifies that quality that characterizes transitional times of life, the betwixt and between experiences when social norms are inverted and even subverted. In itself, liminality is neither good nor bad. It is "mystically potent," and as such is a potentially dangerous element lending itself to the ambiguous and paradoxical.[46] One purpose of ritual is to harness this force for the good.[47] As previously noted, Turner has suggested that growing numbers of westerners sense a need for the liminal. He further states that liminality is a category "suggestive for the understanding of many

---

[42]John B. Polhill, "Circumcision and the Early Church, A Hermeneutical Inquiry" (Th.D. dissertation, The Southern Baptist Theological Seminary, 1968), p. 8, following William E. Hull, "The Relevance of the New Testament," *RevExp*, 62 (1965), 187-200.

[43]Philip Sheldrake, *Spirituality and History* (New York: Crossroad, 1991), pp. 163-184.

[44]Ibid., p. 165.

[45]Ibid., p. 172.

[46]Christopher Crocker, "Ritual and the Development of Social Structure: Liminality and Inversion," in *The Roots of Ritual*, ed. James Shaughnessy (Grand Rapids: Eerdmans, 1973), p. 70.

[47]Ibid., p. 71.

social processes and states found outside of ritual contexts."[48] In this light we suggest the appropriateness of the category of liminality, and humanity's apparently universal need for it, as a possible link between the New Testament world and our own.

By our standards, life in preindustrial societies appears tedious. Ritual, however, interrupts the accepted routine from time to time to carry individuals, groups, and even whole peoples through life's passages. These transitions are characterized by a loosening of the normal social restrictions and obligations that permits creativity and criticism of society and, paradoxically, reinforces peoples' commitments to society. As Turner observes, the need for such transitions is common in the twentieth century as well:

> Many of us have highly stable status roles in massive bureaucratic and professional structures, often on a national or even international scale. Many of us clock in and clock out of factories. Others are tightly bound to the wheel of the market and Stock Exchange. We are held in the grip of *les villes tentaculaires*. But only the observant in churches, sects, cults, and religious movements have well articulated ritual liminality. And these groups, too, become bureaucratized, and to a greater or lesser extent secularized; or else defiantly and rigidly desecularized.[49]

Certain qualities commonly associated with liminality echo the ideals of various strands of Christian spirituality. Among these would be humility, simplicity, obedience, egalitarianism, and acceptance of pain and suffering.[50] Many of these, it will be remembered, figure prominently in the spirituality of Hebrews. Christian authenticity, at least in this tradition, becomes an institutionalized state of liminality where transition has become a permanent condition.[51] Herein lies a clue toward a fuller understanding of the pilgrimage motif of Hebrews. It is "outside the camp," in the liminal realm, that believers meet God (13:13). We have discussed particular practices associated with the spirituality of Hebrews. Now we turn to explore in greater detail the attitudes that arise due to the cultic milieu in which the author expresses his spiritual vision. Biblical

---

[48]Turner, "Liminality," p. 208.

[49]Ibid., p. 212.

[50]Victor Turner, *The Ritual Process* (Ithaca: Cornell University, 1969), p. 106.

[51]Ibid., p. 107.

spirituality oscillates between the two poles of surprise and stability.[52] While most have no problem accepting the stabilizing element of spirituality, the surprising, spontaneous aspect is often underdeveloped. In the following paragraphs we intend to use the category of liminality as our primary point of departure. Other qualities or aspects of a cultic world view would also likely offer fruitful results. At least three overarching spiritual attitudes are apparent.

Attitude toward religious forms. For the author of Hebrews, the major concern was not with the cultic perspectives of his audience but with their valuation of particular cultic *forms.* It is inevitable that religion--any religion--will express itself with external manifestations. This is because of the social and psychological constitution of humanity itself. We must find concrete expressions for our spirituality because only when submitted to this limitation can any human endeavor become fruitful.[53] However necessary these external forms may be, they cannot take the place of the truth they are intended to convey.[54]

Hebrews examines the religious forms associated with the old covenant and finds them insufficient media for living and preaching the authentic gospel. They may effect some positive results on a superficial level, but nothing more (9:9-10; 10:1-2; 13:9). Forms, then, are to be questioned and critically evaluated. Those that fail to measure up to the gospel are to be forsaken.

Hebrews thus posits a spirituality of letting go. Whatever externals we make the focus of our loyalties become our idols and keep us from experiencing God through the mediation of Christ alone. Numerous points of relevance come readily to mind. One would be the danger of religious legalism. Underhill has noted the dangers ritualism and formalism present to a healthy view of outward religious forms.[55] Ritualism is the view that, for any good to come of them, the external expressions must be performed "just so." It is marked by a great attention

---

[52]Pamela J. Scalise and Gerald L. Borchert, "The Bible and the Spiritual Pilgrimage," in *Becoming Christian*, ed. Bill J. Leonard (Louisville: Westminster/ John Knox, 1990), p. 32.

[53]Underhill, *Worship*, p. 13.

[54]Polhill, "Circumcision," p. 212.

[55]Underhill, *Worship*, pp. 34-37.

to the minute details of religious performance to the extent that one loses the overall picture. Formalism is an approach to ritual that concerns itself with simply "going through the motions" with little thought for the significance of the practices. Both forms of legalism deny the proper place of ritual in spirituality because they deny the realities that always lie behind the ritual itself.

Another point of relevance is the area of liturgical reform which continues to be a topic in the churches. Rather than simply reclaiming the old worship forms from previous centuries or creating new forms in the image of Madison Avenue, Hebrews would have us demonstrate critical judgment about the value of the forms we would embrace. Since we humans cannot get away from the external contingencies of worship, we had better choose well the forms we would embrace. As we shall see, these forms will not always be suited to stained glass and pipe organs.

In general terms, the repudiation of slavery to externals involves discerning what are our sources of religious, spiritual, and theological security. Once these are located, they must be put to the test and those that are found wanting must be discarded, no matter how precious they may be. Letting go may in fact lead to doing without, and there may be in Hebrews an apophatic counterpoint that would confess the inadequacy of any sort of external religious practice or assertion. At the very least, the quest for liminality in religious forms should suggest the importance of moving beyond the rationalistic patterns of much of mainline religion. Baer, for example, notes the functional similarities between Quaker silence, high church liturgy, and glossolalia in that all three forms of religious expression tend to transcend the analytical intellect. In so doing, these practices free other aspects of the self for spiritual engagement.[56]

Attitude toward imagination. The author of Hebrews boldly asserts that his readers have in some sense already drawn near to the heavenly realities to which they aspire (12:22-24). However one is to understand this assertion theologically, in practical terms it invites an engagement of the imagination on the part of the

---

[56]Richard A. Baer, Jr., "Quaker Silence, Catholic Liturgy, and Pentecostal Glossolalia--Some Functional Similarities," in *Perspectives on the New Pentecostalism*, ed. Russell P. Spittler (Grand Rapids: Baker, 1976), p. 152.

reader. Rituals operate on the level of symbolism and imagination.[57] They move people, individually and corporately, into a realm where humanity's creative energies are given free rein to renew society. In this sense all rituals are more or less liminal.[58] Similarly, the cultic spirituality of Hebrews seeks to tell us something that cannot be apprehended through rational means.

Authentic spirituality should be about helping to foster the creative, right-brain aspects of existence. Although the content of the Christian message remains the same, it is up to each new generation to embody the tradition in modern, creative, and imaginative ways. We must not confuse imagination with one particular misuse of it, which is fantasy.[59] Fantasy preys on human desires and fears, and is thus earthbound and egocentric. A healthy imagination, in contrast, is self-transcendent. Hebrews models a vital interplay between tradition and imagination that does full justice to both. While the imagination needs the support of a tradition to be fully creative, the tradition also needs new imaginative insights to stay alive. Unfortunately, the spiritual tradition of the West often prefers, like the first audience of Hebrews, to live in the past. Robinson describes the problem in terms that one would easily identify with the crisis in Hebrews:

> Tragically, our spiritual tradition has almost entirely become obsessed with self-preservation and a wholly disproportionate veneration for the achievements of the past. Unless the grain fall into the ground and die . . . A tradition that is not ready to see all its outward structures destroyed, all its conventional forms of expression abandoned, to give room for growth of the new, is already moribund.[60]

Another aspect of this issue is that of "holy leisure." Celebration, play, and even humor have often been a part of ritual in preindustrial cultures. Christian

---

[57]Numerous scholars have taken up the theme of imagination in religious studies in the past decade. See, for example, John J. Collins, *The Apocalyptic Imagination* (New York: Crossroad, 1984); Walter Brueggemann, *Hopeful Imagination* (Philadelphia: Fortress, 1986); Maria Harris, *Teaching and Religious Imagination* (San Francisco: Harper, 1987).

[58]Turner, "Liminality," p. 209.

[59]Edward Robinson, "Enfleshing the Word," *Religious Education*, 81 (1986), 358.

[60]Ibid., p. 364.

worship as well owes itself to be playful from time to time.[61]   Some of this playfulness may be seen even today in the festive, childlike atmosphere moderns inculcate and exult in at major holidays, especially Christmas.

Finally, the role of the arts in the spiritual life deserves a closer analysis. Christians can stimulate the imaginative, creative side of spirituality by fostering a deeper appreciation for drama, music, and the visual arts as means of religious expression and religious encounter.[62]

Attitude toward earthly life. There is indeed an inner sanctum in heaven that Christians may experience proleptically even now. For the moment, however, our lives must be lived on earth, where there is no longer any distinction between sacred and non-sacred space. The context for our current divine encounter is beyond any fabricated sacred enclosure. With no sacred borders, there is no longer a realm of safe haven. We are to live our faith "out there" in the world, where acts of mercy, solidarity with outcasts, and bearing Christ's shame are the components of our liturgy. Life in all its fullness, and indeed in all its worldliness, is thus the milieu in which we draw near to God through Christ (13:13). The spirituality of Hebrews, for all of its dualistic language, does not then represent a retreat from the world. Hebrews ritualizes the practice of spirituality, but does not reduce it to a liturgy that can be performed somewhere and then left behind.

Radcliffe argues that, unlike other Christians, the author of Hebrews "makes the bold move of refusing to offer any alternative experience of the celestial liturgy" than that found in the Jerusalem cultus.[63] While this is true to a certain extent, it misses the author's main point. Heavenly realities are in fact available to believers, but they do not always appear heavenly in their earthly incarnations.

One aspect of the phenomenology of pilgrimage is worthy of mention in this regard. That is that the pilgrim generally goes as one intentionally assuming the role of the stranger. In various traditions pilgrims wear distinctive garb and go

---

[61]Baer, "Functional Similarities," pp. 158-159.

[62]See William L. Hendricks and Robert Don Hughes, "Christian Spirituality and the Arts," in *Becoming Christian*, ed. Bill J. Leonard (Louisville: Westminster/John Knox, 1990).

[63]Timothy Radcliffe, "Christ in Hebrews: Cultic Irony," *New Blackfriars*, 68 (1987), 495.

penniless, or else carry money only to give to the poor.[64] Rather than blending in with the locals, they must be different; and in the process they willingly enter that limbo of statuslessness where authentic life transitions may be accomplished. It is thus no accident that Hebrews insists that believers identify with the poor, the mistreated, and the prisoners.

This sacralization of all of life implies that social action is a fitting expression of one's commitment to Christ. It is not something ancillary or preparatory to spiritual practice: it is an integral part. Furthermore, if all of life is the Christian's act of worship, this suggests we look at the commonplace as an avenue for divine encounter. We must find a place in our spirituality for daily work, so that we might pray with Brother Lawrence, "Lord of all pots and pans and things . . . Make me a saint by getting meals and washing up the plates!"[65] Herein lies an implicit repudiation of the isolationist mentality that sees the church as a fortress against the world. Christians must remember that the Great Commission is for believers to go out into the world, not for the world to come to church.

Conclusion

The cultic motif in the spirituality of Hebrews is intricate, imaginative, and everywhere present. The author reflects the cultic realities of his time, yet from first to last he invites his readers to see something higher, nobler, better. In this masterful sermon he points consistently beyond the cultus that had long been the center of his audience's spiritual life to a single focus: Jesus Christ. Through the language of ritual and priesthood and sanctuary he bids us all to root our spiritualities in the story of Jesus' death and resurrection.

A recent "Family Circus" cartoon depicted a young boy being tucked into bed, saying, "Tell me a story, Mommy, and put me in it."[66] Such is the role of cultus: it tells us a story and assures us that we are not passive hearers but

---

[64]Doris Donnelly, "Pilgrims and Tourists: Conflicting Metaphors for the Christian Journey to God," *Spirituality Today*, 44 (1992), 28,30-31.

[65]Brother Lawrence, *The Practice of the Presence of God* (Old Tappan, NJ: Revell, 1958), p. 11.

[66]Bill Keane, "The Family Circus," *The Courier-Journal*, Thursday, July 23, 1992, sec. E, p. 9.

participants in the action. Such, the author of Hebrews would tell us, is the value of imagining the Christian life in these terms.

BIBLIOGRAPHY

A. Primary Sources

Basore, John W., ed. *Seneca: Moral Essays.* 3 vols. Loeb Classical Library. Cambridge: Harvard University, 1928-1935.

Charlesworth, James H., ed. *The Old Testament Pseudepigrapha.* 2 vols. Garden City: Doubleday, 1985.

Colson, G. H., and G. H. Whitaker, eds. *Philo.* 12 vols. Loeb Classical Library. Cambridge: Harvard University, 1929-1962.

Danby, Herbert, ed. *The Mishnah.* Oxford: University Press, 1933.

Epstein, I., ed. *The Babylonian Talmud.* 35 vols. London: Soncino, 1948-1952.

Freedman, H., and Maurice Simon, eds. *Midrash Rabbah.* 10 vols. London: Soncino, 1951.

Goldin, Judah, ed. *The Fathers according to Rabbi Nathan.* Yale Judaica Series 10. New Haven: Yale University, 1955.

Jonge, M. de, ed. *The Testaments of the Twelve Patriarchs: A Critical Edition of the Greek Text.* Leiden: Brill, 1978.

Lightfoot, J. B., and J. R. Harmer, eds. *The Apostolic Fathers.* 1891; rpt. Grand Rapids: Baker, 1988.

Lohse, Eduard, ed. *Die Texte aus Qumran: Hebräisch und Deutsch.* Munich: Kösel, 1971.

Neusner, Jacob, trans. *Sifre to Deuteronomy: An Analytical Translation.* 2 vols. Atlanta: Scholars, 1987.

_____. *Sifra: An Analytical Translation.* 3 vols. Atlanta: Scholars, 1988.

_____. *Mekhilta according to Rabbi Ishmael: An Analytical Translation.* 2 vols. Atlanta: Scholars, 1988.

Newsom, Carol A. *Songs of the Sabbath Sacrifice: A Critical Edition.* Harvard Semitic Studies 27. Atlanta: Scholars, 1985.

Nickelsburg, George W. E., and Michael E. Stone, eds. *Faith and Piety in Early Judaism: Texts and Documents.* Philadelphia: Fortress, 1983.

Roberts, Alexander, and James Donaldson, eds. *The Ante-Nicene Fathers.* 10 vols. New York: Scribner's, 1899.

Thackeray, H. St. J., R. Marcus, and L. Feldman, eds. *Josephus.* 10 vols. Loeb Classical Library. Cambridge: Harvard University, 1926-1965.

Vermes, Geza, ed. *The Dead Sea Scrolls in English.* 2nd ed. Baltimore: Penguin, 1975.

178

B. Commentaries

Attridge, Harold W. *The Epistle to the Hebrews.* Hermeneia. Philadelphia: Fortress, 1989.

Brown, Raymond. *The Gospel according to John.* The Anchor Bible. Garden City: Doubleday, 1966.

Bruce, F. F. *The Epistle to the Hebrews.* Rev. ed. New International Commentary on the New Testament. Grand Rapids: Eerdmans, 1990.

Buchanan, George Wesley. *To the Hebrews.* The Anchor Bible. Garden City: Doubleday, 1972.

Casey, Juliana. *Hebrews.* New Testament Message 18. Wilmington: Michael Glazier, 1980.

Jewett, Robert. *Letter to Pilgrims: A Commentary on the Epistle to the Hebrews.* New York: Pilgrim, 1981.

Johnsson, William G. *Hebrews.* Knox Preaching Guides. Atlanta: John Knox, 1980.

Lane, William G. *Hebrews.* Word Biblical Commentary. 2 vols. Dallas: Word, 1991.

Levine, Baruch A. *Leviticus.* The Jewish Publication Society Torah Commentary. Philadelphia: Jewish Publication Society, 1989.

Michel, Otto. *Der Brief an die Hebräer.* Kritisch-Exegetischer Kommentar über das Neue Testament. Göttingen: Vandenhoeck & Ruprecht, 1966.

Milgrom, Jacob. *Leviticus.* Vol. 1. The Anchor Bible. New York: Doubleday, 1991.

Moffatt, James. *A Critical and Exegetical Commentary on the Epistle to the Hebrews.* International Critical Commentary. New York: Scribner's, 1924.

Montefiore, Hugh. *A Commentary on The Epistle to the Hebrews.* London: Black, 1964.

Noth, Martin. *Exodus: A Commentary.* Old Testament Library. Philadelphia: Westminster, 1962.

Riggenbach, D. Eduard. *Der Brief an die Hebräer.* Leipzig: Erlangen, 1922.

Sarna, Nahum M. *Exodus.* The Jewish Publication Society Torah Commentary. Philadelphia: Jewish Publication Society, 1991.

Spicq, Ceslaus. *L'Épitre aux Hébreux.* 2 vols. Paris: Gabalda, 1952.

Westcott, B. F. *The Epistle to the Hebrews.* 2nd ed. 1892; rpt. Grand Rapids: Eerdmans, 1955.

C. Books and Monographs

Bouyer, Louis. *History of Christian Spirituality: Vol. 1, The Spirituality of the New Testament and the Fathers.* London: Burns and Oates, 1960.

Brother Lawrence. *The Practice of the Presence of God.* Old Tappan, NJ: Revell,

1992.

Brueggemann, Walter. *Hopeful Imagination: Prophetic Voices in Exile*. Philadelphia: Fortress, 1986.

Campbell, Joseph, with Bill Moyers. *The Power of Myth*. New York: Doubleday, 1988.

Childs, Brevard S. *Myth and Reality in the Old Testament*. London: SCM, 1960.

Cody, Aelred. *Heavenly Sanctuary and Liturgy in the Epistle to the Hebrews*. St. Meinrad, IN: Grail, 1960.

_____. *A History of Old Testament Priesthood*. Analecta Biblica 35. Rome: Pontifical Biblical Institute, 1969.

Cohen, Shaye J. D. *From the Maccabees to the Mishnah*. Library of Early Christianity 7. Philadelphia: Westminster, 1987.

Collins, John J. *The Apocalyptic Imagination*. New York: Crossroad, 1984.

Daly, Robert J. *Christian Sacrifice: The Judaeo-Christian Background before Origen*. The Catholic University of America Studies in Christian Antiquity 18. Washington: Catholic University of America, 1978.

_____. *The Origins of the Christian Doctrine of Sacrifice*. Philadelphia: Fortress, 1978.

Deissmann, Adolf. *Light from the Ancient East*. Trans. Lionel R. M. Strachan. New York: Harper, 1927.

De Young, James Calvin. *Jerusalem in the New Testament: The Significance of the City in the History of Redemption and in Eschatology*. Amsterdam: Kok & Kampen, 1960.

Driver, Tom F. *The Magic of Ritual: Our Need for Liberating Rites that Transform Our Lives and Our Communities*. San Francicso: Harper, 1991.

Dunn, James D. G. *Baptism in the Holy Spirit: A Re-examination of the New Testament Teaching on the Gift of the Spirit in Relation to Pentecostalism Today*. Philadelphia: Westminster, 1970.

Durkheim, Émile. *The Elementary Forms of Religious Life: A Study in Religious Sociology*. Trans. Joseph Ward Swain. New York: Macmillan, 1915.

Eliade, Mircea. *Cosmos and History*. Trans. Willard R. Trask. New York: Harper, 1959.

_____. *The Sacred and the Profane*. Trans. Willard R. Trask. San Diego: Harcourt, 1959.

_____. *Myth and Reality*. Trans. Willard R. Trask. New York: Harper, 1963.

Gennep, Arnold van. *The Rites of Passage*. Trans. Monika B. Vizedom and Gabrielle L. Caffee. Chicago: University Press, 1960.

Grimes, Ronald L. *Research in Ritual Studies: A Programmatic Essay and Bibliography*. ATLA Bibliography Series 14. Metuchen, NJ: Scarecrow, 1985.

Grove, Philip Babcock, et al., eds. *Webster's Third New International Dictionary.* Springfield, MA: Merriam, 1976.

Harris, Chris. *Creating Relevant Rituals: Celebrations for Religious Education.* Newtown, NSW: Dwyer, 1992.

Harris, Maria. *Teaching and Religious Imagination: An Essay in the Theology of Teaching.* San Francisco: Harper, 1987.

Hay, David M. *Glory at the Right Hand: Psalm 110 in Early Christianity.* Society of Biblical Literature Monograph Series 18. Nashville: Abingdon, 1973.

Hermisson, Hans-Jürgen. *Sprache und Ritus im altisraelitischen Kult: zur "Spiritualisierung" der Kultbegriffe im Alten Testament.* Neukirchen-Vluyn: Neukirchener, 1965.

Hughes, Graham. *Hebrews and Hermeneutics.* Society for New Testament Studies Monograph Series 36. London: Cambridge, 1979.

Humphreys, Fisher. *The Death of Christ.* Nashville: Broadman, 1978.

Hurst, L. D. *The Epistle to the Hebrews: Its Background of Thought.* Society for New Testament Studies Monograph Series 65. Cambridge: University Press, 1990.

Isaacs, Marie E. *Sacred Space: An Approach to the Theology of the Epistle to the Hebrews.* Journal for the Study of the New Testament Supplementary Series 73. Sheffield: Academic Press, 1992.

Jones, Cheslyn, Geoffrey Wainwright and Edward Yarnold, eds., *The Study of Spirituality.* Oxford: University Press, 1986.

Jonsson, John N. *Worlds within Religion.* Louisville: Nilses, 1987.

Jung, Carl G., and C. Kerényi. *Essays on a Science of Mythology.* Princeton: University Press, 1969.

Kaiser, Otto, and Werner Georg Kümmel. *Exegetical Method: A Student's Handbook.* Trans. E. V. N. Goetschius. New York: Seabury, 1963.

_____. *Exegetical Method: A Student's Handbook.* Rev. ed. Trans. E. V. N. Goetschius. New York: Seabury, 1981.

Käsemann, Ernst. *The Wandering People of God.* Trans. Roy A. Harrisville and Irving L. Sandberg. Minneapolis: Augsburg, 1984.

Kelsey, Morton. *Prophetic Ministry.* New York: Crossroad, 1984.

Klappert, Bertold. *Die Eschatologie des Hebräerbriefs.* Theologische Existenz heute 16. Munich: Kaiser, 1969.

Kosmala, Hans. *Hebräer-Essener-Christen: Studien zur Vorgeschichte der frühchristlichen Verkündigung.* Studia Post-Biblica 1. Leiden: Brill, 1959.

Kraus, Hans-Joachim. *Worship in Israel: A Cultic History of the Old Testament.* Trans. Geoffrey Buswell. Richmond: John Knox, 1966.

Lane, William L. *Call to Commitment: Responding to the Message of Hebrews.* Nashville: Nelson, 1985.

Leeuw, Gerhardus van der. *Religion in Essence and Manifestation.* Trans. J. E.

Turner. Princeton: University Press, 1963.

Lehne, Susanne. *The New Covenant in Hebrews*. Journal for the Study of the New Testament Supplementary Series 44. Sheffield: Academic Press, 1990.

Lightstone, Jack N. *The Commerce of the Sacred: Mediation of the Divine among Jews in the Graeco-Roman Diaspora*. Brown Judaic Studies 59. Chico: Scholars, 1984.

Lindars, Barnabas. *The Theology of the Letter to the Hebrews*. New Testament Theology. Cambridge: University Press, 1991.

Loader, William R. G. *Sohn und Hoherpriester: Eine traditionsgeschichtliche Untersuchung zur Christologie des Hebräerbriefes*. Wissenschaftliche Monographien zum Alten und Neuen Testament 53. Neukirchen-Vluyn: Neukirchener, 1981.

Manson, William. *The Epistle to the Hebrews: An Historical and Theological Reconsideration*. London: Hodder and Stoughton, 1951.

McDonnell, Rea. *The Catholic Epistles and Hebrews*. Message of Biblical Spirituality 14. Ed. Carolyn Osiek. Wilmington: Glazier, 1986.

Millgram, Abraham. *Jewish Worship*. Philadelphia: Jewish Publication Society, 1971.

Mora, Gaspar. *La Carta a los Hebreos como escrito pastoral*. Barcelona: Herder, 1974.

Morris, Leon. *The Apostolic Preaching of the Cross*. Grand Rapids: Eerdmans, 1955.

Moule, C. F. D. *Worship in the New Testament*. Ecumenical Studies in Worship 9. Richmond: John Knox, 1961.

Mowinckel, Sigmund. *Religion und Kultus*. Göttingen: Vandenhoeck & Ruprecht, 1953.

Nairne, Alexander. *The Epistle of Priesthood: Studies in the Epistle to the Hebrews*. Edinburgh: Clark, 1913.

Otto, Rudolf. *The Idea of the Holy*. 2nd Ed. Trans. John W. Harry. London: Oxford, 1950.

Pedersen, Johannes. *Israel: Its Life and Culture*. Vols. 3-4. London: Oxford University Press, 1940.

Peterson, David. *Hebrews and Perfection*. Cambridge: University Press, 1982.

Pitts, James M., ed. *The Way of Faith: Words of Admonition and Encouragement for the Journey Based on The Letter to the Hebrews*. Wake Forest: Chanticleer, 1985.

Ringgren, Helmer, and Åke V. Ström. *Religions of Mankind: Yesterday and Today*. Ed. J. C. G. Grieg. Trans. Niels L. Jensen. Edinburgh: Oliver & Boyd, 1967.

Scholer, John M. *Proleptic Priests: Priesthood in the Epistle to the Hebrews*. Journal for the Study of the New Testament Supplementary Series 49. Sheffield: Academic Press, 1991.

Schröger, Friedrich. *Der Verfasser des Hebräerbriefes als Schriftausleger.* Regensburg: Pustet, 1968.

Scott, E. F. *The Epistle to the Hebrews: Its Doctrine and Significance.* Edinburgh: Clark, 1922.

Sheldrake, Philip. *Spirituality and History: Questions of Interpretation and Method.* New York: Crossroad, 1992.

Smith, Jerome. *A Priest For Ever: A Study of Typology and Eschatology in Hebrews.* London: Sheed and Ward, 1969.

Smith, Jonathan Z. *Imagining Religion: From Babylon to Jonestown.* Chicago Studies in the History of Judaism. Chicago: University Press, 1982.

Sowers, Sidney G. *The Hermeneutics of Philo and Hebrews.* Basel Studies of Faculty 1. Richmond: John Knox, 1965.

Thompson, James W. *The Beginnings of Christian Philosophy.* Catholic Biblical Quarterly Monograph Series 13. Washington: Catholic Biblical Association of America, 1982.

Thurén, Jukka. *Das Lobopfer der Hebräer: Studien zum Aufbau und Anliegen von Hebräerbrief 13.* Acta Academiae Åboensis, Series A: Humaniora 47, 1. Åbo, Finland: Åbo Akademi, 1973.

Tobin, Thomas. *The Spirituality of Paul.* The Message of Biblical Spirituality 12. Ed. Carolyn Osiek. Wilmington: Glazier, 1987.

Turner, Victor. *The Ritual Process: Structure and Anti-Structure.* Ithaca: Cornell University Press, 1969.

_____. *Process, Performance and Pilgrimage.* Ranchi Anthropology Series 1. New Delhi: Concept, 1979.

Underhill, Evelyn. *Worship.* New York: Harper, 1937.

Vanhoye, Albert. *La Structure littéraire de l'épitre aux Hébreux.* Paris: Desclée de Brouwer, 1963.

_____. *Situation du Christ: Hébreux 1-2.* Lectio Divina 58. Paris: Cerf, 1969.

_____. *Old Testament Priests and the New Priest.* Trans. J. Bernard Orchard. Petersham, MA: St. Bede's, 1986.

Vaux, Roland de. *Ancient Israel: Its Life and Institutions.* Trans. John McHugh. New York: McGraw-Hill, 1961.

Wakefield, Gordon S., ed., *Westminster Dictionary of Christian Spirituality.* Philadelphia: Westminster, 1983.

Williamson, Ronald. *Philo and the Epistle to the Hebrews.* Leiden: Brill, 1970.

Young, Frances M. *The Use of Sacrificial Ideas in Greek Christian Writers from the New Testament to John Chrysostom.* Patristic Monograph Series 5. Philadelphia: Philadelphia Patristic Foundation, 1979.

183

D. Articles and Essays

Abrahams, Israel, and Aaron Rothkoff. "Tabernacle." *Encyclopaedia Judaica*, vol. 15. New York: Macmillan, 1971.

Andriessen, Paul. "L'Eucharistie dans l'Épitre aux Hébreux." *Nouvelle Revue Théologique*, 94 (1972), 269-277.

Alexander, Jon. "What Do Recent Writers Mean by Spirituality?" *Spirituality Today*, 32 (1980), 247-256.

Attridge, Harold W. "Heard Because of His Reverence." *Journal of Biblical Literature*, 98 (1979), 90-93.

Baer, Richard A., Jr. "Quaker Silence, Catholic Liturgy, and Pentecostal Glossolalia--Some Functional Similarities." In *Perspectives on the New Pentecostalism*. Ed. Russell P. Spittler. Grand Rapids: Baker, 1976.

Bamberger, Bernard J., et al. "Angels and Angelology." *Encyclopaedia Judaica*, vol. 2. New York: Macmillan, 1971.

Barrett, C. K. "The Eschatology of the Epistle to the Hebrews." In *The Background of the New Testament and Its Eschatology*. Ed. D. Daube and W. D. Davies. Cambridge: University Press, 1956.

Baumgarten, Joseph M. "Sacrifice and Worship among the Jewish Sectarians of the Dead Sea (Qumrân) Scrolls." *Harvard Theological Review*, 46 (1953), 141-159.

Behm, Johannes, "καινός, κ.τ.λ." *Theological Dictionary of the New Testament*, vol. 3. Ed. Gerhard Kittel. Trans. Geoffrey Bromiley. Grand Rapids: Eerdmans, 1965.

Best, Ernest. "Spiritual Sacrifice: General Priesthood in the New Testament." *Interpretation*, 14 (1960), 273-299.

Bolle, Kees W. "Speaking of a Place." In *Myths and Symbols: Studies in Honor of Mircea Eliade*. Ed. Joseph M. Kitagawa and Charles H. Long. Chicago: University Press, 1969.

Borchert, Gerald L. "A Superior Book: Hebrews." *Review and Expositor*, 82 (1985), 319-332.

Borgen, Peder. "Philo of Alexandria: A Critical and Synthetical Survey of Research since World War II." In *Aufstieg und Niedergang der römischen Welt*, vol. II.21.1. Ed. Hildegard Temporini and Wolfgang Haase. Berlin: Walter de Gruyter, 1984.

Brown, Raymond. "Pilgrimage in Faith: The Christian Life in Hebrews." *Southwestern Journal of Theology*, 28 (1985), 28-35.

Bruce, F. F. "Recent Contributions to the Understanding of Hebrews." *Expository Times*, 80 (1968-1969), 260-264.

Caquot, André. "Le Service des anges." *Revue de Qumran*, 13 (1988), 421-429.

Casey, Juliana M. "Christian Assembly in Hebrews: a Fantasy Island?" *Theology Digest*, 30 (1982), 323-335.

Charles, J. Daryl. "The Angels, Sonship and Birthright in the Letter to the

Hebrews." *Journal of the Evangelical Theological Society*, 33 (1990), 171-178.

Coudert, Allison. "Angels." *The Encyclopedia of Religion*, vol. 1. Ed. Mircea Eliade. New York: Macmillan, 1987.

Cousins, Ewert H. "What Is Christian Spirituality?" In *Modern Christian Spirituality*. American Academy of Religion Studies in Religion 62. Atlanta: Scholars, 1990.

Crocker, Christopher. "Ritual and the Development of Social Structure: Liminality and Inversion." In *The Roots of Ritual*. Ed. James Shaughnessy. Grand Rapids: Eerdmans, 1973.

Crichton, J. D. "A Theology of Worship." In *The Study of Liturgy*. Ed. Cheslyn Jones, Geoffrey Wainwright, and Edward Yarnold. Oxford: University Press, 1978.

Culpepper, R. Alan. "A Superior Faith: Hebrews 10:19-12:2." *Review and Expositor*, 82 (1985), 375-390.

_____. "Editorial Introduction." *Review and Expositor*, 85 (1988), 5-6.

Dahl, N. A. "A New and Living Way: The Approach to God according to Hebrews 10:19-25." *Interpretation*, 5 (1951), 401-412.

Dibelius, Martin. "Der himmlische Kultus nach dem Hebräerbrief." In *Botschaft und Geschichte*, vol. 2. Tübingen: Mohr, 1956.

Doty, William G. "Mythophiles' Dyscrasia: A Comprehensive Definition of Myth." *Journal of the American Academy of Religion*, 48 (1980) 531-562.

Dumbrell, W. J. "'The Spirits of Just Men Made Perfect.'" *Evangelical Quarterly*, 48 (1976), 154-159

Eire, Carlos M. N. "Major Problems in the Definition of Spirituality as an Academic Discipline." In *Modern Christian Spirituality*. American Academy of Religion Studies in Religion 62. Atlanta: Scholars, 1990.

Fass, David E. "How the Angels Do Serve." *Judaism*, 40 (1991), 281-289.

Ferguson, Everett. "Spiritual Sacrifice in Early Christianity and its Environment." In *Aufstieg und Niedergang der römischen Welt*, vol. II.23.2. Ed. Hildegard Temporini and Wolfgang Haase. Berlin: Walter de Gruyter, 1980.

Ferguson, Sinclair B. "The Reformed View." In *Christian Spirituality: Five Views of Sanctification*. Ed. Donald L. Alexander. Downer's Grove: InterVarsity, 1988.

Fischer, Edward. "Ritual as Communication." In *The Roots of Ritual*. Ed. James Shaughnessy. Grand Rapids: Eerdmans, 1973.

Freedman, William. "The Literary Motif: A Definition and Evaluation." *Novel*, 4 (1971), 123-131.

Galley, Hans-Detlof. "Der Hebräerbrief und der christliche Gottesdienst." *Jahrbuch für Liturgik und Hymnologie*, 31 (1987-1988), 72-83.

Gaster, Theodor H. "Angel." *The Interpreter's Dictionary of the Bible*, vol. 1. Ed. George Arthur Buttrick. Nashville: Abingdon, 1962.

185

_____. "Sacrifices and Offerings, OT." *The Interpreter's Dictionary of the Bible*, vol. 4. Ed. George Arthur Buttrick. Nashville: Abingdon, 1962.

Ginsberg, Harold Louis, et al. "Cult." *Encyclopaedia Judaica*. Vol. 5. New York: Macmillan, 1971.

Grässer, Erich. "Der Hebräerbrief 1938-1963." *Theologische Rundschau*, 30 (1964-1965), 138-236.

Grimes, Ronald L. "Ritual Studies." *The Encyclopedia of Religion*, vol. 12. Ed. Mircea Eliade. New York: Macmillan, 1987.

Grintz, Yehoshua M., et al. "Temple." *Encyclopaedia Judaica*, vol. 15. New York: Macmillan, 1971.

Hanson, Bradley C. "Spirituality as Spiritual Theology." In *Modern Christian Spirituality*. American Academy of Religion Studies in Religion 62. Atlanta: Scholars, 1990.

Haran, Menahem, et al. "Priests and Priesthood." *Encyclopaedia Judaica*, vol. 13. New York: Macmillan, 1971.

Hendricks, William L., and Robert Don Hughes. "Christian Spirituality and the Arts." In *Becoming Christian: Dimensions of Spiritual Formation*. Ed. Bill J. Leonard. Louisville: Westminster/John Knox, 1990.

Henninger, Joseph. "Sacrifice." Trans. Matthew J. O'Connell. *The Encyclopedia of Religion*, vol. 12. Ed. Mircea Eliade. New York: Macmillan, 1987.

Herr, Moshe David, and Jacob Milgrom. "Day of Atonement." *Encyclopaedia Judaica*, vol. 5. New York: Macmillan, 1971.

Hine, Virginia H. "Self-Generated Ritual: Trend or Fad?" *Worship*, 55 (1981), 404-419.

Hood, Ralph W. "Mysticism in the Psychology of Religion." *Journal of Psychology and Christianity*, 5 (1986), 46-49.

Hruby, Kurt. "Les Anges dans le culte synagogal et la piété juive." In *Saints et sainteté dans la liturgie: Conférences Saint-Serge XXXIIIe semaine d'études liturgiques, Paris, 22-26 juin 1986*. Ed. A. M. Triacca and A. Pistola. Rome: Edizioni Liturgiche, 1987.

Hull, William E. "The Relevance of the New Testament." *Review and Expositor*, 62 (1965), 187-200.

Hughes, Philip E. "The Blood of Jesus and His Heavenly Priesthood in Hebrews." *Bibliotheca Sacra*, 130 (1973), 99-109, 195-212, 305-314; 131 (1974), 26-33.

_____. "The Christology of Hebrews." *Southwestern Journal of Theology*, 28 (1985), 19-27

Johnsson, William G. "The Cultus of Hebrews in Twentieth-Century Scholarship." *Expository Times*, 89 (1978), 104-108.

_____. "The Pilgrimage Motif in the Book of Hebrews." *Journal of Biblical Literature*, 97 (1978), 239-251.

186

Johnston, George. "οἰκουμένη and κόσμος in the New Testament." *New Testament Studies*, 10 (1964), 352-360.

Jones, Peter Rhea. "A Superior Life: Hebrews 12:3-13:25." *Review and Expositor*, 82 (1985), 391-405.

Jonsson, John N. "Reflection on Geo Widengren's Phenomenological Method: Towards a Phenomenological Hermeneutic of the Old Testament." *Scriptura*, 2 (1986), 21-39.

Kinerk, Edward. "Toward a Method for the Study of Spirituality." *Review for Religious*, 40 (1981), 3-19.

Koester, Helmut. "'Outside the Camp': Hebrews 13:9-14." *Harvard Theological Review*, 55 (1962), 299-315.

Kuss, Otto. "Der Verfasser des Hebräerbriefes als Seesorger." In *Auslegung und Verkündigung*, vol. 1. Regensburg: Pustet, 1963.

Leach, Edmund R. "Ritual." *International Encyclopedia of the Social Sciences*, vol. 13. Ed. David L. Sills. New York: Macmillan, 1968.

Levenson, Jon D. "The Jerusalem Temple in Devotional and Visionary Experience." In *Jewish Spirituality: Vol. 1, From the Bible through the Middle Ages*. World Spirituality. Ed. Arthur Green. New York: Crossroad, 1987.

Levine, Baruch A. "Biblical Temple." *The Encyclopedia of Religion*, vol. 2. Ed. Mircea Eliade. New York: Macmillan, 1987.

_____. "Priesthood: Jewish Priesthood." *The Encyclopedia of Religion*, vol. 11. Ed. Mircea Eliade. New York: Macmillan, 1987.

López Fernández, Enrique. "Sacerdocio ministerial y eucaristía en la Carta a los Hebreos." *Studium Ovetense*, 5 (1977), 99-136.

MacRae, George W. "Heavenly Temple and Eschatology in the Letter to the Hebrews." *Semeia*, 12 (1978), 179-199.

McGinn, Bernard. "Introduction." *Christian Spirituality: Vol. 1, Origins to the Twelfth Century*. Ed. Bernard McGinn, John Meyendorf and Jean Leclerq. World Spirituality. New York: Crossroad, 1989.

McNicol, Allan J. "The Heavenly Sanctuary in Judaism: A Model for Tracing the Origin of an Apocalypse." *Journal of Religious Studies*, 13 (1987), 66-95.

Michel, Otto. "οἶκος, κ.τ.λ." *Theological Dictionary of the New Testament*, vol. 5. Ed. Gerhard Friedrich. Trans. Geoffrey Bromiley. Grand Rapids: Eerdmans, 1967.

Milgrom, Jacob. "Atonement in the OT." *The Interpreter's Dictionary of the Bible*. Suppl. vol. Ed. Keith Crim. Nashville: Abingdon, 1962.

_____. "Sacrifices and Offerings, OT." *The Interpreter's Dictionary of the Bible*. Suppl. vol. Ed. Keith Crim. Nashville: Abingdon, 1962.

Mitton, C. L. "Atonement." *The Interpreter's Dictionary of the Bible*, vol. 1. Ed. George Arthur Buttrick. Nashville: Abingdon, 1962.

Moe, Olaf. "Der Gedanke des allgemeinen Priestertums im Hebräerbrief." *Theologische Zeitschrift*, 5 (1949), 161-169.

Mora, Gaspar. "Ley y sacrificio en la Carta a los Hebreos." *Revista Catalana de Teología*, 1 (1976), 1-50.

Myerhoff, Barbara G., Linda A. Camino, and Edith Turner. "Rites of Passage: An Overview." *The Encyclopedia of Religion*, vol 12. Ed. Mircea Eliade. New York: Macmillan, 1987.

Neusner, Jacob. "Map without Territory: Mishnah's System of Sacrifice and Sanctuary." *History of Religions*, 19 (1979), 103-127.

Newsom, Carol A. "Merkabah Exegesis in the Qumran Sabbath *Shirot.*" *Journal of Jewish Studies*, 38 (1987), 11-30.

_____. "'He Has Established for Himself Priests': Human and Angelic Priesthood in the Qumran Sabbath Shirot." In *Archaeology and History in the Dead Sea Scrolls: The New York University Conference in Memory of Yigael Yadin.* Ed. Lawrence Schiffmann. Journal for the Study of the Pseudepigrapha Supplement Series 8. Sheffield: Academic Press, 1990.

Nikiprowetzky, Valentin. "La Spiritualisation des sacrifices et le culte sacrificiel au Temple de Jérusalem chez Philon d'Alexandrie." *Semitica*, 17 (1967), 97-116.

Omanson, Roger L. "A Superior Covenant: Hebrews 8:1-10:18." *Review and Expositor*, 82 (1985), 361-373.

Oswalt, John N. "A Myth Is a Myth Is a Myth: Toward a Working Definition." In *A Spectrum of Thought: Essays in Honor of Dennis F. Kinlaw.* Ed. Michael L. Peterson. Nashville: Parthenon, 1982.

Oxtoby, Willard G. "Priesthood: An Overview." *The Encyclopedia of Religion*, vol. 11. Ed. Mircea Eliade. New York: Macmillan, 1987.

Peterson, David. "Toward a New Testament Theology of Worship." *Reformed Theological Review*, 43 (1984), 65-73.

Principe, Walter. "Toward Defining Spirituality." *Sciences religieuses/Studies in Religion*, 12 (1983), 127-141.

Rabinowitz, Louis Isaac, et al. "Synagogue." *Encyclopaedia Judaica*, vol. 15. New York: Macmillan, 1971.

Radcliffe, Timothy. "Christ in Hebrews: Cultic Irony." *New Blackfriars*, 68 (1987), 494-504.

Rainey, Anson, et al. "Sacrifice." *Encyclopaedia Judaica*, vol. 14. New York: Macmillan, 1971.

Richardson, Paul A. "The Primacy of Worship." *Review and Expositor*, 85 (1988), 9-18.

Robinson, Edward. "Enfleshing the Word." *Religious Education*, 81 (1986), 356-371.

Ruager, Søren. "'Wir haben einen Altar' (Heb 13,10): Einige Überlegungen zum Thema: Gottesdienst/Abendmahl im Hebräerbrief." *Kerygma und Dogma*, 36 (1990), 72-77.

Rylaarsdam, J. C. "Atonement, Day of." *The Interpreter's Dictionary of the Bible*, vol. 1. Ed. George Arthur Buttrick. Nashville: Abingdon, 1962.

188

Schenke, Hans-Martin. "Erwägungen zum Rätsel des Hebräerbriefes." In *Neues Testament und christliche Existenz: Festschrift für Herbert Braun zum 70. Geburtstag am 4. Mai 1973*. Ed. Hans Dieter Betz and Luise Schottroff. Tübingen: Mohr, 1973.

Schlier, Heinrich. "παρρησία, παρρησιάζομαι." *Theological Dictionary of the New Testament*, vol. 5. Ed. Gerhard Friedrich. Trans. Geoffrey Bromiley. Grand Rapids: Eerdmans, 1967.

Schneider, Johannes. "ἔρχομαι, κ.τ.λ." *Theological Dictionary of the New Testament*, vol. 2. Ed. Gerhard Kittel. Trans. Geoffrey Bromiley. Grand Rapids: Eerdmans, 1964.

Schneiders, Sandra M. "Theology and Spirituality: Strangers, Rivals, or Partners?" *Horizons*, 13 (1986), 253-274.

_____. "Spirituality in the Academy." In *Modern Christian Spirituality*. American Academy of Religion Studies in Religion 62. Atlanta: Scholars, 1990.

Schrage, Wolfgang. "συναγωγή, κ.τ.λ." *Theological Dictionary of the New Testament*, vol. 7. Ed. Gerhard Friedrich. Trans. Geoffrey Bromiley. Grand Rapids: Eerdmans, 1971.

Schröger, Friedrich. "Der Gottesdienst der Hebräerbriefgemeinde." *Münchener Theologische Zeitschrift*, 19 (1968), 161-181.

Schüssler Fiorenza, Elisabeth. "Cultic Language in Qumran and in the New Testament." *Catholic Biblical Quarterly*, 38 (1976), 159-177.

Seesemann, Heinrich. "πανήγυρις." *Theological Dictionary of the New Testament*, vol. 5. Ed. Gerhard Friedrich. Trans. Geoffrey Bromiley. Grand Rapids: Eerdmans, 1967.

Silberman, Lou H. "Prophets/Angels: LXX and Qumran Psalm 151 and the Epistle to the Hebrews." In *Standing before God: Studies on Prayer in Scriptures and in Tradition with Essays in Honor of John M. Oesterreicher*. Ed. Asher Finkel and Lawrence Frizzell. New York: Ktav, 1981.

Silva, Moisés. "Perfection and Eschatology in Hebrews." *Westminster Theological Journal*, 39 (1976), 60-71.

Smothers, Thomas G. "A Superior Model: Hebrews 1:1-4:13." *Review and Expositor*, 82 (1985), 333-343.

Snell, A. "We Have an Altar." *Reformed Theological Review*, 23 (1964), 16-23.

Songer, Harold S. "A Superior Priesthood: Hebrews 4:14-7:28." *Review and Expositor*, 82 (1985), 345-359.

Spicq, Ceslaus. "La Panégyrie de Hebr. XII,22." *Studia Theologica*, 6 (1952), 30-38.

Strathmann, H. "λατρεύω, λατρεία." *Theological Dictionary of the New Testament*, vol. 4. Ed. Gerhard Kittel. Trans. Geoffrey Bromiley. Grand Rapids: Eerdmans, 1967.

_____, and R. Meyer. "λειτουργέω, κ.τ.λ." *Theological Dictionary of the*

New Testament, vol. 4. Ed. Gerhard Kittel. Trans. Geoffrey Bromiley. Grand Rapids: Eerdmans, 1967.

Stewart, R. A. "The Sinless High-Priest." *New Testament Studies*, 14 (1967-1968), 126-135.

Swetnam, James. "Christology and the Eucharist in the Epistle to the Hebrews." *Biblica*, 70 (1989), 74-95.

Talbert, Charles H. "The Myth of a Descending-Ascending Redeemer in Mediterranean Antiquity." *New Testament Studies*, 22 (1976), 418-440.

Thüsing, Wilhelm. "'Laßt uns hinzutreten . . .' (Hebr 10,22): Zur Frage nach dem Sinn der Kulttheologie im Hebräerbrief." *Biblische Zeitschrift*, 9 (1965), 1-17.

Turner, Victor. "Myth and Symbol." *International Encyclopedia of the Social Sciences*, vol. 10. Ed. David L. Sills. New York: Macmillan, 1968.

_____. "Ritual, Tribal and Catholic." *Worship*, 50 (1976), 504-526.

_____. "Liminality, Kabbalah, and the Media." *Religion*, 15 (1985), 205-217.

_____. "Rites of Passage: A Few Definitions." *The Encyclopedia of Religion*, vol. 12. Ed. Mircea Eliade. New York: Macmillan, 1987.

Vanhoye, Albert. "L'οἰκουμένη dans l'épître aux Hébreux." *Biblica*, 45 (1964), 248-253.

Vicent Cernuda, Antonio. "La introducción del Primogénito, según Hebr 1,6." *Estudios Bíblicos*, 39 (1981), 107-153.

Weiss, Konrad. "φέρω, κ.τ.λ." *Theological Dictionary of the New Testament*, vol. 9. Ed. Gerhard Friedrich. Trans. Geoffrey Bromiley. Grand Rapids: Eerdmans, 1974.

Wenschkewitz, Hans. "Die Spiritualisierung der Kultusbegriffe: Tempel, Priester und Opfer im Neuen Testament." *Αγγελος* 4 (1932), 70-230.

Williamson, Ronald. "The Eucharist and the Epistle to the Hebrews." *New Testament Studies*, 21 (1975), 300-312.

_____. "The Background of the Epistle to the Hebrews." *Expository Times*, 87 (1975-1976), 232-237.

Wills, Lawrence. "The Form of the Sermon in Hellenistic Judaism and Early Christianity." *Harvard Theological Review*, 77 (1984), 277-299.

Winston, David. "Philo and the Contemplative Life." In *Jewish Spirituality: Vol. 1, From the Bible through the Middle Ages*. Ed. Arthur Green. World Spirituality 13. New York: Crossroad, 1987.

Ydit, Meir, and Hanoch Avenary. "Avodah." *Encyclopaedia Judaica*, vol. 3. New York: Macmillan, 1971.

Young, N. H. "The Gospel according to Hebrews 9." *New Testament Studies*, 27 (1980-1981), 198-210.

Zuesse, Evan M. "Ritual." *The Encyclopedia of Religion*, vol. 12. Ed. Mircea Eliade. New York: Macmillan, 1987.

190

E. Unpublished Sources

Casey, Juliana. "Eschatology in Hebrews 12:14-29: An Exegetical Study." S.T.D. dissertation, Catholic University of Louvain, 1976.

Cason, Durward Veazey. "Ἱερεύς and Ἀρχιερεύς and Related Contexts in Hebrews." Ph.D. dissertation, The Southern Baptist Theological Seminary, 1931.

Dukes, James Graydon. "Eschatology in the Epistle to the Hebrews." Th.D. dissertation, The Southern Baptist Theological Seminary, 1956.

Gordon, Victor Reese. "Studies in the Covenantal Theology of the Epistle to the Hebrews in Light of Its Setting." Ph.D. dissertation, Fuller Theological Seminary, 1979.

Johnsson, William G. "Defilement and Purgation in the Book of Hebrews." Ph.D. dissertation, Vanderbilt University, 1973.

Jonsson, John N. Conversations with author. October 2 to November 13, 1991.

Maxey, Lee Zachary. "The Preacher as Rhetorician: The Rhetorical Structure and Design of Hebrews 12:4-13." Paper read at the Society of Biblical Literature Annual Meeting, November 24, 1991.

Minor, Mitzi Lynn. "The Spirituality of the Gospel of Mark." Ph.D. dissertation, The Southern Baptist Theological Seminary, 1989.

Polhill, John B. "Circumcision and the Early Church, A Hermeneutical Inquiry." Th.D. dissertation, The Southern Baptist Theological Seminary, 1968.

Schneiders, Sandra Marie. "The Johannine Resurrection Narrative: An Exegetical and Theological Study of John 20 as a Synthesis of Johannine Spirituality." 2 vols. S.T.D. dissertation, Pontificia Universitas Gregoriana, 1975.

Sharkey, Sarah Ann. "The Background of the Imagery of the Heavenly Jerusalem in the New Testament." Ph.D. dissertation, The Catholic University of America, 1986.

Taylor, Charles Duey. "A Comparative Study of the Concept of Worship in Colossians and Hebrews." Th.D. dissertation, The Southern Baptist Theological Seminary, 1957.

Walker, William Oliver, Jr. "Cultus and Tradition: A Contribution to the Problem of Faith and History in the Old Testament." Ph.D. dissertation, Duke University, 1962.

INDEX

I. OLD TESTAMENT
(including Apocrypha)

II. NEW TESTAMENT

196

III. PHILO

IV. RABBINIC CORPUS

V. DEAD SEA SCROLLS

DATE DUE

JUL 3 1 2001			
			Printed in USA